Visual Basic 2005 Express Edition For Dummies®

Cheat Sheet

Standardized Naming Conventions

Some programmers like to use a set of standard abbreviations for variable types and controls to make their programming easier to read. For example, instead of using the default name `TextBox1`, they would change its `Name` property in the Properties window to something more descriptive and prepend the identifying abbreviation *txt* — for example, `txtUsersPhone` for a TextBox into which the user types his phone number. The following table illustrates some of the standard prefixes that programmers use when naming variables and controls.

Prefix	Corresponding Object	Example	Prefix	Corresponding Object	Example
Acd	ActiveDoc	AcdMainPage	Hpl	HyperLink	HplURL
Chk	CheckBox	ChkBoldface	Lbl	Label	LblContents
Cbo	ComboBox	CboDropper	Lst	ListBox	LstNames
cm	ADO command (database)	cmMyCommand	Pag	Page	PagTurn
Cmd	CommandButton	CmdExit	Pgf	PageFrame	PgfRule
Cmg	CommandGroup	cmgSelectOne	Prj	ProjectHook	PrjSuzerine
Cn	Connection (database)	CnMyConnex	Rb	RadioButton	RbBlueBackground
Con	Container	CntFramed	Rs	Recordset (database)	RsTotalSales
Ctr	Control	CtlSeeThis	Sep	Separator	SepZone
Fld	Field (database)	FldTitles	Spn	Spinner	SpnWatch
Frm	Form	FrmColors	Txt	TextBox	TxtAddress
Frs	FormSet	FrsTypeIn	Tmr	Timer	TmrAnimation
Grd	Grid	GrdGoods	Tbr	ToolBar	TbrDropThis
Grc	Column (in grid)	GrcQuantity	Tbl	Table (database)	TblTitles
Grh	Header (in grid)	GrhYearsResults			

D1605169

Shortcut Keys Used in the VB Express Edition

These shortcut key combinations — some of them traditional in word processing — can speed things up when you're writing, editing, or testing code in the VB Express Code window.

Command Name	Shortcut Key(s)	Behavior
`Edit.Copy`	Ctrl+C / Ctrl+Insert	Copies the currently selected item to the Clipboard.
`Edit.Cut`	Ctrl+X / Shift+Delete	Removes the currently selected item, but saves a copy in the Clipboard in case you want to paste it somewhere.
`Debug.Step Into`	F8	Starts debugging in step mode. Moves execution to the next line of code.
`Debug.Step Over`	Shift+F8	Same as F8, except if you are about to single-step into a procedure, Step Over executes the procedure all at once, rather than step by step.
`Edit.Paste`	Ctrl+V / Shift+Insert	Pastes the contents of the Clipboard at the insertion point.
`Edit.Redo`	Ctrl+Y	Restores a previously undone action.

(continued)

For Dummies: Bestselling Book Series for Beginners

Visual Basic 2005 Express Edition For Dummies®

Cheat Sheet

(continued)

Command Name	Shortcut Key(s)	Behavior
Edit.SelectionCancel	Esc	Cancels the current operation, deselects text, or closes a dialog box.
Edit.Undo	Ctrl+Z	Reverses the last editing action.
File.SaveAll	Ctrl+Shift+ S	Saves all documents in the current solution (application).
File.SaveSelectedItems	Ctrl+S	Saves the currently active form.
View.ViewCode	F7	Displays the selected file (in Solution Explorer) in the Code window.
View.ViewDesigner	Shift+ F7	Displays the selected file in the Design window. (It's easier to just double-click the filename in Solution Explorer.)
View.PropertiesWindow	F4	Displays the Properties window.
View.FullScreen	Shift+Alt+Enter	Toggles between normal and full-screen view in the Code window.

Visual Basic Express Data Types

Visual Basic Data Type	Storage Size	Value Range (Data This Variable Type Can Accommodate)
Boolean	2 bytes	True or False
Byte	1 byte	0 to 255 (unsigned)
Char	2 bytes	0 to 65,535 (unsigned)
Date	8 bytes	January 1, 0001 to December 31, 9999
Decimal	16 bytes	+/–79,228,162,514,264,337,593,543,950,335 with no decimal point; +/–7.9228162514264337593543950335 with 28 places to the right of the decimal; smallest non-zero number is +/–0.0000000000000000000000000001
Double (double-precision floating-point)	8 bytes	–1.79769313486231E+308 to –4.94065645841247E–324 for negative values; 4.94065645841247E–324 to 1.79769313486231E+308 for positive values
Integer*	4 bytes	–2,147,483,648 to 2,147,483,647
Long (long integer)	8 bytes	–9,223,372,036,854,775,808 to 9,223,372,036,854,775,807
Object	4 bytes	Any type can be stored in a variable of type Object
Short	2 bytes	–32,768 to 32,767
Single (single-precision floating-point)	4 bytes	–3.402823E+38 to –1.401298E–45 for negative values; 1.401298E–45 to 3.402823E+38 for positive values
String (variable-length)	Depends on implementing platform	0 to approximately 2 billion Unicode characters
Structure (user-defined type)	Sum of the sizes of its members	Each member of the structure has a range determined by its data type independent of the ranges of the other members. A structure is a complex, programmer-defined variable composed of multiple elements.

* Several variations on the integer type are now available. In addition to the common Integer, Short, and Long types described in the table above, there is a signed (permit negative numbers) SByte (1 byte) type. Unsigned types are: UShort (2 bytes), UInteger (4 bytes), and ULong (8 bytes).

For Dummies: Bestselling Book Series for Beginners

Visual Basic® 2005 Express Edition

Express Edition

FOR

DUMMIES®

Visual Basic® 2005 Express Edition

FOR DUMMIES®

by Richard Mansfield

Wiley Publishing, Inc.

Visual Basic® 2005 Express Edition For Dummies®

Published by
Wiley Publishing, Inc.
111 River Street
Hoboken, NJ 07030-5774

www.wiley.com

For general information on our other products and services, please contact our Customer Care Department within the U.S. at 800-762-2974, outside the U.S. at 317-572-3993, or fax 317-572-4002.

For technical support, please visit www.wiley.com/techsupport.

Wiley also publishes its books in a variety of electronic formats. Some content that appears in print may not be available in electronic books.

Library of Congress Control Number: 2005927625

ISBN-13: 978-0-7645-9705-3

ISBN-10: 0-7645-9705-1

Manufactured in the United States of America

10 9 8 7 6 5 4 3 2

1B/QZ/RR/QV/IN

About the Author

Richard Mansfield's recent titles include *Office 2003 Application Development All-in-One Desk Reference For Dummies, CSS Web Design For Dummies, Visual Basic .NET Weekend Crash Course, Visual Basic .NET Database Programming For Dummies, Visual Basic .NET All-in-One Desk Reference For Dummies,* and *Visual Basic 6 Database Programming For Dummies* (all from Wiley).

From 1981 through 1987, he was editor of *COMPUTE! Magazine,* during which time he wrote hundreds of magazine articles and two columns. From 1987 to 1991, he was editorial director and partner in Signal Research and began writing books full-time in 1991. He has written 37 computer books since 1982. Of those, four became bestsellers: *Machine Language for Beginners* (COMPUTE! Books), *The Second Book of Machine Language* (COMPUTE! Books), *The Visual Guide to Visual Basic* (Ventana), and *The Visual Basic Power Toolkit* (Ventana, with Evangelos Petroutsos). Overall, his books have sold more than 500,000 copies worldwide and have been translated into 11 languages.

Dedication

This book is dedicated to my mother, Florence Mansfield.

Author's Acknowledgments

I'd like to thank the following people for their contributions to this book. Acquisitions Editor Katie Feltman is always a pleasure to work with — knowledgeable, enthusiastic, and good with authors (at least this one, anyway). Project Editor Becky Huehls also deserves praise for her thoroughgoing edit, and the many improvements to the book that resulted.

Technical Editor John Mueller is a highly regarded author in the computer book field (and a friend, and coauthor of previous titles with me). I feel lucky that he agreed to review my manuscript for errors in both the code and the concepts. His considerable depth of knowledge contributed to the quality of the book. If you disagree with some of my technical or theoretical observations, assume that John did too, but I wasn't wise enough to take his advice and change my remarks.

I also want to thank Copy Editor Andy Hollandbeck for making many improvements. Andy not only knows how to write good English, he's also more familiar than most copy editors with computer programming. Plus, he seems like a good guy in the bargain. Happily, Andy seems to have pretty balanced views about the great serial comma debate, and the current conflict over gerunds.

To these, and all the good people at Wiley who contributed in so many additional ways to this book, my thanks for the time and care they took to ensure its quality every step along the way from original idea to final publication.

Publisher's Acknowledgments

We're proud of this book; please send us your comments through our online registration form located at www.dummies.com/register/.

Some of the people who helped bring this book to market include the following:

Acquisitions, Editorial, and Media Development

Project Editor: Rebecca Huehls

Acquisitions Editor: Katie Feltman

Copy Editor: Andy Hollandbeck

Technical Editor: John Mueller

Editorial Manager: Leah Cameron

Permissions Editor: Laura Moss

Media Development Specialist: Travis Silvers

Media Development Manager: Laura VanWinkle

Media Development Supervisor: Richard Graves

Editorial Assistant: Amanda Foxworth

Cartoons: Rich Tennant (www.the5thwave.com)

Composition Services

Project Coordinators: Adrienne Martinez, Kathryn Shanks

Layout and Graphics: Carl Byers, Andrea Dahl, Lauren Goddard, Stephanie D. Jumper, Barry Offringa, Mary Gillot Virgin

Proofreaders: Leeann Harney, Carl William Pierce, TECHBOOKS Production Services

Indexer: TECHBOOKS Production Services

Publishing and Editorial for Technology Dummies

Richard Swadley, Vice President and Executive Group Publisher

Andy Cummings, Vice President and Publisher

Mary Bednarek, Executive Acquisitions Director

Mary C. Corder, Editorial Director

Publishing for Consumer Dummies

Diane Graves Steele, Vice President and Publisher

Joyce Pepple, Acquisitions Director

Composition Services

Gerry Fahey, Vice President of Production Services

Debbie Stailey, Director of Composition Services

Contents at a Glance

Table of Contents

Expanding Your Program 28
Frightening Yourself with the "Starter" Kits 32
Checking Out Additional Resources 33

Chapter 3: At Your Service: Loads of Built-In Helpers **35**
IntelliSense Is Available 36
Reusing Code Snippets 38
Automatic math: Snippets in action 38
Improving the code in code snippets 39
Customizing code snippets 40
Customizing the Way You Work 41
Automatic windows 42
Controlling your keyboard 42
Changing toolbars 44
Your IDE, your way 44
Aligning and Sizing Controls 45
Using Help 46
Error or "Exception" Helpers 48

Chapter 4: Tackling Essential Tools **51**
Introducing the Toolbox and Its Controls 51
Adjusting a Control's Properties 53
Changing a property in the Properties window 54
Some important properties (and many that aren't) 55
Enabling Users to Change Properties 65
Working Around Application Settings 66
A more complex but flexible Application Settings workaround 67
Storing persistent data: Its various hideouts 68
Changing a property with the Application Settings feature 70
Understanding the Solution Explorer 72
Adding other files 72
Finding your solution 73

Part II: Programming the Practical Way **75**

Chapter 5: Common Tasks **77**
Mastering Events 77
Using Subroutines 78
Writing a simple sub 79
Passing parameters 79
Using Functions 80
Understanding Scope 81
When variables are local 82
Public: The greatest scope of all 84
Scoping procedures 85

Introduction

_{...}

Welcome to the world of VB Express programming. Microsoft has put many of its best technologies and tools into this powerhouse package, and this book shows you how to get the most out of them.

VB Express sits on top of a huge, very powerful technology called .NET. And the full power of the .NET code library (the Framework) is available to every VB Express programmer. That's quite a bargain, considering it's free. However, Microsoft states that its primary goal when building VB Express was that it be easy for beginners and amateurs to use. In my view, they only partially succeeded.

The .NET Framework itself can be difficult to maneuver. It's quite large, and the classification system employed is only partly successful. You will want to read the suggestions in this book that help you manage and navigate through this immense and diverse library of procedures (functions you can use in your programs, if you get the syntax and punctuation right). Please take a little time to read the discussion of the very helpful — I'd say essential — intellisense technology built into VB. You can find that information in Chapter 3.

Also, commonly needed libraries, such as `system.data`, must be added to your program by you. This can be confusing to a beginner, and some of the error messages you'll see can be perplexing. See Chapter 13 for a quick review of this technique if you aren't familiar with it.

I'm torn about announcing that perhaps the greatest problem faced by newcomers to VB is its own documentation. Torn because my book looks so much better by comparison, but also disheartened because people who don't have your foresight, Dear Reader, didn't buy my book. Therefore, they are likely to attempt to learn VB from the Help documentation and the sample programs Microsoft is providing — and they're likely be mightily discouraged by the "help" offered.

I've been a great fan of VB since its inception in the early 1990's, and it really saddens me to think of all the potential VB users who are likely to be confused by the built-in documentation. They should come to this language with excitement and achievement — writing programs quickly and having lots of fun getting the computer to do what they want it to do.

You, though, have this book, and I think you'll quickly see why programming in VB can be easy to do but can also produce impressive results.

I've made every effort to ensure that this book *is* understandable:

- ✔ **The programming examples in this book are short and to the point.** Too many VB Express Help code examples are far too large — too much of the programming code isn't related to the topic being illustrated.

- ✔ **This book is written by an experienced writer.** VB Express's built-in Help documentation is full of technospeak written by people who have far more programming experience than writing skill. Consider, for example, this paragraph from VB Express Help: "Every structure has an implicit public constructor without parameters. This constructor initializes all the structure's data members to their default values." I can't imagine who thinks that this is information a beginner needs to know, much less believes that a beginner could possibly understand.

  I believe that Microsoft developers are aware of this problem, and they're working on it. So check the online Visual Studio Express Web pages for updated documentation and sample applications at `http://msdn.microsoft.com/vstudio/express`.

- ✔ **This book has been carefully reviewed by several editors to ensure that it is both clear and technically accurate.** I know how frustrating it is to be unable to get a code example up and running.

Understanding Visual Basic

During the 1990s, far more programmers chose to use Visual Basic than all other programming languages combined. Estimates range from 3 million to 6 million active VB developers.

In spite of its popularity — or perhaps partly *because* of it — some programmers lifted their noses into the air, sniffed, and claimed that VB wasn't a "serious" language. In other words, the languages they used were more difficult (strange punctuation, bizarre vocabulary, confusing syntax, and so on) and sometimes required much more time than VB to finish a project.

But in the early days, those languages did have a significant advantage: They could be used to build programs that accomplished some jobs faster and better than VB. In fact, some tasks were simply impossible in VB. Using the Windows Crypto API to encrypt files, for example, required an expert C++ guru. Now, though, you can use VB Express to quite easily tap into more security power than the Crypto API ever offered. No gurus required.

Visual Basic was the first, and I believe is still the best, *rapid application development* language. Nevertheless, some programmers complained that VB didn't qualify as a "real" programming language until it had true inheritance, multi-threading, and other features that some power programmers love. VB now has those dubious tools. VB Express's technology is equivalent to all other professional programming languages. In fact, all the .NET languages compile into the *same* executable code result. So, snobs, lower your noses.

Tapping into the Power

VB Express is both powerful and diverse. Almost anything you want to do with Windows or Internet programming can be done with VB Express. But, best of all, many of Visual Basic's features are very easy to use. The tools include hundreds of efficiencies, step-through wizards, and shortcuts. For example, even if you have no experience at all in adding a database to an Internet Web page, you can discover how to do just that in about two minutes (see Chapter 14).

Of course, other tasks are not as rapidly accomplished. Otherwise, this book would be five pages long, and people wouldn't be paid to write programs.

Nonetheless, if you want to create a Web page, design a brand-new database, or leverage your programming skills in general, this is the book for you. And VB Express is the language for you. It's really the only computer language left that's specifically geared to novices, amateurs, and small businesses.

Some jobs do take longer than slapping a database connection onto a Web page (but in VB Express, they often don't take much longer). Precisely *how* much longer depends on what you want your Web page to do, how complex your database is, and if you want to get into object-oriented programming (OOP). But if you can click a mouse, write ordinary Visual Basic programming, and follow straightforward directions, you can usually do the job. This book shows you, in clear English, how to create effective Windows applications and Web pages.

About This Book

My main job in this book is to show you the best way to master the various techniques that, collectively, put you on the path to VB Express programming expertise. If a task requires hands-on programming, I show you, step-by-step, how to write that programming. In other cases, I tell you about a simpler, better way to accomplish a job. Otherwise, you could spend days hand-programming something that's already been built — something you can create by clicking a simple menu option, adding a prebuilt component, firing up a wizard, or using a template.

Because VB Express is so huge, you can easily overlook the many shortcuts it contains. I've been on the betas for VB for about 14 years now, and I was on the VB Express technical beta from its start. I've also written many books on Visual Basic. All modesty aside, I do know Visual Basic well.

I've been exploring VB .NET several hours a day for five years — since its debut in July 2000. I've written five books on the topic. You'd think I would have pretty much mapped out the .NET world by now, but no. As you will discover yourself, .NET is a gigantic collection of interrelated technologies, and even at this late date you can find yourself boldly going where no one has gone before.

I hope that all my work these past years will benefit you — showing you the many useful shortcuts and guiding you over the rough spots. I won't pull any punches: I confess it took me several hours of wrestling with VB Express to figure out how to get data successfully displayed in a grid. Now I can show you how to do it in just a few minutes.

Also, unlike some other books about Visual Basic programming (which must remain nameless) as well as the VB Express Help system, this book is written in plain, clear English. You will find sophisticated tasks made easy: The book is filled with step-by-step examples that you can follow, even if you've never written a line of programming or designed a single computer application before.

Visual Basic Express does require some brains and practice to master, but you can handle it. To make this book as valuable for you as possible without writing a six-volume life's work on all of Visual Basic's features and functions, I geared this book toward familiarizing you with the most useful tools to use with the most common programming tasks. You can use most of these tools to create either Windows or Web applications. (The approach to both platforms is quite wonderfully similar, thanks to the WebForms and "code-behind" features you explore in Part IV.)

VB Express gives you dozens of ways to get a job done, but one way nearly always proves to be the best, most sturdy, most effective, and, often, most efficiently programmed. I show you those best ways throughout the book.

How to Use This Book

This book obviously can't cover every feature in VB Express. Instead, as you try the many step-by-step examples in this book, you'll become familiar with the most useful features of Visual Basic programming and many shortcuts and timesaving tricks — some that could take years to discover on your own. (Believe me, some of them have taken me years to stumble upon.)

Whether you want to create stunning Web sites or impressive Windows applications, this book tells you how to get the results you're after. Here are just a few of the goals that you can achieve with this book:

- ✔ Build professional-looking, effective programs.
- ✔ Understand how to build database programs.
- ✔ Create Web pages.
- ✔ Discover how to best use many features built into VB Express.
- ✔ Get the most out of VB Express's new My object, DataView control, Visual Web Developer, .NET Framework, and other great tools.
- ✔ See how to use, test, and deploy your own VB Express programs.

Many people think that programming is impossibly difficult and that Internet programming is even more difficult. It doesn't have to be. In fact, many common programming jobs have already been written for you in VB Express, so you don't have to do the programming at all.

If you're smart, you don't reinvent the wheel. Sometimes, all you need to know is where in VB Express to find a particular component, wizard, template, or other prebuilt solution. Then, drop it into your application. And when you do need to program by hand, this book's code examples can often help you get the job done more quickly than you could do it all by yourself. Because the .NET technology is so large and, to many programmers, so daunting (at least at first), you must learn your way around. This book can be your key to unlocking .NET's secrets.

This book tells you whether a particular wheel has already been invented. It also shows you how to save time by using or modifying existing components or Help code to fit your needs instead of building new solutions from scratch. But if you're doing something totally original (congratulations!), this book also gives you step-by-step recipes for tackling many common tasks from the ground up.

Foolish Assumptions

In writing this book, I had to make a few assumptions about you, dear reader. I assume that you know how to use Windows and understand the elements of computing in general (the various ways to use a mouse, how to navigate menus, and so on).

I also assume that you don't know much, if anything, about VB Express programming. Perhaps most importantly, I assume that you don't want lots of theory or extraneous details. You just want to get the programming jobs done.

How This Book Is Organized

The overall goal of *Visual Basic 2005 Express Edition For Dummies* is to provide an enjoyable and understandable guide for the Visual Basic Express programmer. This book is accessible to developers and programmers with little or no programming experience.

The book is divided into five parts, with several chapters in each part. But the fact that the *book* is organized doesn't mean *you* have to be. You don't have to read the book in sequence from Chapter 1 to the end, just as you don't have to read a cookbook in sequence.

In fact, if you want to know, for instance, how to save and load disk files, or find out about the new My tool, go right to Chapter 6. You're not expected to know what's in Chapters 1 through 5 before you can get results in Chapter 6. Similarly, within each chapter, you can often scan the headings and jump right to the section covering the task that you want to accomplish. There is no need to read each chapter from start to finish. I've been careful to make nearly all the examples self-contained — they don't depend on previous examples. And each of them works, too. They've been thoroughly tested.

All of the source code for all the examples in this book is downloadable from this book's Web site at: www.dummies.com/go/visualbasic2005express

The following sections give you a brief description of the book's five main parts.

Part I: The Basics of Visual Basic Express

This part of the book introduces VB Express, explaining its purposes, elementary features, and why it exists in the first place. After all, Visual Basic .NET is quite similar to VB Express. But as Chapter 1 points out, VB .NET has met with resistance from the programming community.

In this part, you see how common tasks are accomplished and discover the elements of .NET programming. You're introduced to the main features of Visual Basic Express's generous suite of programming tools. You see how to use some of Visual Basic's primary tools, such as IntelliSense and the Toolbox, to make most any programming job easier. You get a taste of VB Express programming by working with the main subdivisions within the Editor — the Properties window, Code window, Toolbox, Design window, and so on.

Part II: Programming the Practical Way

Part II covers the fundamentals of programming itself: using procedures, programming inside events, managing scope, looping, and branching. You also explore the new My object, a shortcut when programming some common tasks — particularly file and directory management. You also work with variables, arrays, printing, debugging, and deployment.

Part III: Dealing with Databases

Experts estimate that around 80 percent of all programming involves databases. That's not surprising when you consider that computers are sometimes called *data processors*. In this part, you see how tables, rows (also called records), and columns (fields) work together to organize data and make it more easily sorted and retrieved. You also master the elements of the important DataSet, a way of detaching a table (or several) from a database to avoid the overhead of having to maintain a continual connection to the central database itself. It's more practical, in the same way that checking books out of a library is more efficient than forcing the entire town to read them only in the library building itself.

Part IV: Programming for the Web

This part covers the various ways to build a Web site, including how to use the new Visual Web Developer tools to get your Web pages up and running quickly. You find out how to work with ASP.NET technology to build intelligence into your Web site programs, and you discover other important programming techniques unique to Web sites, such as how to store variables, connect a Web page to a database, deal with cookies, and communicate back and forth between your site's server and the computers used by visitors to your site.

Part V: The Part of Tens

Here's a fun section. Each of two chapters contains brief (mostly) tips, techniques, and resources that, as an active VB Express programmer, you'll surely want to know about. Some of the topics covered include using random numbers, using the Upgrade Wizard to translate older BASIC (pre-.NET) programs into .NET, keystroke detection, registry access, customized controls, online resources, the menu builder, and other topics. You'll likely find some useful ideas here.

Appendixes

This book comes with two appendixes. Appendix A covers everything you need to know about the CD that comes with this book: the content you'll find, the system requirements, and more.

On this book's Web site (www.dummies.com/go/visualbasic2005express), you'll find Appendix B — a huge, book-length Appendix that is a dictionary of traditional VB programming commands and their VB Express equivalents. Those who have prior VB programming experience can look in Appendix B for a command that they already know (such as InStr), and see how that job is done the VB Express way. But those readers who are not familiar with traditional VB will also find this searchable appendix useful. If you want to quickly find out, for example, how to change a property of Form1 from within Form2, search the dictionary and you get your answer.

Every line of code that you see in this book is also available for download from the *For Dummies* Web site. Take advantage of this handy electronic version of the code. You can then just copy and paste the source code instead of typing it by hand. It saves lots of time and avoids pesky typos.

Conventions Used in This Book

This book is filled with step-by-step lists that serve as recipes to help you cook up a finished product. Each step starts off with a boldface sentence or two telling you what you should do. Directly after the bold step, you may see a sentence or two, not in boldface, telling you what happens as a result of your bold action — a menu opens, a dialog box pops up, a wizard appears, whatever.

A primary convention used in this book is that I've tried to make the step-by-step examples as general as possible, but at the same time make them specific, too. Sounds impossible, and it wasn't easy. The idea is to give you a concrete, specific example that you can follow and understand, while also giving you a series of steps that you can apply directly to your own real-world projects.

Also, note that a special symbol shows you how to navigate menus. For example, when you see "Choose File⇨New⇨Project," you should click the File menu, click the New submenu, and finally click the Project option.

When I display programming code, you see it in a typeface that looks like this:

```
Dim pfont As Font
pfont = New Font("Times New Roman", 12)
```

And if I mention some programming code within a regular paragraph of text, I use a special typeface, like this: `Dim pfont As Font`.

What You Need to Get Started

To use this book, you need only two things: a computer and a copy of VB Express. (This book does not require the high-end, industrial-strength "professional" team programming versions of Visual Basic.) So all you need is VB express itself, and, for the chapters on Web page programming, the Visual Web Developer. You can use the trial version of the software provided on this book's CD or download it from `http://msdn.microsoft.com/vstudio/express`.

Icons Used in This Book

Notice the eye-catching little icons in the margins of this book. They mark certain paragraphs to emphasize that special information appears. Here are the icons and their meanings:

The Tip icon points you to shortcuts and insights that save you time and trouble.

A Warning icon aims to steer you away from dangerous situations.

The Technical Stuff icon marks short journeys into hyper-specific or jargon-filled areas of programming. You can safely skip text marked with this icon, but the information is there if you feel the need to satisfy your inner geek.

The Remember icon prompts you to review a concept that I think you'll want to remember.

Where to Go from Here

Where you turn next depends on what you need. If you want the lowdown on Visual Basic Express's fundamental tools, as well as some important terms and concepts, turn to Part I. If you're looking for the answer to a specific problem, check the index or the table of contents and then just turn directly to the appropriate section.

I hope you find programming with VB Express as useful, and as much fun, as I do.

Part I
The Basics of Visual Basic Express

The 5th Wave   By Rich Tennant

@RICHTENNANT.com

Gee, Richard, you'll have to show me where on the toolbar you found an icon labeled "Overkill".

In this part . . .

Visual Basic Express is likely to remain for some time the only computer programming language for beginners, hobbyists, and small-business people. Part I introduces you to this new, streamlined version of the famous Visual Basic language. You find out why VB Express was created — the audience Microsoft expects and its goals for the language. You also explore the elements of VB, its features, tools, and editing environment. You see how to accomplish common tasks and learn the elements of .NET programming — the new technology that Microsoft introduced in 2000 and that has had a major effect on the programming community. You also explore VB Express programming by working with the main subdivisions within the Editor — the Properties window, Code window, Toolbox, Design window, and so on.

Chapter 1

What It's All About: Visual Basic Express Takes a Bow

*V*isual Basic Express is the only popular computer programming language available today. By *popular,* I mean "for the people" — novices, small-business people, amateurs — anyone other than professional programmers. VB Express is the language for the rest of us.

There are far more small-business people, beginners, and enthusiasts than there are professionals, just as amateur cooks outnumber professional chefs. That's why VB Express's predecessor, Visual Basic, was for a decade the world's most popular computer language by a wide margin.

Small-business people need an efficient, understandable programming language to write quick utilities to solve problems unique to their work. A surfboard maker may often need to calculate polyester catalyst ratios, or dad might want to write up a quick history quiz to help with Laura's homework. A hobbyist may enjoy creating a coin collection management program.

Whatever your personal needs, knowing how to program a computer — and thus how to perfectly *customize* its behavior — is a useful and often enjoyable skill.

Something Happened in Orlando

Before you get started writing programs with VB Express, you may find it helpful to understand why Visual Basic Express was even created. After all, Visual Basic .NET already existed, so why this new express version of VB? In the following sections, I explain how VB has changed over the years, so that you can understand just how VB Express fits into the picture and what VB Express can do for you.

Visual Basic through the years

When Microsoft introduced Visual Basic in 1991, VB was primarily a proce- dure- oriented language (organizing its programs via Events, subroutines, and functions).

To make it easily understood, Visual Basic was designed to be as close to English as possible. Its punctuation, diction, and syntax are familiar — easily understood, remembered, and read — because VB is like a natural human language. Someone creating VB would choose the word *stop*, for example, when they wanted the computer to stop. Makes sense to me.

But in July 2000, something astonishing happened in Orlando. Visual Basic .NET was unveiled in front of an audience of many of the world's best Visual Basic programmers. But VB .NET was so unlike what Basic has always stood for that I heard people around me gasp as the .NET features were described.

VB .NET changed Basic from its traditional role as the fastest route from idea to application to a more powerful — but less organized — language. Where previously simplicity had been the guiding principle, now OOP (object-oriented programming) became a primary goal. And in the process, some needless complexities were introduced.

Visual Basic today

Visual Basic *was* the world's most popular programming language for over a decade, but when Visual Basic .NET appeared, things changed. Because of the .NET framework's added complexity, Visual Basic became less appealing to many for beginning, amateur, and small-business programmers. Its popularity has declined. In this newest iteration of Visual Basic — Visual Basic Express 2005 — Microsoft has tried to win back this segment of programmers.

Visual Basic 2005 comes in two versions: Visual Basic 2005 for Developers and Visual Basic 2005 Express Edition. Because you bought this book, I assume you have the Express Edition.

VB for Developers focuses on technologies that assist people working in groups on the same program (OOP has many such features). But for people programming alone, VB Express should be everything you need. VB Express is a subset of VB for Developers, but little of significance is left out for those programming solo.

What Does Visual Basic Express Have to Offer?

Nobody knows whether it's too little, too late, but VB Express is designed to rescue Visual Basic, and maybe it will. I hope so. The world needs a computer language for the rest of us — for those who aren't professional programmers. (For professionals, complexity and obscurity often help ensure job security.)

VB Express *is* simpler on the surface than its big brother Visual Basic .NET, but the entire, massive .NET Framework (library of objects) is at your disposal in VB Express. So you'll find all the power you need under the hood.

The Express initiatives

I believe Microsoft understands that there is a problem (how many copies of VB .NET are selling?). Is VB Express the answer? I hope so. VB Express interacts with beginning programmers differently than VB .NET does, but with varying degrees of success:

✔ The `My` object achieves some abstraction (reducing your need to write huge amounts of code to accomplish some common tasks), as you can see in Chapter 6.

✔ The startup screen (see Figure 1-1) appears to contain welcomed simplifications and assistance. But I find much of the content behind the links on this "Welcome to Visual Basic Express" portal deceptive. The "Create Your First Program" step-through leads you to think that you can create "powerful programs . . . quickly and easily." The example browser trick is hardly a *program.* The My Movie "starter kit" is far from useful or easy as a learning tool. It's quite advanced actually, and certainly off-putting to all but the Einsteins among novice programmers.

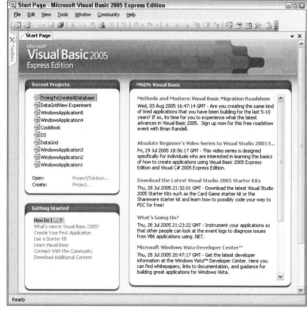

Figure 1-1:
Looks inviting, but are the examples understandable and promises kept?

✔ The menus in VB Express are abbreviated. For example, the macro feature available on the Tools menu in ordinary VB .NET is missing from VB Express. This is similar to what happens when you first install Microsoft Word — presumably not to frighten and confuse beginners with too many features all at once. But in Word you can opt to restore the full menu. In VB Express, the shortening of menus actually represents the removal of features. For example, the macro feature isn't available. Perhaps you're expected to get comfortable using VB Express and then move on up to the more advanced version if you want features such as macros. But don't be too concerned about this — you'll likely find everything you really need in VB Express.

✔ Error messages are being improved. Some of them are now more precisely descriptive of the actual error (rather than offering vague, misleading statements about OOP complexities). And now, useful suggested fixes to the code are sometimes offered. But many error messages remain simply alarming and/or useless. Take a look at Figure 1-2

Figure 1-2:
This is a
VB error
message.
Can you
understand
what it's
trying to
tell you?

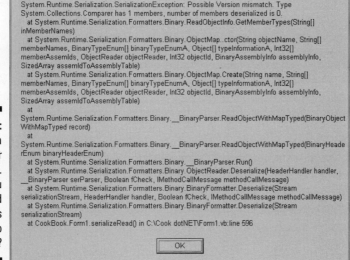

CookBook

System.Runtime.Serialization.SerializationException: Possible Version mismatch. Type System.Collections.Comparer has 1 members, number of members deserialized is 0.
   at System.Runtime.Serialization.Formatters.Binary.ReadObjectInfo.GetMemberTypes(String[] inMemberNames)
   at System.Runtime.Serialization.Formatters.Binary.ObjectMap..ctor(String objectName, String[] memberNames, BinaryTypeEnum[] binaryTypeEnumA, Object[] typeInformationA, Int32[] memberAssemIds, ObjectReader objectReader, Int32 objectId, BinaryAssemblyInfo assemblyInfo, SizedArray assemIdToAssemblyTable)
   at System.Runtime.Serialization.Formatters.Binary.ObjectMap.Create(String name, String[] memberNames, BinaryTypeEnum[] binaryTypeEnumA, Object[] typeInformationA, Int32[] memberAssemIds, ObjectReader objectReader, Int32 objectId, BinaryAssemblyInfo assemblyInfo, SizedArray assemIdToAssemblyTable)
   at System.Runtime.Serialization.Formatters.Binary.__BinaryParser.ReadObjectWithMapTyped(BinaryObjectWithMapTyped record)
   at System.Runtime.Serialization.Formatters.Binary.__BinaryParser.ReadObjectWithMapTyped(BinaryHeaderEnum binaryHeaderEnum)
   at System.Runtime.Serialization.Formatters.Binary.__BinaryParser.Run()
   at System.Runtime.Serialization.Formatters.Binary.ObjectReader.Deserialize(HeaderHandler handler, __BinaryParser serParser, Boolean fCheck, IMethodCallMessage methodCallMessage)
   at System.Runtime.Serialization.Formatters.Binary.BinaryFormatter.Deserialize(Stream serializationStream, HeaderHandler handler, Boolean fCheck, IMethodCallMessage methodCallMessage)
   at System.Runtime.Serialization.Formatters.Binary.BinaryFormatter.Deserialize(Stream serializationStream)
   at CookBook.Form1.serializeRead() in C:\Cook dotNET\Form1.vb:line 596

OK

> As you can see in Figure 1-2, this monstrously unhelpful mass of jargon cannot be considered a useful message to the ordinary programmer. Sometimes more is less.

Yet I remain somewhat hopeful. Though not yet accomplished, the initiatives listed here are worthy goals. Perhaps VB Express will evolve into a popular language.

Finding help

Although efforts have been made to improve the VB Help feature since the introduction of VB .NET, unfortunately, much remains to be done before Help is uniformly helpful. In my view, *writers* didn't write the Help examples (neither the code nor the narratives that describe them). Programmers did. And what's worse, I think that many if not most of those programmers are familiar with C languages and only vaguely, if at all, acquainted with Visual Basic. As a result, you often find bizarre code examples in the Help documentatation that are a mixture of VB and C styles, accompanied by explanations that defy understanding. As a result, Help too often remains very little help indeed.

For example, imagine a beginner trying to better understand what a *subroutine* is. After all, subs are a major feature in every VB program. So our apprentice — with dewy eyes and a hopeful heart — looks it up in the VB Express Help index and is inundated with confusing jargon, some words that even most advanced VB programmers don't understand: *containing class, interface, structure, Implements keyword, access modifiers, attributes, protected, derived class, ProtectedFriend, assembly, overloading , overriding, redeclares, NotOverridable, MustOverride, shadows, generic procedure*, and on and on. And you're treated to "explanations" like this (send me a translation if you know what they're talking about):

> The Implements statement must include the interface specified by
> interface. However, the name by which the interface defines the Sub (in
> definedname) does not have to be the same as the name of this procedure
> (in name).

Get it? And this nonsense is supposed to be a *help* document for beginners and novices, the purported audience for VB Express. Sounds to me more like page 439 of the government handbook on assembling a card table.

My advice to you is to use this book as your guide instead (and also take advantage of the many code examples in the extensive online Appendix described in this book's Introduction). This book and the huge online Appendix are written by me, a Visual Basic programmer and a writer. You can understand this book and the Appendix. Also, although the VB Express Help system doesn't yet have much to offer (keep checking online to see if it improves), some of VB's features can be quite useful. Chapter 3 introduces some excellent built-in helpers such as IntelliSense, and Chapter 10 explains how to use debugging tools to track down errors.

A couple years ago I offered myself to Microsoft's VB team, like the Aztec virgin that in my heart I am. And I've written them lengthy suggestions, talked to them in person, and had e-mail conversations back and forth with them. They've assured me that they're working on improving the Help system and making other changes.

Taking a First Look

Usually when you start writing a Windows program in VB Express, you begin by adding components (controls from the Toolbox, see Chapter 4) to a form. This creates the user interface on the *form* — the window that the user interacts with. There can be other windows, but many shorter programs have only a single form. You can move the toolbox, shown in Figure 1-3, like most features of the editor (or IDE, see Chapter 2), but most people leave it on the left side.

Figure 1-3:
The Toolbox
holds lots of
powerful,
prebuilt
components
that you just
drag and
drop onto
your VB
Express
forms.

Creating a user interface helps organize your project

Adding components and thereby defining what the user sees helps you organize your programming into logical categories. A button that you label Open File becomes the location where you write code to load a file from the user's hard drive. If you put a Button control on a form and then double-click that button, a little VB Express magic happens. You're switched to the code window "underneath" the form — or behind the scenes. The user doesn't see the code, but they certainly appreciate that you wrote some programming behind the button so it actually does its job. The Code window is illustrated in Figure 1-4.

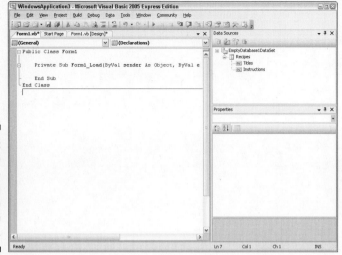

Figure 1-4:
You write
your pro-
gramming
here in
the code
window.

Programming for the Web

Internet programming differs somewhat from ordinary Windows programming, but VB Express offers some great tools for this task, too. Part IV covers
these topics. You use an editor similar to the IDE for Windows programming,
but optimized for Web use — including a specialized set of controls in the
Toolbox. The Visual Web Developer Express Edition — a free download — is
shown in Figure 1-5.

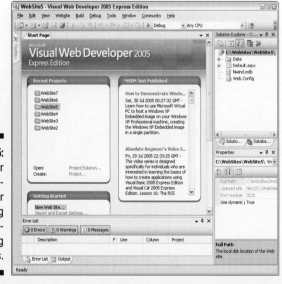

Figure 1-5:
This editor
is opti-
mized for
designing
and pro-
gramming
Web pages.

Chapter 2

Up and Running

*I*t's time to get your feet wet and see what you can do with VB Express. First, you explore some of the steps Microsoft has taken to accommodate amateur, hobbyist, and novice programmers — the intended audience for VB Express and the other Express languages, such as Visual Web Developer and SQL Server 2005 Express. Then you create and test your first VB Express program — a milestone in some people's lives because they realize that communicating with a computer can be tremendous fun. (It amplifies your brain.) Then you go on to modify your gem of a program, discovering how to tweak its qualities, add textures, and insert graphics. Finally, you're exposed to the dubious educational value of the *starter kits* — Microsoft's idea of what's helpful for beginning VB programmers. Are these kits of any use to you? Read on.

Finding Resources from Microsoft

As you get started using VB Express, you might like to know what resources and features Microsoft has designed with the novice programmer in mind:

✔ **Simplified interface:** The VB Express editor (or IDE, *integrated design environment*) where you write your programs is somewhat simplified — or as Microsoft describes it, *streamlined* — compared to Visual Basic .NET, Express's big brother. The menus in VB Express are shorter, so you're not overwhelmed by too many choices. Some of the more exotic, rarely used features have been hidden or removed. After all, some .NET editor features are designed for the heavy-duty industrial programming typically tackled by large groups of advanced programmers.

✔ **Starter kits:** Another attempt to entice the novice and amateur programmer audience into the Express product line is the starter kits: prewritten applications that you can learn from or modify to suit your own needs. They can be downloaded from

```
http://lab.msdn.microsoft.com/vs2005/downloads/starterkits
```

A couple of these kits are described at the end of this chapter. But be warned: In my view, these kits are hardly for beginners. The Movie Collection project, in particular, is obviously far too advanced for a novice programmer.

✔ **Webcasts:** You can also find some Webcasts (online video tutorials), such as *Coding4Fun,* with its Prince-inspired, hip-hop spelling. Beyond that, you can watch 10 hours of video for VB Express beginners at

```
http://lab.msdn.microsoft.com/express/beginner
```

✔ **The Express home page on Microsoft's site:** You can find the latest documentation, downloads, and other information on this page, which you can find at

```
http://lab.msdn.microsoft.com/express
```

Building a Basic VB Program

Traditionally, a beginner's first program does something extremely simple. It's a birth announcement — the birth of a new programmer. You might as well get your feet wet with VB Express from this famous starting place.

Your goal: to display the message *Hello World* to the user who runs your program. But because this is Visual Basic — where you can add powerful features by merely dragging and dropping — I show you how to enhance this classic "Hello World" application with a few quick mouse moves. In the process, you see some basic maneuvers you can use for just about any program you want to write.

To create your first VB Express program, follow these steps:

1. **If you haven't yet downloaded and installed VB Express, go to Microsoft's Web site and complete the installation process.**

   The correct Web page may change from the following address; if you don't find VB Express here, search Google for "Visual Basic Express Download."

   ```
   http://lab.msdn.microsoft.com/express/vbasic/default.aspx
   ```

2. **Run VB Express.**

   You see the startup screen in the editor, as shown in Figure 2-1.

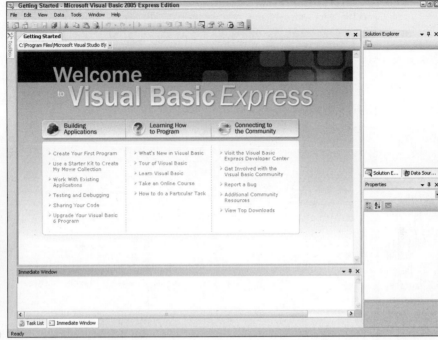

Figure 2-1:
You see this
welcome
screen,
loaded with
options,
when you
first fire up
VB Express.

3. Choose File⇨New Project.

The New Project dialog box opens, as shown in Figure 2-2.

Figure 2-2:
When you
choose
New Project
from the File
menu, you
see this
dialog box.

4. Double-click the Windows Application icon.

The dialog box closes and a new, empty VB Express project appears in
the editor, as shown in Figure 2-3.

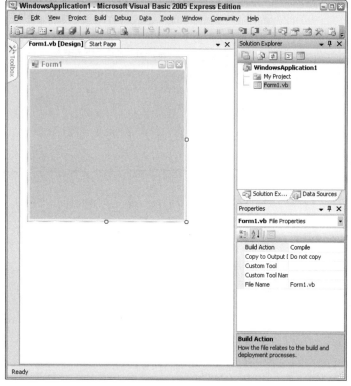

Figure 2-3:
This form
is your
primary
visual
design
surface;
it's where
you write
your pro-
gramming
code.

Notice Form1 in Figure 2-3. While you're creating your program (it's called *design time*), you can drop prebuilt controls like buttons, text boxes, and many other useful tools onto this form. Quite a few of these tools are for your user, allowing whoever uses your VB Express application to interact with it by clicking buttons, entering text, and so on. When your program is executed (run by the user during *run time*), the form turns into a window.

5. **Double-click the form.**

The editor switches from *design view* to *code view*, as shown in Figure 2-4.

Notice the `Private Sub Form1_Load` line at the top of the screen in Figure 2-4. This is an *event*. It *triggers* or *fires* when something happens in the program. This particular event is triggered when Form1 is first loaded — in other words, when the program first runs.

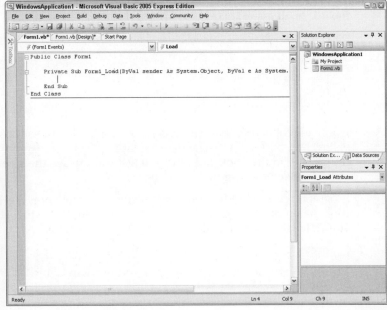

Figure 2-4:
This code
window
is where
you type in
your pro-
gramming.

This window (Form1) is the first thing the user sees when starting your program — and its Load event is a good place to put any programming code that you want to run when the program starts. Form1_Load is also a good place to test your programming code because all you have to do to see the effects is press F5 to execute the code. So in this book, example code is frequently put into Form1_Load for you to test and experiment with.

You can safely ignore the `(ByVal sender As System.Object, ByVal e As System.EventArgs) Handles MyBase.Load` nonsense. You could program for 10 years without ever needing to employ or modify this stuff more than a few times. This jargon has bubbled up from the lower levels of VB's current runtime engine. It was hidden in most previous versions of VB — and we can hope will be removed in some future version. But don't delete it — you'll cause bugs. "Those who know best" have decided to add it to every event in VB Express. Just try to ignore it.

There's a blank line between `Private Sub` and `End Sub`, but you can make more space if you want by pressing Enter a few times (while your blinking insertion cursor is located on that blank line). Try it now.

6. Type the following programming code (shown in boldface) into the Form1_Load event:

```
Private Sub Form1_Load(ByVal sender As System.Object, ByVal e As
        System.EventArgs) Handles MyBase.Load

    MsgBox("Hello World")

End Sub
```

Ignore anything else that happens (a prompt might appear in a light yellow box, and other distractions might pop up). You explore these things later in the book. For now, you just want to see the splendid effects caused by your programming.

Programs written in VB Express are tested by simply pressing F5, which runs the program — just as it will behave and appear to the user after you've finished creating it. Go ahead. Don't be bashful, . . .

7. . . . press F5.

You see the result — your message — as shown in Figure 2-5. You've done it!

Figure 2-5:
Your first
program in
VB Express
works
perfectly!

8. Click OK.

Your message window closes, but the Form is still displayed because the program is still running.

9. Click the red X in the upper-right corner of Form1.

The window (Form1) closes, and, because it's the "startup" object for this application, the application itself also shuts down. You're back in the editor, in code view, ready to add new features to your program, which is the topic of the next section.

Expanding Your Program

After you build a basic program, you get to experiment a bit, giving yourself a sense of the power beneath the surface of VB Express. You can add a texture, a photo — any graphic you want — to create an attractive background for your forms. To see how easy it is to modify the appearance of your VB Express programs, follow these steps:

1. **Using the program you wrote in the previous section, click the tab named Form1.vb [Design] at the top of the code window.**

   You are switched back to the design window. It's easy to move back and forth between the programming (code) window and the design window.

   Notice the Properties window, most likely located in the lower-right corner of the editor.

2. **If you don't see the Properties window, press F4 to display it.**

   You can use the Properties window to change many qualities of a form or the controls in the Toolbox, such as buttons, sliders, and so on.

3. **Scroll down the Properties Window and select the BackgroundImage entry, as shown in Figure 2-6.**

Figure 2-6:
The Properties Window is one of VB Express's most useful tools.

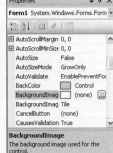

4. **Click the BackgroundImage label in the Properties Window.**

   The property you clicked is now highlighted (selected), as shown in Figure 2-6. You also see a description of the property's purpose, but often the description isn't too helpful because it merely repeats the name of the property. Oh well . . . this feature sometimes adds information you can use

5. **Click the small ellipsis (. . .) button that appears to the right of the now-highlighted BackgroundImage entry in the Properties window.**

   A dialog box opens (see Figure 2-7), showing you any graphics files already located in your project's folder. (There are none yet, so it's blank.)

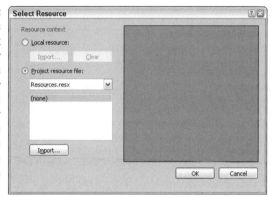

Figure 2-7:
This dialog box shows any resources currently loaded into your project's folder. There are none yet in this project.

6. **Click the Import button in the dialog box.**

   A typical Windows Open dialog box opens, as shown in Figure 2-8.

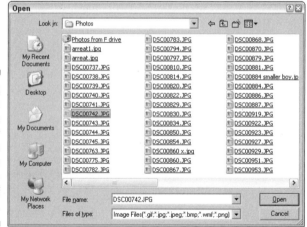

Figure 2-8:
Locate a graphics file on your hard drive to decorate the background of your form.

Image editors, such as Photoshop, let you create textures that look great as backgrounds.

7. **Double-click a graphics file's name in the Open dialog box.**

You're allowed to import the following graphics file types: .gif, .jpg, .jpeg, .bmp, .wmf, and .png. However, if you want to use a different file type, most image editor applications can quickly translate the image into the .jpg format for use with VB.

The graphic you selected is copied to your project's directory as a "resource" to be used as often as you wish in your project. A sample of the graphic is displayed in the Select Resource dialog box, as shown in Figure 2-9.

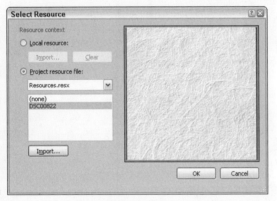

Figure 2-9:
This texture will look good as a background, in my opinion. Your opinion might differ.

If you give your program to someone else to use (this is called *deploying an application*), you just copy the application's folder, and your graphics file goes right along with the rest of the resources and elements in the project (of course you might have to ensure you have copyright permission for the graphics file — particularly if you're planning to *sell* your VB application or something). Having copies of resources all together like this in the same parent folder really simplifies deployment.

8. Click OK.

The Select Resource dialog box closes and the background of your form now displays the image you chose, as shown in Figure 2-10.

With a little extra work, you could expand this program further into a custom, personalizable graphics file viewer. In fact, after you've built up your VB Express skills with this book, you can come back to this project and find expanding it both easy and fun. Too bad all programming languages aren't as efficient and enjoyable as Visual Basic.

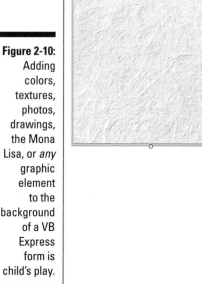

Figure 2-10: Adding colors, textures, photos, drawings, the Mona Lisa, or *any* graphic element to the background of a VB Express form is child's play.

Frightening Yourself with the "Starter" Kits

I certainly won't use the phrase out of touch to describe the faction at Microsoft that thinks it understands how to communicate with novices via "starter" kits. But we've all had a teacher or two who overwhelmed us with too much detail, too many ideas all at once, and too little time to absorb them.

Becoming comfortable with new things requires a bit of sensible pacing. With that in mind, take a look at one of the "starter" kits offered to you in VB Express. I find the programming in these kits difficult to follow, and I've written a dozen books on Basic during the past 25 years. How are beginners supposed to use these complex programs as a way to learn Visual Basic? The answer: They aren't. Only a few absolutely brilliant beginners are likely to find the starter kits a helpful way to learn VB.

To see the *My Movie Collection Starter Kit,* and give yourself a good scare, choose File⇨New Project and then double-click the *My Movie Collection Starter Kit* icon.

As you scroll down the starter kit, you're first given some tasks that are quite easy to manage. You're shown how to use the program (add new data, and so on), and you're invited to try your hand at changing a text property, adding a graphic, and a few other simple adjustments to customize your Movie Collection program. So far, so good.

But suddenly, you're not just pushed into the deep end. You're expected to look at datasets, binding, and other database-related topics so complex and advanced that I wrote an entire book about them (*Visual Basic .NET Database Programming For Dummies,* published by Wiley). And you're supposed to "dissect the functionality of the application by examining the source code," including such advanced topics as Web programming and UserControls.

Perhaps you're a budding programming genius who'll glide right through all this. Perhaps you can dissect the functionality, as they say. But if you're like most people, you'll be flailing pretty quickly.

If you want to see some of the other "starter" kits, go here:

```
http://lab.msdn.microsoft.com/vs2005/downloads/starterkits/
```

If you're like most people, you might want to *use* some of these programs for what they can do. They're sophisticated, complex applications — well-designed graphically and complicated programmatically. They're good applications. But can you, a beginner, *learn from them?*

My advice is not to be discouraged. Normal people — even most highly intelligent people like you and me — find these programs far too advanced to serve as teaching tools. So rather than learn from *them,* just thank yourself that you had the brains to buy this book and keep reading. I promise not to throw snarky looks at *you* or drop a massive, intricate, and difficult program in front of you and suggest that you *start with this.*

Checking Out Additional Resources

Here are two additional resources you might want to check out. The first is a video series aimed directly at the absolute novice. Find it at:

```
http://lab.msdn.microsoft.com/express/beginner/default.aspx
```

The second resource is a set of examples located at:

```
http://lab.msdn.microsoft.com/vs2005/downloads/101samples/def
        ault.aspx
```

Many of these examples are beyond even intermediate programmers' under-standing, but some of them might help you understand aspects of VB (partic-ularly the examples that focus on ways to exploit the excellent set of VB controls, such as the RichTextBox, DataGridView, SplitContainer, and so on).

Microsoft has recently added a number of new starter kits. Perhaps some of these kits will prove more accessible to beginners than the kits I've discussed in this chapter. However, I've reviewed the seven kits currently available, and none is understandable to anyone but the rare genius beginner. Perhaps that's you! See them at:

```
http://lab.msdn.microsoft.com/vs2005/downloads/starterkits/
```

Chapter 3

At Your Service: Loads of Built-In Helpers

*V*isual Basic, in all its versions since 1990, was designed to be a readable, clear language — as close to English as possible. Since 2000, Visual Basic has strayed from that mandate, though it's not yet as full of twisted syntax and redundant punctuation as the C-languages, such as Java and C++.

Another reason for BASIC's famous efficiency is the many add-ons, wizards, prebuilt controls, and other assistance that Microsoft provides for this language. Given that the vision for VB *Express* is a return to the clarity and efficiency of pre-.NET versions of BASIC, you might expect Express to include lots of useful assistants. It does. This chapter explains how to get help in various ways while coding and how to reuse code, customize the editor, and otherwise streamline your programming environment.

IntelliSense Is Available

Some of your best programming assistance comes from *IntelliSense* — a set of helpful features. They're built into the VB Express editor and are on by default. Among the most helpful IntelliSense features are the ones that

- ✔ Fill in the remainder of your line of code as you type the beginning of that line — a process called *auto-statement completion*
- ✔ Provide fixes when VB finds an error
- ✔ Drop lists of properties, methods, or arguments while you're filling in a line of code, which is called *auto-list members*

In our brave new world, tens of thousands of objects in the .NET Framework are available to VB Express programmers. Most of these objects have, in turn, many methods and properties (called the *members* of an object).

Because nobody can memorize all these commands, the *auto-statement completion* and *auto-list members* features of IntelliSense are essential. Gone are the days when programmers could remember all the classes and their members, much less the parameters (the *arguments* — the data in parentheses following some commands) that each of them can take. This gazillion-possible-functions (methods) effect is even worse now that so many functions are *overloaded*, which means that a function behaves differently depending on which of several possible argument lists is used. For example, the simple `Console.Writeline` function has 18 different possible argument lists.

To see these IntelliSense features in action, try this example:

1. In the VB code window, type this line inside a procedure (in a Sub):

```
console.
```

As soon as you type the period (.), an IntelliSense list shows you the members (properties and methods) of the *console* class, as shown in Figure 3-1.

Properties in this list are symbolized by an icon of a hand holding a VCR tape; *members* are symbolized by a flying eraser — as you expect. I've always associated flying erasers with members — *haven't you?*

2. Continue until you have typed this:

```
console.WriteLine(
```

As soon as you type the opening parenthesis, a box pops out suggesting 1 of 18 possible argument lists that apply to the `WriteLine` method, as shown in Figure 3-2.

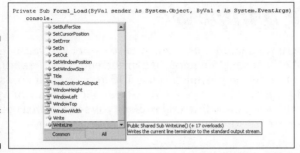

Figure 3-1:
IntelliSense
provides a
list of the
members of
an object.

Figure 3-2:
See all the
ways
to pass
data —
arguments —
to this
WriteLine
method by
clicking the
arrows.

```
Private Sub Form1_Load(ByVal sender As System.Object
    console.writeline(
    ▲1 of 18 ▼ WriteLine ()
    Writes the current line terminator to the standard output stream.
```

3. **Press your up or down arrow keys to see all 18 argument lists. To select an option from the list of possibilities, click it.**

There you have them: auto-list members and auto-statement completion — two extremely valuable assistants in this world of millions of members. (Well, maybe I exaggerate a bit, but what's a little exaggeration among friends?)

Turning on your IntelliSense

To be sure that the IntelliSense features are turned on, follow these steps:

1. Choose Tools⇨Options⇨Text Editor⇨All Languages.

2. In the Statement Completion options on the right side of the Options dialog box, make

sure the Auto List Members and Parameter Information check boxes are selected.

Although I recommend keeping IntelliSense turned on, you can deselect the check boxes if you find that it gets in your way.

Reusing Code Snippets

After you've written a function that works well, why not just reuse it the next time you need the same task accomplished in some future program? For example, some programs first display a User ID/Password InputBox that the user must fill in before being allowed to use the application. If you write a password utility that does this job well, why not save the source code and reuse it if you need password-protection for another program later?

VB Express simplifies reusing code examples by collecting little pieces of source code that perform common functions into *IntelliSense code snippets*. These snippets are nothing more than a semi-automated way of inserting or pasting pre-written code into your program. In addition to the IntelliSense snippets, you can find lots of other code snippets sprinkled all through the VB Help system, and these snippets can be copied and pasted, too. But the IntelliSense code snippets have been selected because, presumably, they represent 500 or so common programming tasks. You can also add your own snippets to the built-in collection or share them with others. In the following sections, you can see how it works.

This concept — code reuse — is a primary feature of *object-oriented programming* (OOP), but reusing code in OOP requires entering the confusing jungle of OOP inheritance and polymorphism. VB Express keeps reusing code easy and straightforward: Its code snippets employ the copy-and-paste approach, which is code reuse at its simplest.

Automatic math: Snippets in action

According to Microsoft, snippets perform a *complete action,* such as sending an e-mail or, as in the example below, calculating mortgage payments.

To see how to use code snippets, assume that your program needs to calculate the monthly payment amount for a mortgage. Follow these steps:

1. **Double-click a Form in design mode to open the Form_Load event of a VB project.**

2. **Right-click a blank line in the Form_Load event.**

3. **Choose Insert Snippet from the context menu.**

   A list of the various categories of snippets from which you can narrow your selection appears, as shown in Figure 3-3.

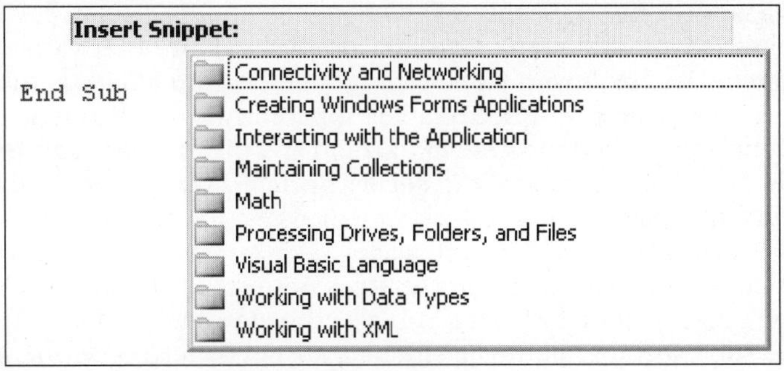

Figure 3-3:
Code
snippets are
organized
into sub-
categories
for your
conve-
nience.

```
Insert Snippet:

End Sub          Connectivity and Networking
                 Creating Windows Forms Applications
                 Interacting with the Application
                 Maintaining Collections
                 Math
                 Processing Drives, Folders, and Files
                 Visual Basic Language
                 Working with Data Types
                 Working with XML
```

4. Double-click the Math category.

A list of the available snippets relating to mathematical tasks appears.

5. Double-click the Calculate a Monthly Payment on a Loan entry.

The code in Listing 3-1 is inserted into your Form_Load event.

Listing 3-1: The Monthly Mortgage Payment Snippet

```
Dim loanAmount As Double
Dim annualPercentRate As Double
Dim futureValue As Double = 0
Dim payment As Double
Dim totalPayments As Double

loanAmount = CDbl(InputBox("How much do you want to borrow?"))
annualPercentRate = CDbl(InputBox("What is the annual percentage rate of your
            loan? Enter 8% as .08."))
totalPayments = CDbl(InputBox("How many monthly payments will you make?"))
payment = Pmt(annualPercentRate / 12, totalPayments, -loanAmount, futureValue,
            DueDate.EndOfPeriod)
MsgBox("Your payment will be " & payment.ToString("C") & " per month.",
            MsgBoxStyle.OKOnly, "Payments")
```

You can execute this code as-is. It works, though a bit clumsily. It displays
three InputBoxes that the user can respond to. Then, it displays a MsgBox
with the answer — the monthly payment for the mortgage that the user
described in the first three InputBoxes. I explain how you might improve the
code in the next section.

Improving the code in code snippets

To improve the user's experience, you can adjust the code so it's more efficient.
Also, some of the code snippets — at the time of this writing anyway — are a

bit half-baked. Notice in Listing 3-1, for instance, that `futureValue` is set to 0, but the other variables aren't. Setting variables to 0 or other variations on *null* is a reflexive habit with many C programmers, though it's actually not done in VB (it's simply not necessary). Apparently, a C programmer wrote this snippet, as is often the case in VB Help and other areas. This programmer seems to have resisted setting *every* declared variable to 0, so that's an improvement, I guess.

VB automatically initializes local variables to their default values (*local variables* are those declared within a Sub, like those used in Listing 3-1). Every time the Sub executes, all those variables are set to zero — so there's no point in setting them to zero yourself.

Customizing code snippets

After you insert a snippet, you likely see lines of code highlighted in green by default. (You can adjust the color by using Tools⇨Options⇨Environment⇨ Fonts and Colors.) In my example snippet (refer to Listing 3-1), the three InputBox lines are highlighted. If you hover your mouse pointer over a highlighted line, you get a "hint" about what you might want to do to improve the code.

In this example, the hints for all three lines say the same thing: "Replace with code that returns a Double for the . . ."

From what I've seen, the highlighted suggestions in most snippets usually merely tell you to replace the snippets' parameters with your own, as shown in Figure 3-4.

Figure 3-4:
The suggestions about highlighted text are not generally much use to you.

```
Private Sub Form1_Load(ByVal sender As System.Object, ByVal e As System.EventArgs)

    Dim loanAmount As Double
    Dim apr As Double
    Dim futureValue As Double = 0
    Dim payment As Double
    Dim totalPayments As Double

    loanAmount = CDbl(InputBox("How much do you want to borrow?"))
    apr = CDbl(InputBox("What is the annual percentage rate of your loan? Enter 8% as .08."))
    totalPayments = CDbl(InputBox("How many monthly payments will you make?"))
    payment = Pmt(apReplace with code that returns a Double for the number of payments.alue, DueDate.EndOfPeriod)
    MsgBox("Your payment will be " & payment.ToString("C") & " per month.", MsgBoxStyle.OKOnly,

End Sub
```

Here's another example: The following snippet draws a rectangle. When you insert this snippet, VB Express highlights `Color.Red` and tells you to "replace with the brush color." I think you could have figured this out for yourself.

```
Dim aBrush As New SolidBrush(Color.Red)
```

 My suggestion is that you view code snippets as a specialized section of Help, a collection of what Microsoft considers examples of common programming jobs. Of course, you could claim that figuring monthly mortgage payments isn't all that common a task, but what the heck; it's a start. And, for beginners, the section in the snippets titled Visual Basic Language does, indeed, include several often-used techniques, such as looping.

 "Wow! How can I remember the proper names for all the .NET classes, functions, and arguments?" You can't. However, VB IntelliSense features can help you figure out the proper programming syntax and diction for all those tens of thousands of built-in functions by providing you with suggestions — lists that pop up while you type a line of code in the code window, as illustrated earlier in this chapter with the `console.writeline` command.

Customizing the Way You Work

VB Express offers you a somewhat "lightened" version of the Visual Studio Editor — a powerful, well-seasoned, very convenient programming environment. I believe there's nothing better this side of heaven for writing computer programs than this IDE (integrated design environment). And, of course, it's highly customizable. The following sections walk you through some key customizations you may want to make.

Automatic windows

Microsoft does extensive usability testing, spending quite a bit of time with focus groups, poring over user-submitted wish lists, and employing other tactics to ensure that its applications and utilities are easy to use and include the features people want. To my mind, this is why its products usually succeed — why, for example, people migrated to Microsoft Word and Internet Explorer from the initially more popular competitors, WordPerfect and Netscape.

Another wise tactic Microsoft employs is to assume that it doesn't know everything (though there are certainly exceptions to this wisdom). Therefore, even if people in focus groups vote overwhelmingly for a particular feature, Microsoft generally makes that feature the default but also allows you to turn it off if you prefer. That's what many of the items in the Tools➪Options menu are: options defaulting to the general preference. But it's up to you if you want to change the default settings.

One example is that when you test a VB project by pressing F5, the Output window does not automatically pop open to show you the progress of the compilation. The Error List window, however, does open by default. These are sensible defaults for novices, perhaps, but if you don't like this behavior, you can change the defaults by following these steps:

1. **Choose Tools➪Options➪Environment (in the left pane of the Options dialog box).**

2. **Click Projects and Solutions in the left pane.**

3. **Select the Show Output Window When Build Starts check box, and the Output window automatically appears whenever you test a VB project — you rebel you.**

4. **Likewise, if you wish, uncheck the Error List option directly below the Output Window option. See if any other options suit your style.**

If you're unclear about what a given option does and would like addition help, click the ? symbol in the upper-right corner of the Options dialog box and then click the option you're unsure about.

Controlling your keyboard

As you may know, .NET represents a grand unification scheme — an attempt to bring all computer languages (or most surviving languages anyway) into the same editor; to make their objects and components usable by any other language in the group; to make them work harmoniously within the same IDE; and to provide, as much as is practical, common protocols, techniques, and tools.

Among the benefits of this drive toward unification is that the features of various applications are becoming standardized (and none too soon, either). For example, Word has offered users the capability of redefining the default keyboard shortcuts for years, and VB Express offers this same capability as well.

I've always found it useful to redefine the default behavior of the F10 key. I like to make it save all opened files. It's a quick way to ensure that my work is safe from power outages, crashes, and other computer-age annoyances. I just hit the F10 key now and then, and my work is saved.

All Microsoft applications ship with various default keyboard shortcuts. Ctrl+O, for example, usually displays the Open File dialog box. Collectively, a set of shortcuts is known as a *mapping scheme*. Clearly, life is easier if the same scheme can be used in all your applications. That's why I define the F10 key in the VB IDE as Save All Files.

Redefining keys is easy; the process in VB Express is similar to the one for Word and other Microsoft applications. The following steps explain how to customize the F10 key, and you can use a similar process to customize any other keyboard shortcut that's helpful to you:

1. **Choose Tools⇨Customize.**

   The Customize dialog box opens.

2. **Click the Keyboard button.**

   You see the Keyboard option, as shown in Figure 3-5:

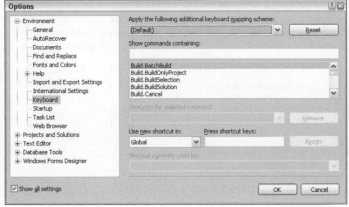

Figure 3-5:
The dialog box that you use to redefine the IDE keyboard.

3. **Scroll the list of actions and select `File.SaveAll`.**

   Note that the menu items are listed in the format *MenuTitle.Action* — in this case, the File menu and the Save All action.

4. **Click in the Press Shortcut Key(s) textbox.**

   The textbox gets the focus (the insertion cursor blinks within the textbox).

5. **Press F10.**

   `F10` appears in the Press Shortcut Key(s) textbox, and because F10 is already assigned to `Debug.Stepover`, you see that action listed in the Shortcut Currently Used By list box.

6. **Click Assign.**

7. **Click OK.**

   Now, whenever you press F10, all open files are saved.

Changing toolbars

VB permits you to add and remove items from toolbars, as well as add and remove entire toolbars from the IDE. To do this, choose Tools⇨Customize and then click a tab based on what you want to do:

- ✔ **The Commands tab** lets you manage individual items within toolbars.
- ✔ **The Toolbars tab** lets you manage entire toolbars.

Your IDE, your way

Many programmers like to arrange the IDE as shown in Figure 3-6. This layout is practical for many programmers and is close to the VB default layout — so Microsoft's focus groups must have indicated its popularity. This layout keeps only the Solution Explorer and Properties windows always visible, and the Toolbox is tabbed on the left side so that you can quickly access it.

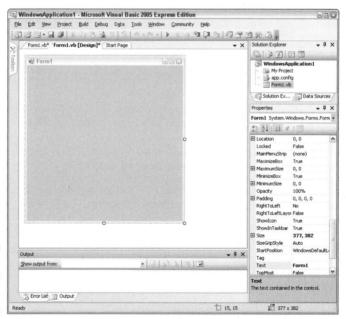

Figure 3-6:
A popular
layout.

I like to give myself even more coding room. I select the Auto Hide option from the context menus that appear when I right-click the title bar of the Solution Explorer, Properties window, and Output window. This hides them, but exposes a tab, just like the Toolbox. In this way, you have the maximum screen space for your primary work area: the design/code window.

Going back to the default layout

You can manipulate the windows within the IDE and their behaviors in various ways by dragging them or by choosing options on the Windows menu. You can tab, tile, or dock various windows and position them in various ways. If you become hopelessly confused, you can reset the layout to the default VB arrangement by choosing Tools⇨Options⇨Environment⇨ General. Click the Reset Windows Layout button to restore the default.

In that same area of the Options dialog box, you can also choose between tabbed or MDI-style child windows. (MDI stands for *multiple document interface,* and no tabs are involved; instead, you can tile various windows within the IDE.)

You can drag the various child windows around to different positions in the IDE, and you can "dock" them, meaning they attach to each other or to the frame of the IDE. (In Figure 3-6, the Solution Explorer and Properties windows are docked to each other and also to the right side of the IDE itself.) Sometimes you need to drag windows around and drop them in various ways to finally get them to dock where you want them — so you should experiment. Also, use the View menu to display other windows that you want to see.

Aligning and Sizing Controls

To illustrate yet another way that VB assists you while you're programming, take a look at the cool tools that help you position and size controls.

Controls, such as buttons and text boxes, that you add to forms aren't automatically pretty. They aren't necessarily lined up vertically or horizontally, nor are they the same size. But they should be if you want your work to look polished. VB provides some quick ways to format your controls:

- ✔ **Basic lines:** While you drag controls around on a form, lines appear when the controls are aligned, as shown in Figure 3-7.

- ✔ **Snap to Grid feature:** This feature is handy when controls on a form are haphazardly arranged. A grid sits beneath the controls on a form. The Snap to Grid feature forces controls to automatically align to this grid — like magnets jumping onto a refrigerator door.

By default, the Snap to Grid feature is turned off in the Express IDE because, I assume, it scares novices until they realize what it is (though it's also used in the Windows desktop to align icons). Anyway, you should turn it on because it makes it easier for you to drag controls into alignment. To turn the feature on, choose Tools⇨Options⇨Windows Forms Designer. Select SnapToGrid and change its value from False to True. In this dialog box, you can also adjust the size of the grid and its visibility.

Figure 3-7:
Figure 3-7:
Align your
controls by
using visual
hints, like
this line that
indicates
when the
right sides
of the
TextBox and
button are
aligned.

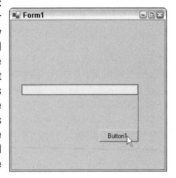

✔ **Make Same Size command:** This command actually aligns and sizes
   selected controls. To use it, drag your mouse around all the controls
   (which selects them as a group) and then choose Format⇨Align and
   Format⇨Make Same Size.

✔ **Keyboard shortcuts:** To align, click one control to select it and then
   press Ctrl+Arrow keys to move it. To resize the control, press
   Shift+Arrow keys.

Using Help

The Visual Studio Help system, to which VB Express has access, is the product of decades of refinement. Most of that refinement is useful and has pro-
duced a huge library of code examples. Alas, along with the refinement has
come some regrettable corruption as well.

Much VB Express Help documentation has been written by C programmers,
and thus the documents aren't examples you should really learn from. Some
examples are fine; others are needlessly complex.

The philosophy that guides VB is *clarity*: Make the diction, syntax,
punctuation — *everything* — as easily understood, as convenient, and as
English-language-like as possible. The C-languages, like C++ and Java, have
the opposite philosophy. They fairly celebrate obscurity, needless complexity, bizarre punctuation, and other inefficiencies that slow up programming,
but do help guarantee job security.

Alas, when you go for Help in VB Express, all too often you find jargon and confusion rather than effective help. The example is probably too long, with lots of unnecessary distractions that don't illustrate the main technique cleanly and directly. Worse, what code you do find is too often written by C programmers, so it's not actually VB code but rather a kind of hybrid somewhere between C and VB. Sure, it sometimes *runs* when you paste it into a program, but try to understand what it does and you can get quickly confused. It's hard to learn from it. And, too often, it *doesn't* run; then you're really up a tree.

That said, *some* code examples are written in a VB-like fashion — and they work — and *some* of the text descriptions are understandable — having been written by non-propellerheads who understand English and Visual Basic and who can write comprehensible sentences. So try searching Help when you run into a problem, and maybe you'll get lucky. Here are some other help resources where you may find answers to your questions:

- **The Start Page in VB Express,** under "Connecting to the Community," offers additional online resources. Click the Start Page tab at the top of the code or design pane and then find the Getting Started area on the left side.

- **In the Help page,** too, you can find links to additional resources, particularly in the Search feature — it looks both locally (on your hard drive) and online for answers to your questions. Two online resources are searched: MSDN (Microsoft Developer Network) and the "Code Wise" community.

- **On newsgroups,** the court of last resort, experts can often answer your questions when you can't find answers anywhere else. To get to the newsgroups, click the Post a Question link on the Search tab, as shown in Figure 3-8.

But don't despair — Microsoft has been trying to make VB Help better since forever — or at least since 2000, when .NET appeared and so many non-VB programmers took over the job of trying, and often failing, to write VB Help examples. Anyway, that's when *I* first noticed the turn toward C-speak in VB Help. For the past five years those in charge of VB at Microsoft have been, I assume, increasing the ratio of VB people to C people working on VB Help. So, perhaps in the future, the majority of VB Help will be written by people who actually know and understand the VB language.

Figure 3-8:
Last-resort
help can
come from
news-
groups.

Error or "Exception" Helpers

When VB Express detects an error, it sometimes points you in the right direction about how to fix the error — or at least gives you ideas about where to look for help.

Following the insipid practice of using C-language jargon, this new feature is called the *Exception Helper* — though what they mean to say is *error*, not *exception*. You can see an example of this use of *exception* in Figure 3-9.

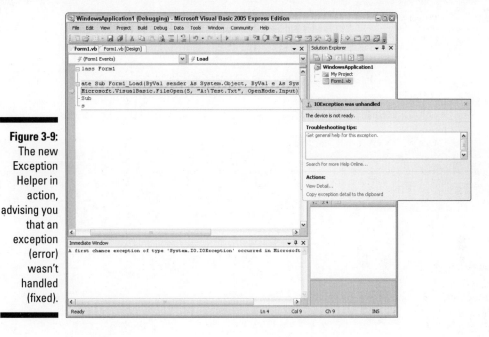

Figure 3-9:
The new
Exception
Helper in
action,
advising you
that an
exception
(error)
wasn't
handled
(fixed).

If you try to access a file that doesn't exist on the hard drive, you get the
error messages shown in Figure 3-9. A closer look at a similar message is
shown in Figure 3-10.

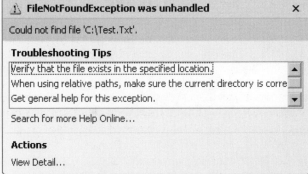

Figure 3-10:
This error is
correctly
identified
and very
good advice
is given
about how
to fix it.

Compared to previous error handlers, the new Exception Helper is a real
improvement. Not only do you avoid having to access More Details, which is
usually *less* helpful, but you also often get an actual specific, helpful description of the error itself.

Chapter 4

Tackling Essential Tools

. . . .

In This Chapter

▶ Understanding the Toolbox

▶ Examining the TextBox

▶ Adjusting properties

▶ Mastering the primary properties

▶ Using the Solution Explorer

. . . .

*T*his chapter is a tour of the primary programming tools in the main VB programming window: the Toolbox, Property window, and Solution Explorer.

Arguably the single most significant improvement in computer programming history took place in the early 1990s with the introduction of the Visual Basic Toolbox. Before that collection of components, programmers had to create the user interface mostly by hand. Buttons, textboxes, tables, and other features were time-consuming to program. With Visual Basic's Toolbox, you just drop completely functional components onto your forms (or as they're known to users, your *windows*).

You use the Property Window to adjust the qualities (the *properties*) of the tools (controls) in the Toolbox. For example, it's in the Properties Window that you can change the font size or text color for a TextBox.

The Solution Explorer is your window into the entire project. This window displays all the projects — you can have more than one — and files in your "solution." It's like a small version of Windows Explorer that's dedicated just to the program you're currently working on.

Introducing the Toolbox and Its Controls

By default, the Toolbox is a tab on the upper-left side of the main programming window. To see it,

1. Start Visual Basic Express and choose File⇨New⇨Project.

2. **Double-click the Windows Application icon.**

   Now you see the Toolbox tab in the upper left. (If you don't, choose View⇨Toolbox.)

3. **Glide your mouse pointer over the tab, and the Toolbox slides out.**

The Toolbox is where the controls (also called *components*) sit, waiting for you to double-click or drag and drop one to place it on a form. For convenience, most of the controls you'll likely use often are available in the Common Controls section in the Toolbox:

- **PictureBox:** Holds a graphic.

- **Label:** Used to add captions to PictureBoxes and other controls. This is read-only at run time; the user cannot edit a label.

- **TextBox:** Doubtless the TextBox is among the most often used Visual Basic components — second only to the Button control, I would guess. TextBoxes are used for both input and output: They display text or accept the user's typed text. However, if you're merely adding a caption to identify the purpose of, say, a CheckBox, use a Label instead. A TextBox would be overkill.

  The TextBox is so important that learning more about it is worth your time. A TextBox behaves like a simple word processor, but it does have its limitations. For instance, at any one time, it displays only a single font and a single type style (such as italics) for the entire contents. Also, it displays only one size of text at a time. You change the font, style, and size by changing the TextBox's properties — but the entire contents of the TextBox then change. You can't change a single word, for example, to italics. It's all or nothing.

  Note that the RichTextBox control on the Toolbox does not suffer from several of the ordinary TextBox's limitations. You might want to experiment with the RichTextBox if your project has special word-processing needs or if you expect to exceed the TextBox's 65,535-character (about 10,000 words) limit.

- **GroupBox:** A zone that contains other controls, most specifically a way to group RadioButtons so they work as a unit.

- **Button:** A very common control that acts like a button on an electronic device, activating something. For example, most message boxes have an OK button on them. You click it to close the message box.

- **CheckBox:** CheckBoxes usually appear in a group, allowing you to select any or all of a set of options. For example, you could display CheckBoxes to allow the user to choose text qualities: italic, bold, or underlined. Any combination of these options is permitted.

- **RadioButton:** Only one RadioButton in a group can be selected at a time, just like the row of buttons on a car radio that choose different stations. Click one button and the previously depressed button is deselected. In other words, use RadioButtons for a set of options which are mutually exclusive, such as a group of RadioButtons allowing the user to specify the text color.

✔ **ComboBox:** Similar to a ListBox, but the user can type text into a ComboBox.

✔ **ListBox:** Presents a list to the users from which they can click a selection.

Unfortunately, not *all* the most common controls are on the default view. You must scroll (click the down-arrow icon at the bottom of the Toolbox) to access the seven highly useful Dialog controls, such as the `OpenFileDialog`. I cover the dialog boxes in Chapters 7 and 10.

Also, some controls are a bit strange: The ScrollBar controls aren't of much use because the TextBox, which is most likely to need scroll bars, includes its own scroll bars. But for every dubious control, you find quite a few really useful ones.

Most controls save you quite a bit of programming time. For example, the DataGridView control is an excellent, full-featured, quick way to connect a database to your application and to display it for user interaction. And you can add many, many other controls to the Toolbox; just choose Tools⇨ Choose Toolbox Items. Precisely what controls are available here depends on various factors, such as what programs you've installed or if you've added third-party controls, for example.

If you're unclear about what a control can do, press F1 and use the Index feature in Help to look it up.

Adjusting a Control's Properties

Many Visual Basic components have quite a few properties — the TextBox has more than most — and you can change these properties, depending on how you want the control to look and work. Before you get started, it's helpful to understand a few points about properties:

✔ **You usually don't have to change very many of the default properties.** In general, each property defaults to its most commonly useful value.

For instance, all VB's controls' `Visible` properties default to `True` rather than `False` because you almost always want your components to be visible to the user. However, some controls, such as the Timer, are used internally by your program and are never made visible to the user. Those few controls have no `Visible` property at all. Also, they are not displayed on your forms. Instead, they are placed on a "tray" just below the form, visible to you, the programmer, only while designing your program.

✔ **You can change different properties at different points in the development process.** Some properties, such as the `Name` property, can be changed only at *design time* (while you're writing your program). Other properties, such as the `Text` property, can be changed during either design time or *run time* (while the program is running). Yet other properties, such as the contents of a ListBox, can be changed *only* during run time — by the programming you write that executes when the user runs the program. Every property you see in the Properties window can be set at design time.

✔ **It's important to understand that components start out with all their properties in one state or another.** The `Width` property, for example, is set to *some* width, and the `Size` property contains two numbers that specify the size of the TextBox. In any case, the conditions of the properties determine what the user first sees or how the component first behaves when the application runs.

Changing a property in the Properties window

The TextBox is such an important component that I use it as an example of how to change a control's properties. Here are the basic steps:

1. **If necessary, click the Windows Forms tab in the Toolbox (which should be selected by default). Then double-click the TextBox icon in the Toolbox.**

   A TextBox appears on your form. Also notice the Properties window in the lower-right corner of the main window.

   Now you've added a TextBox component to your form. After that, you run up against an unfortunate (and happily rare) inefficiency. Somebody back in the beginning made a bad decision about the default font size property setting for the TextBox. It's 8.5 points — way too small for most uses. Use 11 instead.

2. **If the Properties window isn't visible, choose View➪Properties Window or press F4.**

   The restless folk at Microsoft rarely see a phrase they can't "improve." So the language describing programming and other Microsoft technologies isn't stable, or even slow to change. Each new version of Microsoft products brings with it some confusing and unhelpful changes in the vocabulary used to describe the products. Since 1990, a major fixture of Visual Basic programming has been known as the *Property window.* Now, in VB Express Help, you see it described as the *Property Editor.* Perhaps this is an error; perhaps it's yet another pointless name change. You've been warned.

3. **To increase the size of the TextBox's** `Font` **property, click the TextBox to select it.**

   Selecting a control during design time causes its properties to be displayed in the Properties window.

4. **Click the** `Font` **property in the Properties window, and you see an ellipsis (. . .) button appear, indicating that there is more to see.**

5. **Click the ellipsis button to open a dialog box in which you can change several qualities of the font. Change it to 11 in the Size list and then click OK to close the dialog box.**

   Now you've got a good, usable TextBox.

If you're going to use more than one TextBox in a project, you can avoid having to adjust the font size property for each new TextBox. Simply click the TextBox that you just finished cleaning up and press Ctrl+C to copy it. Then press Ctrl+V to paste a new TextBox with all the same properties inherited from its parent. Same size, same color, same font, same everything except its position (the `Location` property specifies that it be slightly down and to the right of its parent, so you can see it) and its `Name` property, which defaults to `TextBox2`. (The original was `TextBox1`.)

Some important properties (and many that aren't)

This section dives into the TextBox's properties, covering each major property in turn. A total of 53 properties appear in the Properties window when a TextBox has the focus (is clicked and therefore is surrounded on the form by a frame with white boxes at each corner). Many of these properties are also properties of other components, as well as being properties of forms. So you're going to find out about the uses and features of some important, common properties by looking through the following descriptions. But don't worry about memorizing most of them. Most of them are — to put it politely — rarefied.

For example, the `BackColor` property is fairly universal — most components have this property so that you can change their color. But a major lesson I hope you internalize from the following in-depth sections is that the majority of properties are rarely used. I tell you which ones are valuable and which ones you can usually just forget.

Some of the TextBox properties, such as the `Font` property, include a set of additional properties (size, bold, underline, and so on). These multi-property collections are indicated in the Properties window by a small + next to the primary property name. When clicked, this + reveals an ellipsis (. . .) button. When you click the ellipsis button, a dialog box opens in which you can edit the settings for the group of properties.

The following list is in the alphabetical order that you see in the Properties window if you click the Alphabetic icon (the little "AZ") at the top of the Properties window, which I suggest you do. After all, the default categorized view is a pretty loose set of often misleading groupings. At least that's my view.

DataBindings

The DataBindings property is used to attach a control to a database. Chapter 12 covers this property in detail.

Name

This is the ID for your component. It's how you specify it when writing code:

```
TextBox1.Text = "Hello"
```

Some programmers like to use the default names that VB gives each control when the control is added to the form. Others like to change the Name property in the Properties window to more accurately describe the purpose of the control, such as ZipcodeField for a TextBox in which the user is supposed to enter her zip code.

In the Properties window, DataBindings and Name are placed within parentheses. The parentheses force these two important properties to the top of the list whether you show the Properties window in Alphabetical or Categorized view.

AcceptsReturn, AcceptsTab

The AcceptsReturn and AcceptsTab properties describe how VB reacts to the user pressing the Enter (Return) and Tab keys. By default, pressing Enter moves you down to the next line in a MultiLine-style TextBox. If you set AcceptsReturn to False, pressing Enter causes a simulated mouse-click on the default button on the form. If you set AcceptsTab to True, a tab (move over five spaces) is inserted into the text when the user presses Tab. If you set it to False, pressing Tab moves you to the next control on the form, according to the TabIndex property (described later in this section).

Accessibility

The three new Accessibility properties provide features for people with disabilities.

AllowDrop

AllowDrop determines whether a TextBox permits drag-and-drop operations.

Anchor

Anchor is a valuable property. It determines whether and how a control stretches if the user stretches the form. The default Anchor value for the TextBox is Top, Left — which means that the TextBox doesn't enlarge or shrink if the user drags the form to resize it. To allow a user to resize a TextBox, click Anchor in the Properties window, click the down-arrow icon, and then click all four of the image map edges. Press F5 to run the program and you can see the TextBox grow and shrink as you drag the form to resize it.

AutoCompleteCustomSource, AutoCompleteMode, AutoCompleteSource

Word and other text-input applications offer users shorthand abbreviations that are automatically completed by the application. For example, in Word, you can choose Tools⇨Autocorrect Options and then do what I do and enter n as the shortcut and Richard Mansfield as the AutoCompletion phrase. That way, every time I need to type my name, I can just type n and press the spacebar. Word substitutes my entire name for the *n*.

AutoCompleteMode works somewhat like that. If you're creating a database program and you expect that users will often have to type in a filepath, Internet address, or some other predictable text, set the AutoCompleteSource property to CustomSource and the AutoCompleteMode to Append or Suggest. Then type some phrases or addresses into the AutoCompleteCustomSource property. At the time of this writing, this feature is not yet activated.

AutoRelocate

Some controls can "bump" themselves out of the way, moving a bit to remain visible if another control is dragged onto them or otherwise overlaps them. This property enables a control to move in such situations. AutoRelocate is not yet working at the time of this writing.

AutoSize

AutoSize determines whether the size of the TextBox changes to accommodate any changes in the font or font size.

BackColor

If you want to, you can change a TextBox's BackColor property to pink or blue or some other color (but it's best to leave it white in most applications). Similarly, you can change the text color by adjusting the ForeColor property. Again, you should probably leave well enough alone. The default black text on a white background is not only more legible, it's also more dignified.

BorderStyle

Leave the `BorderStyle` (formerly `Appearance`) property alone. It provides part of the 3-D framing effect. If you change it to `FixedSingle`, you turn back time so that the user interface looks like it was designed before Windows 95. If you set it to the third option, `None`, you go back even further in time — regressing all the way to DOS.

CausesValidation

The `CausesValidation` property can remain set to `True` with no harm done. When set to `True`, the `Validate` event is triggered when the focus shifts from the TextBox to another component (when the user clicks it or tabs to it). This property comes in handy only with database work — forget about it for now.

CharacterCasing

The `CharacterCasing` property can be set to force all text to be lowercase, uppercase, or mixed.

ContextMenuStrip

You can add context menu controls to your form from the Toolbox. A particular context menu control can be assigned to a control by specifying the context menu's `Name` property in the `ContextMenuStrip` property.

Controls

`Controls` is a new property that represents a collection of any child controls within the current control. `Controls` isn't listed in the Properties window, but it is in the IntelliSense list, the list of properties and methods that pops out when you type the following into the code window:

```
TextBox1.
```

As soon as you type the `.`, VB displays the list of possible members you can add after that period to access qualities (properties) and behaviors (methods, such as Hide or Clear) of the TextBox.

Cursor

The `Cursor` property is what used to be called the `MouseIcon` property, and it determines what the mouse pointer looks like when it is on top of the TextBox. I advise against changing this property unless you're sure you won't confuse the user.

Dock

`Dock` determines whether the control moves to one of several positions within its container (the form). Changing this property also changes the size of the control.

Enabled

The Enabled property, if set to False, prevents users from typing anything into the TextBox (which is said to be *disabled*). Any text already in the TextBox appears light gray rather than the default black to indicate that the TextBox is disabled.

You should disable a component when it makes no sense for the user to try to use it. For example, suppose you have several TextBoxes on a form on which the user is supposed to fill in data about himself, and he fills in the TextBox for his age with 44 years. You could then disable a check box in which he is supposed to indicate whether he is a member of AARP. You have to be over 50 to join AARP, so it makes no sense to leave that check box enabled. Enabled is often used in programming in response to situations like the one described in this AARP example. The code for this is TextBox1.Enabled = False.

Font, ForeColor

Font defines the typeface, such as Times New Roman or Arial. Font also includes such typeface features as boldface and italic. ForeColor defines the color of the text characters.

GenerateMember

This is some more OOP stuff. You'll probably never use it, but I can't promise that. I have no idea what the Help description is trying to say. It uses phrases like "type definition," "root object," "member variables," and "extender property." This kind of talk has lots of meaning to OOP geeks, but is of little use to most of us normal, ordinary programmers. Perhaps, by the time the Help system is finalized, somebody who writes English sentences will have translated the geekspeak so you and I can understand it. Then again, probably not.

HideSelection

The HideSelection property is yet another highly esoteric option. Text can be selected within a TextBox — by programming (as is done by a spell-checker to signal a misspelled word) or by the user dragging the mouse over some text. In either case, the text is highlighted. HideSelection, when set to False, means that selected text in your TextBox remains highlighted, even if the TextBox loses the focus (meaning that the user clicks some other form to give it the focus).

I can't really think of a use for this HideSelection property, and, as you've seen in this chapter, some other properties are just like it: highly specialized. I suggest that you not clutter your brain trying to memorize these rare birds. What you do need to remember is that VB contains hundreds of programming features, and if you want to do something highly specialized, you probably can. The way to find out how to accomplish your specific goal is to press F1, click the Search Tab in Help, and type some words that describe your highly specialized job. Unlike the Help Index feature (which locates major topics), the Search feature reads through the entire Help file, looking for specialized words or phrases.

ImeMode

This handles katakana and other aspects of Japanese writing. If you're like me, you find this a puzzling feature, and have serious doubts about its utility in your future work.

Lines

The `Lines` property is a collection (an array) of the individual lines of text in the TextBox. Each line is distinct from the previous line because the user pressed Enter to move down. You can access the individual lines by using code like this:

```
Dim x as String
x = TextBox1.Lines(2)
```

This example code puts the third line down from the top of the TextBox into variable x. Note that `(2)` represents the *third* line and not the second — it's the old "zeroth" problem in computer language lists: The first line of text is Line 0.

Location

The `Location` property, with its `X` (horizontal position) and `Y` (vertical position) attributes, replaces the previous `Left` and `Top` properties. However, you can still use `Left` and `Top` in your code, oddly enough, but they don't appear in the Properties window, consistency being the hobgoblin of little minds.

You can adjust these `X` and `Y` properties in the Properties window, or, to move a control dynamically during run time, you can add code like this to your programming code:

```
TextBox1.Left = 14
```

Locked

The `Locked` property is similar to, but less drastic than, setting the `Enabled` property to `False`. When set to `True`, `Locked` permits the TextBox's text to be scrolled, and even highlighted, by the user. It also permits you, the programmer, to change the text: `TextBox1.Text = "This new text."` The text is not changed to a gray color. However, as when `Enabled` is set to `False`, the user can't edit the text.

Margin

Specifies the space between the control and other controls on a Form. Try adding a couple of controls to a form and then setting one of their `Margin` properties to 12 or so. See what happens when you try to drag the control near another control (a dotted line appears when the margin is reached). The `Margin` property defaults to 3 pixels.

MaximumSize

`MaximumSize` specifies in pixels how large (width, height) the control can be resized.

MaxLength

The `MaxLength` property lets you specify the maximum number of characters the user can enter into the TextBox. This is useful if you want users to enter information such as a zip code, the length of which you know in advance. The default length is 32,767 characters.

Modified

The `Modified` property tells you whether the text has been changed by the user since the TextBox was created or since you last set the `Modified` property to `False`. `Modified` doesn't appear in the Properties window but can be used in your programming code to detect whether you need to save the contents of the TextBox to disk (because it has been edited by the user).

Modifiers

The `Modifiers` property simply drops down a list of the various scope declaration keywords: `friend`, `public`, and so on. This specifies which categories of other objects can communicate with the control. For details about *scoping*, see Chapter 5.

MinimumSize

Same as MaximumSize, except it specifies how small the control can be.

MouseIcon

The traditional `MouseIcon` property has been renamed `Cursor`, which I discuss earlier in this chapter. I mention this only for experienced programmers who expect to find `MouseIcon` still in the list of properties.

MultiLine

The `MultiLine` property determines whether the TextBox can display more than one line of text. If set to `False`, users can type in as much text as they wish, but the Enter key won't work. If the text grows longer than the width of the TextBox, it scrolls horizontally as the user types.

Padding

This specifies the distance between a control's contents and its frame or border. It defaults to zero pixels, but a TextBox in particular looks more professional if you give it around 5 pixels padding, so the text doesn't butt up against the sides of the box.

PasswordChar

The PasswordChar property lets you specify which character appears when the user types a password. In other words, if you want to use a TextBox as a password entry field for the user, you can type a * symbol as the PasswordChar. If you type in any character as the PasswordChar, the TextBox displays only that character as users type their passwords (for example, **********). You know the routine. (I've always wondered whether this subterfuge is all that necessary — after all, do you have people hovering over your shoulder all the time, just waiting to see your password? I suppose it's better to hide it though — there are lurkers.) Note that the MultiLine property must be set to False for the password feature to work properly. Unless you're specifically using a TextBox for password entry, leave this property alone, empty.

ReadOnly

The ReadOnly property at first seems baffling. When set to True, the text in the TextBox can only be "read," not changed. ReadOnly seems rather unnecessary, given that the Enabled property does the same thing. The difference? With Enabled = True and ReadOnly = False, the text in the TextBox can at least be copied.

RightToLeft

For an English speaker, the RightToLeft property has no value and should be left at its default. However, some languages, such as Arabic and Hebrew, run text from right to left. You would set RightToLeft when using such languages so that vertical scroll bars appear on the left side of a TextBox.

Scrollbars

The Scrollbars property enables you to add a horizontal or vertical scroll bar to your TextBox so that users can scroll through a block of text that is larger than the size of the TextBox. However, even without scroll bars, the user can always press the arrow keys, the PgUp and PgDn keys, the spacebar, and so on to move through text in the TextBox.

ShortcutsEnabled

Defaulting to True, this property allows you to turn off the familiar (and sometimes not so) shortcut key combinations, such as Ctrl+C to copy selected text. Why you would want to deprive users of their accustomed shortcut keys is a mystery to me.

The Cheat Sheet at the front of this book lists the common shortcut key combinations.

Size

The traditional, classic, pre-VB `Height` and `Width` properties are no longer available. They have been replaced with a `Size` property that includes — what shall we call them? — a pair of "subproperties" named `Height` and `Width`. Size is expressed by default in pixels. Experiment by changing the size property to see the effect on a control.

TabIndex

The `TabIndex` property defines the order in which components get focus as the user repeatedly presses the Tab key to move among them.

`TabIndex` is useful because it offers a quick way for the user to move among the input components (TextBoxes, CheckBoxes, and so forth) on a form — all without having to remove his or her hands from the keyboard. However, some components, such as a PictureBox, are not usually employed as user-input devices, so you can set their `TabStop` properties to `False` to eliminate them from the `TabIndex` group. Components such as `Labels`, which can never be used as input devices, simply have no `TabIndex` property in the first place and are therefore never included in the tabbing.

Sometimes, though, you do want to permit a PictureBox to become part of the `TabIndex` list so that the user can interact with it. How can a PictureBox ever be used as an input device, you ask? A simple example is when you put some programming into the PictureBox's `Click` event. When the picture is clicked or, in this case, when the user tabs to it and presses Enter, something happens. You might display several small PictureBoxes, each containing a different image — perhaps a car, a bus, a train, and a plane. When the user clicks one, a phone number for arranging that kind of transportation appears.

Here's a more sophisticated example: Put a map of Italy into a PictureBox in a cookbook application, let users click a location on the map, and then display a list of recipes typical to the locale that was clicked. (The *x* and *y* coordinates for the `MouseDown` event tell you exactly where, on a graphic, the user clicked.)

TabStop

The `TabStop` property, when set to `False`, removes the component from the `TabIndex` list.

Tag

The `Tag` property is a kind of sticky note that you can attach to a component. You can type in some unique text as a way of identifying the component when it is passed to a procedure. `Tag` is also sometimes used like a little cookie — the Internet type, not the scrumptious snack type — holding some information that is supposed to stick with the control and always be available.

Text

The `Text` property contains the text in the TextBox. It's similar to a string variable, and you can programmatically read it:

```
Dim s As String
s = TextBox1.Text
```

or write text to it:

```
Dim s As String = "Here's some text"
TextBox1.Text = s
```

TextAlign

The new `TextAlign` (formerly `Alignment`) property offers three alternatives to the traditional left-justify (default) text alignment. You can center or right-justify the text, but such adjustments are rarely of any use (unless you specialize in wedding invitations, in which the centered alignment is always the necessary style).

UseSystemPasswordChar

This is . . . what shall we call it? . . . *specialized*? If set to `True`, it overrules the `PasswordChar` property (if any) and instead specifies that some other character should be used instead (perhaps a hyphen rather than your `PasswordChar` "*" or whatever). Why this matters at *all* to *anyone* is hard to understand.

UseWaitCursor

The WaitCursor is the small hourglass icon that replaces the normal mouse arrow pointer when the computer is busy, such as when loading a long file. Set this property to `True` in your code if some lengthy process prevents the user from interacting with your application or TextBox. It alerts the user that the computer has not frozen, but is quite busy temporarily. (Of course, if the program *is* locked up, that hourglass still shows up.)

Visible

The `Visible` property determines whether the user can see the TextBox. During design time, components are always visible. But during run time, if you set the `Visible` property to `False`, the user can't see the component. When would you want to make a component invisible? Read on.

Although it's not traditional, Microsoft and other developers recently started employing a new way of interacting with users. For example, if the user clicks a button labeled "Additional Features," the button is set to `Visible = False` and is replaced with two or three `RadioButtons` from which the user can select additional preferences. Those RadioButtons were always sitting there, but their Visible property was False until the user clicked the button, revealing them.

A second use for Visible is when you want to use a feature of a component, but you don't want the user to see that component. The most frequent use of this trick is to employ an invisible ListBox. ListBoxes can alphabetize. You can assign a list of names to a ListBox, set its Sorted property to True, and it organizes the names for you. However, users never need to see this ListBox if they don't need to interact with it. You just wanted to borrow the alphabetizing capability of the ListBox control.

WordWrap

The WordWrap property mystifies me. I can't imagine why you would ever want to set it to False. (Our tech editor, whom I esteem, says he sometimes uses it to make lines of formatted text, such as programming code, easier to read.) Do so, and if users type a line longer than the width of the TextBox, instead of automatically moving to the line below, the text scrolls off to the left to accommodate the super-long line they're typing. This is the way a TextBox behaves if its MultiLine property is set to False. Why you would do it with MultiLine set to True (creating a TextBox that *can* display multiple lines) is beyond me. When WordWrap is set to True, if the user presses Enter, a new line of text begins.

Enabling Users to Change Properties

Many applications allow the user to adjust some of its qualities — the default font, the colors, the position of toolbars, and so on. Obviously, any changes that the user is permitted to make must be stored on the hard drive. If not, the user has to repeat the selection every time the program runs.

Application Settings is a new feature, not found in previous versions of VB, and it's supposed to be a *convenient* way to save information between run times. Here's the problem that the Application Settings feature attempts to solve: Where do you store user preferences?

Also, the application itself might want to store certain types of data separate from the application's own executable file. Adjusting data (such as an Internet address for Help) in a separate file is marginally easier than recompiling the entire application's executable file if that address is embedded within the application's source code. But for this dubious convenience, you pay a pretty stiff price in having to deal with the complicated Application Settings technology.

How do you load and save user or application settings if you want to allow users to change, for example, the color of the text? With the Application Settings feature, it's ridiculously complex. You have to create a class, create properties, import a namespace, and on and on. On top of that, VB itself creates around 60 lines of programming code to help accomplish this simple job. To see this horror story, click the Show All Files icon at the top of the Solution Explorer and then locate and double-click `MySettings.vb` (it's listed under `MySettings.settings`).

Unless Microsoft vastly simplifies it, I suggest you avoid using this monstrous, overwrought Application Settings technology entirely. Unless you're creating a major business application with all kinds of complicated requirements, Application Settings is horrifying overkill. It's one of many evidences that Object Oriented Programming promotes code bloat and makes fantastic, and often pointless, demands on the programmer. If you're merely trying to save some initialization values, using Application Settings is way more effort and difficulty than you need. It's like using a wind tunnel to shuffle a deck of cards. Messy, unnecessary, and, in the final analysis, rather stupid.

Working Around Application Settings

Instead of using Application Settings, just create a little file of your own that stores any initialization information on the user's hard drive. Save the data in a file named, perhaps, `InitInfo.txt` or `Initialization.ini`, in the same folder where the application resides. Then, in the Form1_Load event (the first form that loads when the program executes), just open the file, read in the settings, and apply them to the appropriate controls. Here's an example that shows you how to save and read text size and color information from such a custom file.

```
Private Sub Form1_Load(ByVal sender As System.Object, ByVal e As
        System.EventArgs) Handles MyBase.Load

    TextBox1.Text = "Sample text..."

    Dim a As String

    Dim sr As New System.IO.StreamReader("c:\InitInfo.txt")
    a = sr.ReadLine
    Dim s1 As Single = CSng(a)
    Dim fnt As New Font("Times New Roman", s1)
    TextBox1.Font = fnt

    'get the color
    a = sr.ReadLine
    Dim c As Color
    c = System.Drawing.Color.FromName(a)
    TextBox1.ForeColor = c
```

```
     sr.Close()

     TextBox1.Select(0, 0) 'turn off TextBox selection bug

End Sub
```

And to save the current status of the size and color properties when the program shuts down (in case the user modifies them):

```
Private Sub Form1_FormClosing(ByVal sender As Object, ByVal e As
         System.Windows.Forms.FormClosingEventArgs) Handles Me.FormClosing

    Dim sw As New System.IO.StreamWriter("C:\InitInfo.txt")

    'each time you WriteLine, a carriage return (Enter keypress)
    'is added automatically
    sw.WriteLine("42")
    sw.WriteLine("yellow")
    sw.Close()

End Sub
```

To test this example, use Notepad to create a file and save it as `C:\InitInfo.txt`. This is how the file should look in Notepad:

```
23
blue
```

The first line specifies the font size; the second, the color. Be sure to press Enter after the color to add a carriage return character to the end of the file.

Now press F5 in VB to execute the program. It should read the `23` and `blue` information and change the TextBox's properties. Stop the program, which should cause `42` and `yellow` to replace the original `23` and `blue` in the `.txt` file. Now press F5 to run the program again and see the text change size and color.

A more complex but flexible Application Settings workaround

If you want to get fancy and use the more complicated `TextFieldParser` object — which looks through data separated by any kind of delimiter (separator), not just a carriage return — substitute this next Form_Load code for the simpler StreamReader in the preceding section. Although more complicated, this approach adds flexibility because `TextFieldParser` has features that specialize in parsing text:

```
Private Sub Form1_Load(ByVal sender As System.Object, ByVal e As
        System.EventArgs) Handles MyBase.Load

    TextBox1.Text = "Sample text..."

Using aParser As New System.Text.Parsing.TextFieldParser("c:\ InitInfo.txt")

    aParser.TextFieldType = System.Text.Parsing.FieldType.Delimited

        ' the vbCr means that the data -- size, then color -- are
        'separated by carriage return characters.
        'In other words, each item of data is on its own separate line
        'in the .txt file
        aParser.Delimiters = New String() {vbCr}

        Dim s As String()

        Try
            'get the size
            s = aParser.ReadFields()
            Dim s1 As Single = CSng(s(0))
            Dim fnt As New Font("Times New Roman", s1)
            TextBox1.Font = fnt

            'get the color
            s = aParser.ReadFields()
            Dim c As Color
            c = System.Drawing.Color.FromName(s(0))
            TextBox1.ForeColor = c

        Catch ex As System.Text.Parsing.MalformedLineException
            MsgBox("There was a problem with the data: " & ex.Message)
        End Try
    End Using

    TextBox1.Select(0, 0) 'turn off TextBox selection bug

End Sub
```

Storing persistent data: Its various hideouts

In the beginning of IBM-style computing (mid-1980s), data that needed to be saved for future use was stored in an .INI file (for *ini*tialization, because the program read the settings described in that file when it first started executing). Then the Registry was invented as a way to deal with the problem of users accidentally erasing, renaming, moving, or setting fire to .INI files. The Registry was also supposed to avoid the file inflation resulting from dozens of .INI files.

A little problem with OOP taxonomies

Some contemporary OOP libraries, including the .NET framework underlying VB Express and all the other .NET languages, are rife with nonsense. You often find that to accomplish nearly the same task requires that you write radically different programming code.

One major problem with OOP libraries is that you have to learn new, unique taxonomic "addresses," interrelationships, and coding approaches for each programming task. There's too little consistency, so there are few rules you can study and then apply across tasks. In other words, in the example code in the section, "A more complex but flexible Application Settings workaround," it appears that one set of Microsoft programmers took one approach to changing the Color property of a TextBox, and a different group of programmers took an entirely different approach to changing the FontSize property of a TextBox (and other objects). Although these two tasks are identical, the code you must write to accomplish them is profoundly different.

Compare, if you will, the difference in programming code between the way you change the font size property:

```
Dim fnt As New Font("Verdana", 22)
TextBox1.Font = fnt
```

and the way you change the font color property:

```
Dim c As Color
c = System.Drawing.Color.FromName("blue")
TextBox1.ForeColor = c
```

You're doing *exactly* the same thing in both tasks, namely, changing a property of this

TextBox's text. But you must write programming for these identical tasks in vastly different ways. Each situation must be learned individually. It's horribly inefficient.

To change the size, you

1. Use the New command.
2. Provide an argument list.
3. Don't have to provide a namespace.
4. Apply an object's property.

But to change the color, you:

1. *Don't* use the New command.
2. *Don't* provide an argument list.
3. *Must* provide a namespace.
4. Apply an object's *method*, not a property.

Don't try to understand all the inner workings of the code in this example. (I don't pretend to understand all of it either, and I've been writing books and articles about .NET for 5 years now, and writing about the BASIC language for 20 years.) Studying these variations in syntax won't advance your general understanding of other .NET classes unless you're entirely a novice. Just take a monkey-see, monkey-do approach and plug these code examples into one of your programs if you need to change font size or color. *Don't* try to make sense of these variations in syntax. The system is almost entirely senseless, so you'd be wasting your time.

However, the Registry also has its problems and inefficiencies. What's more, it can be damaged, renamed, destroyed, corrupted, or set ablaze. Lately the fashion has been swinging back again to individualized initialization files (though this time they're kept in the same folder as the application itself, and they usually don't get named .ini).

Similar files are used to hold data between your visits to a Web site. Property "bags" work on the server side, and *cookies* do the job on the user's computer.

Just to be different, VB Express stores its initialization data in files with a .config extension (app.config, for example). I suggest you avoid looking in these files — they're written in XML, which is so verbose that it uses over 1,200 bytes to store the simple size of a TextBox. Size is described like this: 145, 220 — the width and height — and this information *could* be stored in two bytes, but never mind. XML is a current craze among computer professionals. Just ignore it and let VB Express worry about building the XML file for you — it's automatic and way, way too tedious for you to bother trying to do by hand.

But do tell your users not to erase, move, rename, set ablaze, or otherwise touch any files with a .config extension. In fact, the best advice is to tell them to stay the heck away from your folder altogether.

Changing a property with the Application Settings feature

So, the Application Settings "property" stores initialization data, if any. The Applications Settings dialog box displays 46 TextBox properties.

To modify a property during design time (while creating your program rather than while it executes), follow these steps:

1. **Click the + next to (ApplicationSettings) in the Properties window.**

   A new property, PropertyBinding, is revealed in the window.

2. **Click PropertyBinding.**

   An ellipsis button appears.

3. **Click the ellipsis button.**

   The Application Settings dialog box appears, as shown in Figure 4-1.

Figure 4-1:
This new feature stores initialization data for your application.

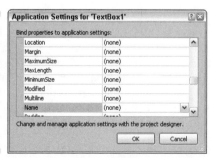

4. **Click the `BorderStyle` property in the dialog box.**

   A down-arrow button appears. This button serves the same purpose as the ellipsis button — it reveals a set of options. However, this is a mini dialog box rather than a group of properties for a component. So apparently a different icon needs to be on the button. Whatever.

5. **Click the down-arrow button.**

   You see a mini dialog box.

6. **Click the New link in the mini dialog box.**

   The New Application Setting dialog box appears, in which you can add an application setting, as you can see in Figure 4-2.

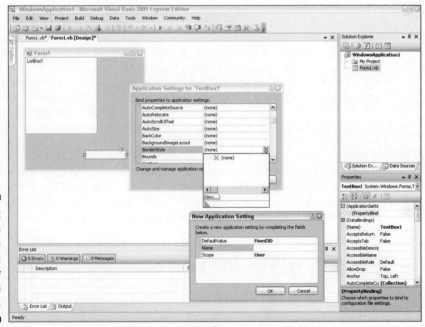

Figure 4-2: Here's where you define a new application setting.

7. **Choose Fixed3D as the default value for your border style.**

8. **Enter a name for this setting.**

   This is similar to choosing a name for a variable or a file. Pick any name that has some meaning to you.

9. **Click OK.**

   The New Application Setting dialog box closes.

10. **Click OK.**

    The ApplicationSetting dialog box closes.

The decision to choose Application or User for the scope option visible in Step 8 above determines how the settings are accessed. An *Application* scope means that the property is set this way for all users of the application, and therefore isn't changeable by the users (who would thus step on each other's toes). A *User* scope is specific to each user, and thus you can give users the option, if you wish, of changing the property.

Understanding the Solution Explorer

Most VB programmers keep three primary windows visible at all times: the design/code window, the Properties window, and the Solution Explorer (see them all in Figure 4-2).

The Solution Explorer is the overall "forest" view of your application's various "trees." It's the largest-scale view. You can have several files associated with each program (or *project,* as they're described by Microsoft) that you write. For example, each form is a separate file, as are other files associated with a project, such as a user.config file, a graphics file for a PictureBox, and so on. The category above files is the *project* — generally a complete utility or application. And above the project is the largest category of all: the *solution.* It can include more than one project.

To see the contents of a file, just double-click it in the Solution Explorer. By default — so as not to confuse you with unnecessary behind-the-scenes details — the Solution Explorer hides most of its support (or *dependency*) files. To see the whole scary group of files, click the Show All Files icon at the top of the Solution Explorer pane.

Adding other files

Most files are added to the Solution Explorer automatically when you start a new project or as you add features to it that require additional files. However, you can manually add various kinds of files to a solution if you wish. They show up in the Solution Explorer along with any of VB's existing files.

For instance, perhaps you want to add a little documentation that describes your solution. To add an ordinary text file to your solution, follow these steps:

1. **Right-click the solution's name in the Solution Explorer (the solution name is always the one in boldface).**

   A context menu appears.

2. **Choose Add⇨New Item from the context menu.**

   The Add New Item dialog box appears.

3. **Double-click the Text File icon.**

   Your new text file appears, ready for you to type into it (and it also appears with the default name `TextFile1.txt` in the Solution Explorer).

Finding your solution

When you add a new file (of any kind) to your project, it is stored on the hard drive in the same directory as all the other files in that project. The directory name is the same as the name of your project (the boldface item in Solution Explorer). A typical path is: `C:\My Documents\Visual Studio\Projects\`*`SolutionName`* (such as `WindowsApplication1`).

Alternatively, you may find the solution in a path like this: `C:\Documents and Settings\Richard Mansfield\My Documents\Visual Studio Projects\WindowsApplication2`. However, you can put your VB.NET projects anywhere you want to. You can even move them to a different computer entirely. Just copy the entire folder and its sub-folders.

To see exactly where a solution is located on a network or your local computer, just choose File⇨Save *Form1.vb.* Then use the Save As dialog box to locate the solution. You could drop the listbox to view the location, or use the dialog box's Up One Level button.

Throughout this book, you work with the Solution Explorer in various ways to view your projects' files and perform other tasks.

Part II
Programming the Practical Way

The 5th Wave   By Rich Tennant

@RICHTENNANT

"You might want to adjust the value of your 'Nudge' function."

In this part . . .

Part II is all about the basics, the fundamentals of Basic programming itself. You discover the major techniques: using procedures, programming inside events, managing scope, looping, and branching. In addition, this part includes an introduction to the new Express My object, a more efficient way to manage various common tasks — particularly file and directory management. You also explore variables, arrays, printing, debugging, and deployment.

Chapter 5

Common Tasks

*I*n this chapter, you see how to handle several very useful, and very common, programming tasks. You find out how to use *procedures* (subroutines, Events, and functions), along with their parameters (also called arguments). You also explore the concept of *range of influence* or *scope*. Finally, you play around with the important techniques of looping (repetitions) and branching (decision-making).

Mastering Events

Functions, subroutines, and Events are all *procedures* — the primary way that programming is organized. Nearly all your programming code is enclosed within procedures — mainly within Events, but sometimes also within subroutines or functions that you write outside the built-in Events.

Much programming is a response to user requests — the user clicks a button, opens a new window (form), or otherwise interacts with your program. Whatever response your program should make to a particular button click, you write that programming in that button's Click event. For example, your form may have a button displaying the word *Exit* that is supposed to end your program if the user clicks it. Double-click this button and put the `end` command inside the procedure:

```
Private Sub Button1_Click(ByVal sender As System.Object, ByVal e As
          System.EventArgs) Handles Button1.Click

End

End Sub
```

Technical Point: Some programmers refer to events as *event handlers*, pointing out that the actual event is the user, for example, clicking a button rather than the event *handler* code that responds to that click. However, for practical purposes, the click and the response are essentially simultaneous, and so feel free to call the programming code *the event*. I do.

Using Subroutines

Sometimes you add your own subroutines to the Event subs that VB automatically inserts into the code window. You can put your own procedures at the very end of a form (but just above the `End Class` line). Simpler, shorter programs can have all their code within Events. You normally add subs, or functions, to larger more complex programs.

`Sub` announces that you are creating a subroutine, a structure that in many ways is like adding a new command to Visual Basic. A subroutine is like a little program within your larger program — it performs some limited task and is available to be called upon to execute that task from anywhere in the program.

Typically, you write subroutines to save yourself from having to repeat the same instructions over and over in various locations in your program. Instead, if there is some task that you'll need to have done repeatedly from different places in your program (such as printing a list), you create a single, general-purpose list-printing routine within a single subroutine — and then just "call" that procedure wherever else in this program the job needs to be done. Thus, writing a subroutine is something like adding a new command to VB, a command that your program needs to use repeatedly but that doesn't come supplied with the language.

You can write your subs at the bottom of a form (just *above* the `End Class` line). Located here, they are easily available for use by any code in their own form. Often, though, you put Subs into Modules by choosing Project⇨Add Module. Find out more about this idea of *availability* (or *scope*) later in this chapter, in "Understanding Scope."

Modules are similar to Forms, but they never become visible and have no Events because they have no Controls. Instead, the purpose of a Module is to contain Subroutines or Functions and to declare Variables or Arrays with the `Public` command. Modules make these available to the entire program, or *global in scope* (as opposed to *local* to a particular form, or even more local to a particular procedure).

Writing a simple sub

You can create a subroutine by simply naming it and entering a line or lines of programming in it. To see how to create a new subroutine, type this line into a form, just above the `End Class` line:

```
Sub testit
```

As soon as you press Enter, Visual Basic makes room for this subroutine and adds both the `End Sub` command and ( ) if you didn't add them. (Every Sub has parentheses in case you'll want to *pass* some information — called an *argument* or *parameter* — to it when you use it.)

Now you can put commands into the Sub structure just as you would into an ordinary Event:

```
Sub testit()
    MsgBox("A new Sub")
End Sub
```

From some other place in the program, you activate this sub merely by using the Sub's name, like this:

```
Private Sub Form1_Load(ByVal sender As System.Object, ByVal e As
          System.EventArgs) Handles MyBase.Load

    testit()

End Sub
```

Press F5 to execute this program, and you see that your sub was triggered and did its job of displaying a message.

Passing parameters

Data is often passed from the "caller" to a procedure. Perhaps your program frequently needs to display message boxes to the user, but the messages differ from time to time. You can make the `testit()` sub more useful, more general purpose, by not including the actual message text in the sub itself. Instead, whenever a caller (code outside the sub) uses the sub, have the caller pass whatever message you need to display. Change the previous example sub to this:

```
Sub testit(ByVal s As String)
    MsgBox(s)
End Sub
```

You don't have to write that `ByVal`. Just type `s as string` and VB automatically inserts the `ByVal` command that someone at Microsoft long ago thought had to be inserted into every argument list. If you go on to become a programming guru, you'll want to investigate the alternative to ByVal (which is called ByRef). For now, just ignore it.

When you're writing a procedure, you can list item(s) of data that are to be sent (or "passed") to that procedure. This data is called the procedure's *arguments*. If more than one argument is being sent, it's called an *argument list*.

Just to spice things up, when you send data (from the command that calls the procedure), that passed data isn't called arguments, it's called the parameters that you're passing. This distinction — rather a fine distinction, to be sure — nonetheless helps you identify the behavior in your source code. In other words, are you currently *sending* a parameter or *receiving* an argument?

Now try an experiment where you change the caller (the line of code that "calls" or employs a procedure) to *pass the parameter* (or *argument*), which means passing some data. In this case, the data is "Call Home":

```
Private Sub Form1_Load(ByVal sender As System.Object, ByVal e As
            System.EventArgs) Handles MyBase.Load

    testit("Call Home")

End Sub
```

Using Functions

Functions are essentially the same as subroutines, but functions not only accept parameters (incoming data), they can also optionally *send data back to the caller.*

Many functions are built into Visual Basic, but they're now called *methods.* For example, the entire .NET Framework is made up of tens of thousands of functions you can use, along with some subroutines as well. But the Framework is mostly functions. For example, the simple MsgBox command — like most other commands you use in the VB Express language — is a function. You just use its name, MsgBox, provide it with some data (the argument, such as "Hello!"), and the function (or method) does its job:

```
MsgBox ("Hello")
```

This particular built-in function doesn't return any data, but consider the InputBox function, which does return something:

```
Dim s As String

s = InputBox("What's your name?")

Debug.WriteLine(s)
```

Run this, and whatever name the user enters into the InputBox is returned to your program, as can be proven by writing it into the Intermediate window with Debug.Writeline.

If you need to return data to the caller, use a function. You can of course, write your own functions, the same way you can write your own subroutines. Note too that you can pass as many parameters (items of data) *to* a function as you wish, but you can only pass *one* item of data back from a function.

Understanding Scope

VB programs are subdivided into zones, similar to the way that the United States is divided into states, counties, and cities. And, just as law enforcement agents have different size jurisdictions (city cops, state troopers, but the FBI can go anywhere), so do VB lines of programming have ranges of influence. This range of influence, called *scope,* mostly applies to variables but can also apply to procedures — subs and functions — as well as to entire classes.

Often you want to query or change the value in a variable, but whether or not that variable is accessible to you depends on its scope. For example, you can always access a variable from within the same procedure. To see how this works, type this into your code module:

```
Private Sub Form1_Load(ByVal sender As System.Object, ByVal e As
        System.EventArgs) Handles MyBase.Load

    Dim N As String = "This"
    MsgBox(N)

End Sub
```

Press F5 and notice that the MsgBox has no problem displaying the value of the variable N. It displays "This". Now type another sub just below the Form1_Load sub in the code window:

```
Public Sub TryIt()

    MsgBox(N)

End Sub
```

Notice that there is a sawtooth line under the variable N in the TryIt sub. Hold your mouse pointer on top of the sawtooth line and VB displays an error message telling you that Name 'N' is not declared.

This error message means that *none* of the lines of code here within the TryIt sub (between Public Sub and End Sub) can *read* (get the value of) *or write* (change) the variable N. N was declared (with the Dim command) in *a separate procedure*, and so the scope of N (its range of accessibility) is limited to lines of code within its same procedure. (The sawtooth line is one of several debugging tools, which I discuss in more detail in Chapter 10.)

Although Dim is the most commonly used, there are seven additional declaration commands you can use: Static, Public, Protected, Friend, Shared, Protected Friend, and Private. These additional commands specify *scope* (from which locations in your program a variable can be accessed).

If you avoid using VB's OOP features to organize your programs (which I suggest you do), you can limit yourself to using only Static, Private and Public. And there's no particular reason you'd want to use Private — why hide code from yourself? (If you're programming in a group with others, Private can be useful to forbid the others from using code you think they have no need to access.)

To sum up: When you declare a variable inside a procedure, the variable works only within that procedure. When the program executes the procedure (or event), the variable comes to life, does its thing, but then dies (disappears) as soon as the End Sub line is executed. These are called *local variables*.

When variables are local

Variables that live only within a single procedure are called *local variables*. Local variables have two qualities that you need to remember:

✔ No programming outside a local variable's own procedure can interact with that variable, either to read its value (contents) or to change that value. A local variable's scope is limited to its own procedure.

✔ When VB finishes executing the procedure in which local variables reside, their values evaporate. If that procedure is executed a second time, whatever value the local variable once contained is no longer there. One execution of the procedure is the variable's "lifetime." There are some situations in which you do want a local variable's value to be preserved. Recall that in those cases, you use the `Static` command rather than the `Dim` command, like this:

```
Private Sub Form1_Load(ByVal sender As System.Object, ByVal e As
            System.EventArgs) Handles MyBase.Load

    Dim n As Integer
    Static x As Integer

End Sub
```

In this example, the variable n loses its value when the `End Sub` is executed. However, the variable x retains its value until the program is shut down. Another way of putting it is this: When you use the `Static` command with a local variable, the value of that variable is preserved for the lifetime of your application. (*Lifetime* means how long something is in existence in a program.)

What do you think would happen if you put two Buttons on your Form and then ran the program and clicked Button1 first, and then clicked Button2, in this next program?

```
Private Sub Button1_Click(ByVal sender As System.Object, ByVal e As
            System.EventArgs) Handles Button1.Click

    Dim X As Integer
    X = 12
    X = X + 5

End Sub

Private Sub Button2_Click(ByVal sender As System.Object, ByVal e As
            System.EventArgs) Handles Button2.Click

    Dim X As Integer
    MsgBox(X)

End Sub
```

The message box displays nothing. The variable X in Button1's Click event is a completely different variable from the X in Button2's Click event. They are *local* in scope and simply have no relationship to each other, no more than two strangers named Mike who happen to live in the Bronx and never meet.

But what if you want both of these procedures to be able to access and manipulate *the same variable*? To do this, you define the variable *outside your procedures*. Try it. First delete the `Dim X as Integer` lines currently in each event.

Then click just above your first procedure (just above the line `Private Sub Form1_Load`) in the code window to move the insertion cursor there. Now type:

```
Dim x As Integer
```

That's where you want to put any variables that you want to give *form-wide* scope — in other words, to permit all the procedures in that form (Form1 in this case) to be able to read and modify the variable. The area where you put form-wide variables is sometimes called the *General Declarations* area. It's outside any procedure, but is within the form, `Class Form1`.

Now, with that X variable `Dim`med up there above (outside) all the subs and other procedures, when you run the same program, click Button1 and then click Button2, you see the result you want to see: 17. By declaring X to be form-wide in scope, the two buttons can access that variable X. Delete the two `Dim` statements that previously declared X within those two Button events. Now `X = X + 5` and `MsgBox(X)` both refer to *the same variable named X.*

When a variable has form-wide scope, it's then available to all the procedures in that form. It's *not* available, however, to the procedures in any *other* forms in the project.

Public: The greatest scope of all

What if you want to make a variable available to *all* the procedures in *all* your forms in a given project? In such a case, you have to use the `Public` command rather than `Dim`. What's more, you have to put this `Public` declaration into a *module*, not a form. Variables declared `Public` in a module are visible *from anywhere in your project.*

It's considered good programming practice to try to avoid using `Public` variables whenever possible, at least so say the OOP theorists. They claim that variables with that much scope can make your programming harder to debug (though I've never had a problem with them — they're talking about 25 programmers working on a huge, complex program).

Looking at the status of variables is one of the primary ways to find out where a problem is located in a program. If you use a local variable, any problem involving that variable can be found in its procedure, which does narrow your search for a bug. By contrast, you have more code — probably much more code — to search and analyze if there's a bug involving a form-wide (or worse, project-wide) variable. However, there are times when you'll find use for form-wide, or even project-wide, scope.

Scoping procedures

Not just variables, but also procedures, have scope. By default, VB makes its events Private (`Private Sub Button1_Click`). If you don't want to permit code outside your current form to access a procedure, declare it `Private`. If you do want to permit outside code access, declare the procedure as `Public`.

There's another scope declaration command, coyly called *Friend*. Friend scope is similar to Public, but only code within its *project* (or application) can access a variable or procedure declared with `Friend`. This means that another, separate application cannot access a `Friend`. (Separate applications *can* make use of `Public` variables or procedures.) Don't worry about this scope until you start writing enormous "solutions" (remember the Solution Explorer?) and need to organize them into multiple programs all working together. Right now, you're just writing programs — which can be quite large themselves without having to grow into "solutions."

VB .NET adds these nine additional procedure declaration commands related to scope: `Overloads`, `Overrides`, `Overridable`, `NotOverridable`, `MustOverride`, `Shadows`, `Shared`, `Protected` and `Protected Friend`. The majority of these commands involve *inheritance,* an OOP technique which I suggest you avoid.

Going Round and Round in Loops

Often a job requires repetition until a result is achieved: Polish your boots until they shine, or add spoonfuls of sugar one at a time until the lemonade tastes good. This kind of repetitious behavior is handled with *looping* in a computer program.

Looping means repeating a task until a condition is met.

Repetition is often needed in computer programs, and the most common loop structure is `For...Next`.

Using a For...Next loop

Between the `For` and the `Next` are *program lines,* which are instructions that get carried out repeatedly. The number of times that the computer executes the loop is defined by the two numbers listed right after the `For`:

```
Sub Iterate()

Dim I, A As Integer

For I = 1 To 4
    A = A + I
Next I

MsgBox(A)

End Sub
```

In this example, the loop's counter variable is named I. (There's a tradition to use the variable I in For...Next loops.) The important thing to understand is that the counter variable is incremented (raised by 1) each time the program gets to the Next command.

The Next command does three things.

✓ Adds 1 to the variable I

✓ Checks whether I has reached the limit set in the For statement (4 in this example) and makes sure the limit has not been exceeded

✓ *Loops* — that is, it sends the program back up — to the For statement to repeat the code one more time. The lines of programming code within the loop are executed each time the loop cycles.

The answer displayed by the message box in the previous example is 10. Try single-stepping through the execution of this loop (press F8 repeatedly), pausing your mouse cursor over the counter variable I and also over the variable A each time you go through the loop. You'll see that the first time through, I is 1. (Look at For I = 1 To 4; the counter starts with 1.) The variable A is empty, but as soon as its line of code is executed, it contains the value of I plus whatever was in A. The second time through the loop, A first has a 1 in it, but the value of I is 2, so A then contains 3. The third time through the loop, 3 is added to 3, resulting in 6. Finally, the last time through the loop, I has a value of 4, which, when added to 6, becomes 10. The program then exits the loop and displays the MsgBox.

Using the Step command with For...Next

Step is an optional command that works with For...Next. You can attach Step at the end of the For line to skip numbers — in other words, to "step" past them. When the Step command is used with For...Next, Step alters the way the loop counts.

By default, a loop counts by 1:

```
Sub Iterate()

Dim a As String


For i = 1 To 12
   a = a & i & " "
Next i

MsgBox a
End Sub
```

And results in 1 2 3 4 5 6 7 8 9 10 11 12.

However, when you use a `Step` command, you change how a `For...Next` loop counts. For example, use `Step 2` to count every other number:

```
Sub Iterate()

Dim a As String

For i = 1 To 12 Step 2
   a = a & i & " "
Next i

MsgBox a
End Sub
```

And results in 1 3 5 7 9 11.

If the mood strikes you, you can even "step" every 73rd number (`Step 73`), count backward (`For I = 10 to 1 Step -1`), or count by fractions (`Step .25`).

Although you can use any numeric expression with `For...Next`, as you get into more complex looping, remember that the range that you're counting must be possible. For example, the following is not possible:

```
For i = -10 To -20 Step 2
   MsgBox "loop"; i
Next
```

This loop does nothing. It can't. You're asking it to count downward, but your `Step` command is positive. As any intelligent entity would when confronted with a senseless request, Visual Basic does nothing with these instructions. It ignores you. You have to make the `Step` negative with `-2` before something will happen.

Nesting For...Next loops

For...Next loops can be nested, one inside the other. At first, this sort of structure seems confusing (and it often remains confusing): The inner loop interacts with the exterior loop in ways that are instantly clear to only the mathematically gifted, although a couple of beers also helps.

Essentially, the inner loop does its thing the number of times specified by its own counter variable, multiplied by the counter variable of the outer loop. Got it? It's like the moon. It's revolves around the Earth, but both are simultaneously revolving around the sun. So the moon's path resembles a corkscrew. To make matters worse, the entire solar system is revolving around the galaxy, but let's not get into that.

When working with nested loops, simply keep substituting counter numbers (and maybe moving code from one loop to the other) until things work the way you want. One meaning of *hacking* to a programmer is similar to what carving is to a sculptor: messing around until the desired result emerges. In this example, I want to display two sets of numbers: 1 2 3 and 1 2 3. After a frosty, cool one, I finally figured how to do it. The outer loop (I) should loop twice, and the inner loop (J) should loop three times. And the value of J should be used each time to display the numbers that I want. Here's the code:

```
Sub Nested()

Dim a, cr As String
Dim I, J As Integer

cr = vbCrLf ' move down one line

For I = 1 To 2
    For J = 1 To 3
        a &= " " & J & cr
    Next J
Next I

MsgBox(a)

End Sub
```

Early exits from loops

If you want to exit the loop before the counter finishes, use the Exit For command. The Exit For command is rarely used, but here's an example of when you'd want to use it. Suppose you're filling an array that should hold only 500 items, and you don't want to overflow it. (I discuss arrays in Chapter 8.) You avoid this by making a provision for an early exit from the loop if necessary. If the Exit For is carried out, execution moves to the line of code following the Next command.

```
If n > 500 Then Exit For
```

You can use Exit Do (for Do loops), Exit Function, Exit Property, and Exit Sub commands as well.

Working with Do loops

Sometimes you might prefer the Do...While loop structure to For...Next; in fact, some programmers favor it over For...Next because it can be a bit more flexible. Do loop structures can be handy in special looping situations. Read on.

Choosing Do...While over For...Next loops

In its most common use, Do...While employs a comparison operator at the start of the loop to test something (is it = or =>, and so on). If the comparison succeeds, the statements in the loop are executed at least once. However, the first time the comparison fails, the loop is skipped, and execution continues on the line following the Loop command. The Loop command signals the end of the Do...While structure, just as the Next command signals the end of the For...Next loop structure.

```
Sub Iterate()

Dim a, cr As String
cr = vbCrLf ' move down one line

Dim y As Integer

Do While y < 11
    y = y + 1
    a = a & y & cr
Loop

MsgBox(a)

End Sub
```

Remember that you must do something in the code within the loop that changes the comparison value. Otherwise, you create an endless loop. Also note that if y in the preceding example already holds a value of 11 or more when the program reaches this loop, the loop never executes. Because the exit test will fail the very first time the loop is encountered, none of the code within the loop will execute at all.

Using Do...Until loops

A version of Do...While is Do...Until. It's just another way of expressing the same idea, but you might find it a little clearer. Do...While loops as long as the comparison is True, but Do...Until loops until the comparison is False:

```
Do Until y = 11
'Some behaviors
Loop
```

Using Loop While and Loop Until

If you want to put the loop exit test at the end of the loop structure, here are two additional ways to construct a Do loop:

```
Do
'Some behaviors
Loop While Y < 11
```

This works the same way as the earlier Do...While example. The difference is that when you put the test at the end, the loop always executes at least once, no matter what value is in the variable Y when you enter the loop.

```
Do
'Some behaviors
Loop Until Y = 11
```

Until works the same as While, but just expresses the condition in an alternative way.

Which of these four structures should you use? Use Do...While or Do...Until if you don't want the loop to execute even once if the exit test fails at the start. As for the difference between the While and Until styles, it's often a matter of which one seems to you to be more readable or which one works better with the exit test. Many times, it's merely a semantic distinction: the difference between *Do the dishes while any are still dirty* versus *Do the dishes until all are clean.*

Exploring While...Wend: A simple loop

Finally, at your disposal is the While...Wend structure, although it's rarely used. It's simple but relatively inflexible:

```
While X < 7
'Some behaviors
Wend
```

As you can see, this looping technique is comparatively elementary. While...Wend has no Exit command (like the Exit Do command). While...Wend is limited to an exit test at the start of the loop, and it does not permit you to use the alternative command Until. The Wend specifies the end of the While code block.

For...Each: Looping in object collections

Moving through a collection of objects is an easy job for programmers, because the collection itself "knows" how many objects it contains. With collections, you can use the For...Each structure.

To see a list of available fonts, you can iterate through the System.Drawing.FontFamily object, like this:

```
Private Sub Form1_Load(ByVal sender As System.Object, ByVal e As
        System.EventArgs) Handles MyBase.Load

Dim F As System.Drawing.FontFamily

For Each F In System.Drawing.FontFamily.Families
    Debug.WriteLine(F.Name)
Next

End Sub
```

The results appear in the Immediate window.

For...Each is a quick and clean way to loop because you don't have to specify a literal number or some other exit test, as in most loops.

Making Decisions via Branching

Branching means choosing between different paths, based on a condition (in other words, allowing the program to make a decision). Making decisions is central to any intelligent behavior, so the If...Then structure is one of the most important features in any computer language — indeed, in any kind of language.

If...Then is the most common way that decisions are made. After the decision is made, you write code to respond appropriately to the decision. A program is said to *branch* at this point because the path it was following splits into more than one trail. The branch that the program chooses is decided here at the If...Then junction. For each of the branches, you write code appropriate to that path.

Many times a day, we do our own personal branching, using a similar structure: If you're hungry, you eat. If it's nice weather, you don't wear a jacket. If the car windows are fogged up, you wipe them off. This constant cycle of testing conditions and then making decisions based on those conditions is what makes our behavior intelligent and adaptive. This same kind of testing is what makes computer behavior intelligent, too.

Understanding If...Then

You put If...Then structures into a program so it reacts appropriately to various kinds of user input, as well as such additional events as incoming data from a disk file, the passage of time, or other conditions.

Here's a simple example of how If...Then is used:

```
Sub Branching()

Dim response, m As String

    Response = InputBox("How many calories did you take in today?")

If Response > 2200 Then
    m = "Keep that up and you'll have to buy new pants. Your bad self."
    Else
        m = "Good self-control on your part."
End If

MsgBox(m)

End Sub
```

The line of code starting with If tests whether something is True. If so, the code on the line or lines following the If are carried out. If the test fails (the test condition is not true), your program skips the line(s) of code until it gets to an Else, ElseIf, or End If command. Then the program resumes execution. Put another way, the If test determines whether some lines of code will be executed.

Notice that if you're making a simple decision (either/or) with only two branches, you can use the Else command. In the preceding example, if the user's response is that he ate more than 2,200 calories, the first message is displayed. Or, if the opposite happened and he ate less that 2,200 calories, the message following the Else command is displayed.

What if you want to branch into more than only two paths? Easy! You can use the `ElseIf` command:

```
If X = "Bob" Then
    MsgBox "Hello Bob"
ElseIf X = "Billy" Then
    MsgBox "Hello Billy"
ElseIf X = "Ashley" Then
    MsgBox "Hello Ashley"
End If
```

In a way, using `ElseIf` is like using several `If...Then`s in a row. But for situations in which you want to test multiple conditions, the better solution is to use the `Select Case` command, as you find out later in this chapter.

As with loops, it's traditional to provide a visual cue by indenting all lines of code that are carried out inside the `If...Then` structure. Also, you can use a simple, one-line version of `If...Then` if your test is simple enough (`True`/`False`) and short enough to just put all on a single line. In that case, you do not use an `End If`. (The `If...Then` structure is assumed to be completed by the end of the line of code.) The computer knows that this is a single-line `If...Then` because some additional code follows the `Then` command. (In a multiline `If...Then` structure, the `Then` command is the last word on the line.) Here's an example of the single-line structure:

```
Sub Branching()

Dim Reply As String, Password As String = "sue"

    Reply = InputBox("What is the password?")

If Reply <> Password Then MsgBox("Access Denied") : End

    MsgBox("Password verified as correct. Please continue.")

End Sub
```

Notice the colon that appears at the end of the `If...Then` line in the preceding example code. The colon is used to combine separate programming statements (logical lines of code) on the same physical line. This is a rarely used technique, but you should be aware of it. It's handy for single-line `If...Then` code, as this example illustrates. You want to do two things should the password fail the test:

✔ Show a message box.

✔ End the program.

Normally, the `End` command has to be on a line of its own in the code. When you use the colon, VB reads the code that follows it as a separate logical line of code. Recall that you can use the space-underscore characters to break a single, long, logical line of code into two physical lines. (*Logical* here means *what VB acts on,* and *physical* means *what you see onscreen.*) Using a colon is the opposite of the space-underscore. A colon allows you to place two logical lines on the same physical line. (You can even cram more than two logical lines on one physical line: `X=X+1:A=B:N="Hi."`, for example.)

Remember that the condition you test with `If` is an expression, so it can involve variables, literals, constants, and any other valid combination of components that can make up an expression. For instance, you can use a function in an expression:

```
If InputBox("Enter your age, but it's optional") <> "" Then

    MsgBox("Thank you for responding")

End If
```

The `InputBox` function is executed, and its result is tested to see whether it does not equal (<>) an empty string (""). If it is empty, the user failed to type anything into the `InputBox` and the MsgBox is not displayed.

Multiple choice: The Select Case command

`If...Then` is great for simple, common testing and branching. But if you're testing for more than two branches, `If...Then` becomes clumsy. Fortunately, an alternative decision-making structure in VB specializes in multiple branching.

Use `Select Case` when several outcomes are possible and several tests need to be run.

The main distinction between `If...Then` and `Select Case` looks something like this:

```
If CarStatus = burning, Then get out of the car.
```

But the `Select Case` structure tests many and various situations:

```
Select Case CarStatus
    Case Steaming
        Let radiator cool down.
    Case Wobbling
        Check tires.
    Case Skidding
```

```
            Steer into skid.
    Case Burning
            Leave the car.
End Select
```

`Select Case` works from a list of possible answers. Your program can respond to each of these answers differently. There can be one, or many, lines of code within each case:

```
Dim Response As String = InputBox("What's your favorite color?")

Select Case LCase(Response)
    Case "blue"
        MsgBox("We have three varieties of blue")
    Case "red"
        MsgBox("We have six varieties of red")
    Case "green"
        MsgBox("We have one variety of green")
    Case Else
        MsgBox("We don't have " & Response & ", sorry.")
End Select
```

This example illustrates that you can use any expression (variable, literal, function, compound expression, or other kind of expression) in the `Select Case` line. Here I used a literal.

In this example, I use the `LCase` command to reduce whatever the user typed to all lowercase letters. (That way you can ignore capitalization.) Then VB goes down the list of cases and executes any lines in which the original expression on the first line matches one of the `Case` lines. Note that the final case is special: The optional `Case Else` command means that if there were no matches, execute the following code.

Using the Is command with Select Case

You can use the special `Is` command with each case to use comparison tests on each case:

```
Dim X As Integer = InputBox("Your weight, please?")

Select Case X
    Case Is < 200
        '(put one or more commands here)
        MsgBox("Good for you")
    Case Is < 300
        '(put one or more commands here)
        MsgBox("Not too bad.")
End Select
```

In the preceding example, if the number is lower than 200, the first block of code lines executes; then execution jumps to the line of programming following End Select. If the number is lower than 300, the second block of code executes (any code between Case Is < 300 and End Select).

Note that as soon as one of the cases triggers a match, no further cases are even checked for a match. The Case structure is merely exited. This order of testing can be important. In the preceding example, if you put the 300 comparison first, the test would pass for any weight less than 300, which is not your intention.

Using the To command with Case Select

If you want to check a range of values, use the To command. It can be a numeric range (Case 4 To 12) or an alphabetic range (based on the first letter of the string being tested):

```
Dim Reply As String = LCase(InputBox("Type in your last name."))

Select Case Reply
    Case "a" To "m"
        MsgBox("Please go to the left line.")
    Case "n" To "z"
        MsgBox("Please go to the right line.")
End Select
```

You can also combine several items in a Case, separating them with commas:

```
Case "a" To "l", "gene", NameOfUser
```

This is an *or* type of test: that is, take action if

✔ The answer begins with a letter between a and l.

Or

✔ It's gene.

Or

✔ It matches the value in the variable NameOfUser.

Chapter 6

It's All about My

My is an object that simplifies .NET programming, allowing you to accomplish some common programming tasks with less bloated (that is, .NET-style) code and with more understandable, more readable programming. Of course, many VB programmers see .NET as seriously damaging the VB language — contrary to the spirit and ideal of clarity and efficiency that has been the hallmark of the Basic language for decades. The My feature in VB Express is an attempt to restore some clarity and efficiency to VB.

In this chapter, I explain how My fits into the picture as VB evolves and how you can put My to use in your programs.

Comparing My to Classic VB and .NET

VB Express (and other Express products) is designed to be less threatening than .NET. In other words, the menus include fewer options, and, though the full .NET Framework is available to VB Express, the surface is at least less "frightening" to novices and amateur programmers.

Part of this move to a simpler, easier user interface is the My object — a somewhat streamlined way to access some of the .NET Framework. The idea is that some Framework experts figure out the best approach to a particular job — file access, for example — and slip it into the My object for your use. That way, you don't have to figure out too many details. For file input/output (I/O), use the My version. This is somewhat similar to historical VB, which had only one way to access files, and it was pretty straightforward and easy to use.

A quick examination of the three versions — the classic simple VB way to open a file, the nightmare .NET way, and the latest My way — will illustrate the My object's use. As you see in the following examples, My isn't as simple as it could be (you still have to use multiple qualifying categories).

Classic VB

In classic VB, you open a file like this:

```
Open "C:\Test.Txt" As 5
```

A .NET version

VB .NET gives you multiple ways to do the job of opening a file; here's one:

```
Dim strFileName As String = "C:\Test.Txt"
Dim objFilename As FileStream = New FileStream(strFileName, FileMode.Open,
            FileAccess.Read, FileShare.Read)

Dim objFileRead As StreamReader = New StreamReader(objFilename)
```

Now, to see how VB .NET reads in the data from the file, enter this code:

```
While (objFileRead.Peek() > -1)
    textbox1.Text &= objFileRead.ReadLine()
End While

objFileRead.Close()
objFilename.Close()
```

And finally, to deselect the text which, by default, strangely, is selected, you type

```
TextBox1.Select(0, 0)
```

The new My version

This My version streamlines the process of reading in a block of text, compared to the lengthy and confusing .NET version above:

```
TextBox1.Text = My.Computer.FileSystem.ReadAllText("C:\Test.Txt")

    TextBox1.Select(0, 0)
```

As you can see, using the My object, while not a return to the classic simplicity of pre-.NET VB, is nonetheless a start in that direction. Some of the verbose, bloated code required by C and object-oriented programming goes back under the hood where it belongs when you use the My object.

Getting Familiar with My

You should familiarize yourself with the shortcuts (relative to .NET anyway) offered by My. The easiest way to do that is to look in Help. This section explains how to get to help and offers an overview of the major My categories.

Browsing through My help

To browse through the My categories in Help, follow these steps:

1. **Click Contents in the VB Express Help Toolbar, as shown in Figure 6-1.**

2. **Dig down to Express Library for Visual Studio⇨Visual Basic Express⇨Visual Basic Reference⇨Keywords and Members by Task⇨My Reference (see Figure 6-1).**

   Unfortunately, some My features are listed by their OOP classifications, which aren't usually very helpful. But go ahead and have look.

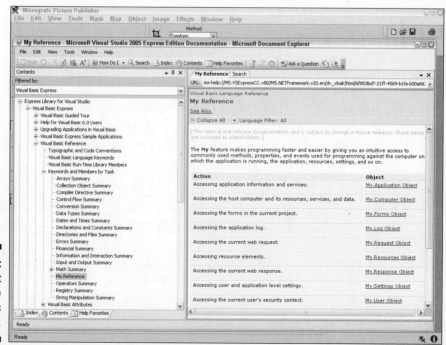

Figure 6-1:
Find out about the My features here in Help.

3. **Click `My.Computer` Object under Objects, then scroll down to view a group of links (underlined in blue). Here you see some general categories that `My` can be used with.**

By maneuvering through this list of objects, you can get an overview of the kinds of jobs that My can help you with. For example, you can use My.Computer to access the Audio, Clipboard, Clock, FileSystem, Info, Keyboard, Mouse, Name, Network, Ports, Registry, and Screen objects. In short, you can control many of the functional Windows features from a central location.

The major My categories

When you try to use My, you find that it has the following six major subcategories. Most of them are pretty useless, but you do want to focus on one of them: the `Computer` category contains almost all the useful features of the My collection. It's the real workhorse of the My group. A distant second is the `Application` category, having only a little to offer you. The `Forms` category has some specialized uses when communicating between forms in a project that uses more than one form. The others, well . . . why are they included in a feature that supposedly streamlines and simplifies? Only the mystery people at Microsoft know the answer. Why did they include the "resources" or "user" cateogies, for example? You tell me.

Here is an overview of the major categories:

✔ **Application:** The program you're writing. You can get information about which directory the application resides in, and a few other details.

✔ **Computer:** The machine the program is running on, providing access to peripherals such as the mouse, screen, and keyboard; plus important capabilities for dealing with the hard drive and its directories and files.

✔ **Forms:** The forms in the current project. Relatively useless for most programming jobs, but loads of access to a form's properties and methods.

However, the current form (`Form1` in the following example) cannot use a reference to itself. If you try to center the form on the screen like this:

```
My.Forms.Form1.CenterToScreen()
```

you're informed that OOP forbids it. Instead, you must refer to the *current* form (the one you're writing this code in at the time) as Me, not My, like this:

```
Me.CenterToScreen()
```

This illustrates the caprice, the random damage, so often characteristic of OOP. Why should you, the programmer, care about these silly categories that the designers of the language use to keep things straight when writing the VB Express language? Both of those ways of centering the form ought to work for the programmer. The reason that the first approach doesn't work is entirely bogus from a programmer's point of view — no matter how much sense this taxonomy might make to the language designers at Microsoft as they try to keep the vast Framework straight in their minds.

✓ **Resources:** The stuff you find here has to do with writing programs in various foreign languages and some OOP technicalities. You can ignore this unless you specialize in OOP or plan to write programs for other cultures (in which case your work is too advanced for My anyway).

✓ **User:** A few specialized security-related things you can ignore.

✓ **WebServices:** Advanced Internet programming. Ignore it.

Using My While Programming

While you're programming, remember to use the IntelliSense feature to see whether My can help you with a job. To understand how this works, assume that you want to copy a file named text.txt from your C:\ root directory to a directory name C:\temp.

Rather than struggle with the .NET approaches, perhaps there's a simpler, more elegant My version of code for this task. Follow these steps:

1. **Start a new VB Windows style project and double-click the form.**

   You see the Form_Load event in the code window.

2. **Type My.. (My followed by a period.)**

   You see a list of the major categories under My..

3. **As usual, you can probably find what you're after in the Computer category, so double-click it.**

   The word Computer is added to My. in your source code.

4. **Type a period after the word Computer.**

   A list of the Computer object's members drops down.

5. **Double-click FileSystem.**

   That word appears in your code string.

6. **Type a period after the word FileSystem.**

   A list of members appears for the FileSystem object.

7. Scroll through the list of members until you see `CopyFile` and then double-click it.

That word appears in your growing list of `My` qualifiers. You're narrowing things down now! Keep up your spirits, you're almost there.

8. If you now press Enter or move your cursor down off this line of code, VB Express inserts a pair of parentheses. Also, that jagged blue line appears.

This blue line means that VB is *not happy* with the line of code. Something is wrong — the line will not work as is. You need to provide some *arguments* — details about which file to copy and where.

9. Delete the right parenthesis ()).

You now are allowed to view the helpful IntelliSense feature that shows you the possible "argument list" variations.

C/OOP programmers describe a function with more than one possible argument list as being *overloaded,* and many functions in the .NET Framework are overloaded.

Figure 6-2 illustrates the four possible variations on the file-copying feature. For example, one of them permits you to overwrite an existing file. But all you're doing is copying to a different folder, so the arguments (source file name, target file name) will work just fine.

Figure 6-2:
The most common arguments are usually shown as the first option, but click the black arrows to see alternatives.

```
My.Computer.FileSystem.CopyFile (|
  ▲ 4 of 4 ▼   CopyFile (sourceFileName As String, destinationFileName As String, showUI As Microsoft.VisualBasic.FileIO.UIOption,
                          onUserCancel As Microsoft.VisualBasic.FileIO.UICancelOption)
  sourceFileName:
    String. The file to be copied. Required.
```

How My could be improved

How could My be better (besides expanding it to include a greater number of common programming tasks)? How about eliminating that tedious and entirely unnecessary OOP classification scheme? In other words, VB Express can easily look up the location of the CopyFile function in the Framework. All you, the programmer, *really* need to use is the word CopyFile. After all, this function is not going to jump into some other area of the Framework — so why should you always have to specify the address in the Framework? The programmer is uninterested in, and has no need of, the OOP classification scheme represented by the redundant part of this code: My.Computer.FileSystem.

Your entire programming should look like this:

```
CopyFile("c:\test.txt",
         "C:\temp\test.txt")
```

In addition, there should certainly be a My feature that simplifies access to your printer. That's a pretty common programming task, but in VB Express it's pretty complex (see Chapter 9).

10. **Just type the two required arguments and press F5 to see your file copied to the C:\temp directory:**

```
My.Computer.FileSystem.CopyFile("c:\test.txt", "C:\temp\test.txt")
```

Simple enough. (Of course, it would be an improvement to eliminate the superfluous OOP part of this code by dropping the class references — like this: CopyFile("c:\test.txt", "C:\temp\test.txt" — but in this version of VB, it just doesn't work that way.)

Chapter 7

Whose Type Are You: Managing Variable Types

*V*ariables are an essential aspect of computing. They're a bit like our human short-term memory. You use a variable to hold some bit of information, such as the user's area code or the number of trains currently running in New Jersey. These facts can change while your program is executing; they can *vary* — hence the name *variable*. For example, the variable `NumberOfTrains` changes as soon as one of the trains stops in Newark. A variable's data also might be different the next time you run the program.

A variable's contents persist only while the program is executing. As soon as someone stops the program, poof! — the data in variables evaporates. Therefore, saving the data in variables is a common job in computer programming. It's the equivalent of our human long-term memory. If you want to store information for a longer time, you usually save the information to the hard drive; that way, it doesn't disappear when the program stops running.

If your program needs to know the user's area code next time the program runs (so the user doesn't have to keep typing it in each time she uses your program), you should make sure that you save that area code information to a database or other file on the hard drive. (Chapter 6 covers saving and loading disk files.)

This chapter is all about variables in VB 2005 Express. Variables are essential to computer programming, just as they are in many other aspects of life. Any container with a label is the real-world equivalent of a variable. And you're surrounded by named containers — they are fundamental to data processing. You also discover how to handle variables when they're grouped together into *expressions*, such as `FirstVariable + SecondVariable`.

Two Main Kinds of Data

Computing is often called *data processing* or *information processing*. The *data* is the pieces of information, such as area codes or the ingredients in a recipe. The *processing* is the actual computing that is done by manipulating the data. For example, when you follow the instructions in a recipe, you are manipulating the raw ingredients to make a cake.

All data breaks down into two primary categories: strings and numbers. You can see this distinction in the following recipe:

```
1 1/2 cup flour, 3 tablespoons cocoa, 1 teaspoon baking soda, 1 cup sugar,
    1/2 teaspoon salt, 5 tablespoons salad oil, 1 tablespoon vinegar,
    1 teaspoon vanilla, 1 cup cold water
```

Notice that some of this data is numeric (1 1/2, 3, and so on) and other data is text (vinegar, vanilla, and so on). A text datum — such as the word *vinegar* — is usually referred to in computer lingo as a *string*.

By the way, here's the data processing part of this recipe:

```
Mix all dry ingredients and put into greased 9x9 cake pan. Then add in
    the wet ingredients, beating with a spoon until mixed. Cook at 350 degrees
    for 1/2 hour.
```

Try it; it's good.

Strings are like words

A *string* is letters strung together: "Don Wilson", "vanilla", "b" (a string can be a single letter), and "454-5001 ext. 23" are all strings. When you assign some literal text to a string variable in a program, the text is enclosed in quotation marks:

```
Dim MyVariable As String
MyVariable = "This is Tuesday."
```

If there's enough memory in your computer, and an application permits large strings, you can hold the entire phone book in a single string if you wish. By contrast, "" is an empty string (empty strings are sometimes useful).

A string can be a single character, a really huge number of characters, empty, or anything in between. It can contain letters of the alphabet, symbols such as * or @, and even digits such as "2".

Note, however, that a *digit* is not the same as a true *number*. A digit is just a character (string) representation. You can't do math with strings.

You *can* concatenate (combine) strings. Try this experiment:

1. **Run VB Express and choose File⇨New Project.**

   The New Project dialog box opens.

2. **Double-click the Windows Application icon in the dialog box.**

   The dialog box closes, and a brand new VB Express project is displayed. You see Form1.

3. **Double-click Form1.**

   The Code window for Form1 opens, where you can write your programming. The Form1_Load event is displayed.

4. **In the Load event — between the two lines beginning with `Private Sub` and `End Sub` — type this programming, shown in boldface:**

```
Private Sub Form1_Load(ByVal sender As System.Object, ByVal e As
         System.EventArgs) Handles MyBase.Load

    Debug.Print("fluor" & "ide")
    Debug.Print("2" + "3")

End Sub
```

5. **Press F5.**

   The program is built and executed. You see the results *fluoride* and *23* displayed in the Immediate window.

`Debug.Print` is a quick way to test something. The results are displayed in the Immediate window, as shown in Figure 7-1. If the Immediate window isn't visible, choose View⇨Other Windows⇨Immediate.

`Debug.Print "fluor" & "ide"` displays `fluoride`. `Debug.Print "2" + "3"` displays `23` (not 5, which is the result when you add numeric variables or literals, such as `2 + 3`, rather than strings). Obviously you can't multiply or subtract or do other math on strings.

Also, VB prefers that you use the `&` symbol to concatenate strings and reserves + for adding numbers. So I should have written that line `Debug.Print "2" & "3"`.

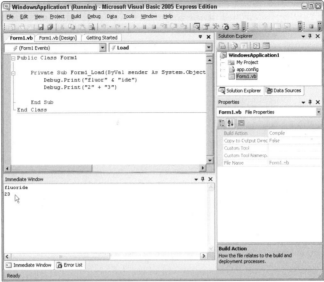

VB usually accepts + with strings, but it doesn't like it. Besides, using + may confuse you into thinking that you are adding numeric variables:

```
Dim n As String = "5"
Dim m As String = "20"
Dim o As String
o = n + m
```

The final line of this code could be mistaken for addition, but no math is happening here. So, to make it absolutely clear that you are *concatenating* two strings, use the ampersand rather than the plus sign, like this:

```
o = n & m
```

You can do math with numbers

You've seen how to work with strings. Numbers are the other kind of data, and they operate inside the computer just as they do in real life: You can do all kinds of math with them.

As I mention in the preceding section, there's a difference between true numbers and numbers stored as strings (digits). Programmers sometimes store numbers as strings, though, if they don't expect to do math with those numbers. Your zip code ("27244") and phone number ("336-555-0123") make better sense stored as strings. You're never going to multiply them, are you?

What's more, some kinds of numeric information simply can't be stored as a numeric variable. You can't store a phone number as a numeric variable if you want to include those hyphens in it. Symbols such as hyphens *must* be stored in a string. If you leave the quotation marks off a phone number, such as 336-555-0123, Visual Basic thinks you want to subtract real numbers, and it calculates the value, -342.

Understanding Variables

Variables are a way of storing information — sometimes quite briefly (because the contents of a variable can *vary,* as the name implies). Nonetheless, you are talking about storing data when you discuss variables. Here's how it works:

1. A program asks the user to type in how much they're willing to pay for a new TV.

2. The user obliges and types 299.

3. What happens then? The computer must remember that information. It stores the information in a *variable.*

In the following sections, you find out how storing this information in a variable works and what considerations to keep in mind when you decide how a variable is stored.

Assigning a value to a variable

After the user types in *299* (called a *value*), the program assigns the value to the variable. If the user types the answer into TextBox1, the following source code assigns the value (whatever value the user types in) to the variable:

```
Dim TopTvPrice As Integer
TopTvPrice = TextBox1.Text
```

The content of the TextBox, the value, is copied into the variable TopTvPrice. Remember that if you don't first *declare* your variable's type (in this case you Dim the variable As Integer), VB Express displays a sawtooth line under the variable's name, indicating an error. And when you move your mouse pointer onto the sawtooth line, an error message appears saying Name TopTvPrice is not declared. You find out more about declaring variables in the section "Creating a Variable," later in this chapter.

Storing string or numeric variables

Does the programmer want to store the `299` described in several previous paragraphs as a string or as a numeric variable? Probably numeric, because it may be necessary to do some math on it (comparing it to the cost of other models, calculating sales tax, adding it to other purchases, and so on).

Although VB generally sees any value with letter characters in it as a string and any value with only digits as numeric, something interesting happens when you type a number like 299 into a TextBox. Anything typed into a TextBox is automatically viewed by VB as a *string*. The `TextBox.Text` property can hold only a string. However, notice that our program assigned that string to a *numeric* (integer) variable:

```
Dim TopTvPrice As Integer
TopTvPrice = TextBox1.Text
```

How can a numeric variable hold a string? It can't. VB *converts* the string `299` into an integer before storing it in the numeric variable `TopTvPrice`.

Some programming languages — such as C — forbid permitting languages to change a data type automatically (only programmers can do it, and they must *explicitly* change the type by writing the necessary programming). If you prefer to be strict about data type conversions, type `Option Strict On` at the very top of the code window. With that option on, VB 2005 Express displays an error message if you try to assign a string to a variable declared `As Integer`, as shown in Figure 7-2.

Figure 7-2:
IntelliSense
warns you
here of an
Option Strict
violation.

```
Private Sub Form1_Load(ByVal sender As System.Object, ByVal
    Dim TopTvPri[Option Strict On disallows implicit conversions from 'String' to 'Integer'.]
    TopTvPrice = TextBox1.Text
                                    ⊙
```

In other words, if the variable `TopTvPrice` has been declared as an `Integer` type and you write the line of code `TopTvPrice = TextBox1.Text`, VB 2005 Express flags this as an error, displays the sawtooth error indicator under `TextBox1.Text`, and when you mouse over that line, you see a pop-up message, and VB puts the following message in the Task List for you: `Option Strict On disallows implicit conversions from ' 'String to 'Integer'`.

If you want to leave `Option Strict On`, you must force conversions in your programming and not simply trust that VB 2005 Express does it for you. You see how to force conversions of variable types later in this chapter. My advice is that beginners leave this option turned off (the default for VB Express). That way you have one less thing to worry about when you're learning to program. Later on, you can turn it on to avoid some relatively rare kinds of bugs that can be caused by implicit conversion. (To turn it on permanently, choose Tools⇨Options⇨Project to make Option Strict On the default, so you don't always have to type it in.)

Naming Variables

Each variable has a name that the programmer gives it. Usually, programmers like to use memorable variable names — something easily recognized, such as `UsersTopTvPrice`.

Underscore characters are allowed in variable names, so some programmers make the name even more readable this way: `Users_Top_Tv_Price`.

You must observe several rules when making up a name for a variable (otherwise, VB protests):

- ✔ **It must start with a letter, not a digit.**
- ✔ **It can't be one of VB's own command words, such as `For` or `Dim`.**
- ✔ **It can't contain any punctuation marks or spaces.**

Creating a Variable

When you create a variable, you can do so explicitly or implicitly. By default VB wants all variables to be explicitly declared and wants their variable types to be specified in that variable declaration, like this:

```
Dim UsersAge as Integer
```

This means that when you use a variable in a program, you *can't* simply type in a name for it, and *voila*, the variable comes into existence. *That* would be *implicit declaration*. VB by default now frowns on this kind of thing for two reasons:

- ✔ One reason that forcing explicit declaration is so highly regarded by many programmers is that when you look later at the code you wrote and you're trying to figure it out, you can see a list of all the variables right there at the top of the procedure or at the top of a class (if you want the variable to apply to the entire class — not just to a single procedure).
- ✔ A second reason, to avoid certain kinds of bugs, is covered at the end of this chapter.

Declaring variables explicitly

Explicit declaration requires more effort. However, many programmers swear by it, and VB Express defaults to it. You use the `Dim` command to explicitly declare the variable:

```
Dim UsersAge As Integer
UsersAge = InputBox ("How old are you?")
```

If you're going to use several variables in the procedure, `Dim` each of them:

```
Dim UsersAge, UsersHeight As Integer
Dim UsersName, Nickname As String
```

Notice that you can combine several declarations on a single line, as long as they are the same variable type. That's why the `String` variable names are not declared in the same line as the `Integer` types in the preceding code example.

Or, if you use the `As` command, you can combine types on the same declaration line:

```
Dim UsersName As String, UsersHeight As Integer
```

VB also permits you to declare a variable *and* assign a value to it on the same line:

```
Dim UsersAge As Integer = 21
```

If you are declaring multiple variables on a single line, you need to use the `Dim` statement only at the start of the line and then just separate the variable names on the rest of the line by commas. Now do you see one reason why you can't use punctuation in variable names? Visual Basic uses various kinds of punctuation to mean various things in a line of code, like those commas. Recall that the single-quote symbol (`'`) means that you're making an annotation (a comment) and VB should ignore everything following the `'` on that line. The `*` means multiply, `&` means concatenate text, and so on.

Notice that the line of code beginning with `Dim` ends with an `As` clause that specifies the variable's type.

VB has nine fundamental variable types, but thousands of objects that you can use as *types*. You get to know fundamental types later in this chapter. For now, just note that each declared variable must be explicitly typed (*typed* here means given a data type, not pressing keys on the keyboard).

Thanks to OOP, everything is an object (even the integer variable type) and, as you can see in Figure 7-3, everything is a variable (even objects like ListBoxes are manipulated as *object* variables). Because OOP uses mad taxonomic systems, traditional usable categories have been blown to bits. If *everything* is in the same category, then that category serves no real purpose, right?

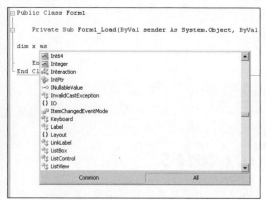

Figure 7-3:
You might
be amazed
at how
many
"variables"
are listed
when you
use Dim
to declare
a new
variable.

Dim stands for *dimension*, an old computer term for "set aside some memory for this." Although Dim is the most commonly used, there are seven additional declaration commands: Static, Public, Protected, Friend, Shared, Protected Friend, and Private. Recall that these additional commands specify either *scope* (from how many locations in your program the variable can be accessed) or *lifetime* (how long the variable holds its value — only while the procedure within which it is declared is executing, or while the entire program is running). See Chapter 5 if you need a refresher on scope and lifetime.

Declaring variables implicitly

If you're a radical and want to use *implicit* declaration (no declaration needed), you can type this at the very top of your code window (above any Imports statements):

```
Option Explicit Off
```

To make this the default, so you don't have to type it into each program, choose Tools⇨Options⇨Project and uncheck the Option Explicit check box.

Here's an example of implicit declaration: Perhaps your program displays an InputBox that asks the user how old he or she is. The variable in which you want to store his or her answer (the value) can be named UsersAge (I know, I know; it should be User'sAge, but you can't use punctuation in variable names):

```
UsersAge = InputBox ("How old are you?")
```

As soon as the user types 44, or whatever, and closes the InputBox, the value 44 is assigned to the variable UsersAge. The value is stored. When your program later wants to process that data, it knows where to look. It merely uses the variable name. Say you want to find out if the user is eligible for AARP (the < symbol means "is less than"):

```
If UsersAge < 50 Then MsgBox ("You're too young to join AARP, pup.")
```

Notice that you use the variable name as you use any other number in this programming. When the program executes, whatever number the user typed in is compared to 50 in this line of code.

Manipulating Variables

Classic variables hold only one value at a time. But the value can change as necessary (hence the name *variable*). For example, you could write the following code (although it makes no sense to do so):

```
Dim TVShow as String
TVShow = "Barney"
TVShow = "Five-O"
```

When this program executes, VB assigns the text Barney to the variable TVShow but immediately dumps that value and replaces it with Five-O. When a new value is assigned to a variable, the previous value in that variable simply no longer exists.

You can assign *literal* values ("Barney" or 299, as illustrated previously), but you can also assign one variable's value to another. When you assign a variable to another variable, the variable on the left of the equals sign (=) gets the value held in the variable to the right of the =. At this point, both variables contain the same value. This is like making a copy of the value. In this next example, the contents (the value) in the variable PopularShow are copied into the variable MyTVShow:

```
MyTVShow = PopularShow
```

One practical and common use of copying one variable into another was illustrated earlier in this chapter with this line:

```
TopTvPrice = TextBox1.Text
```

In this code, the user's typed input is assigned to a variable, identifying that input's meaning in the program. You can more easily understand the meaning of TopTvPrice than TextBox1.Text when you read the code.

Packing several values into an array

Sometimes, a variable's ability to hold only one value at a time is limiting. If you need to collect a whole group of values together in one package, you need to use a special way to group values: You give them one "variable name," but you give each individual value a unique index number. This is similar to the way that all your neighbors share the same road name but are distinguished from each other by house numbers: 12 Elm, 13 Elm, 14 Elm, and so on.

A group of values sharing the same name, but with different index numbers, is called an *array*. An array is somewhat like a mini-database, holding related pieces of information that are indexed for easy manipulation.

Arrays are so important — and have been so enhanced from classic versions of VB — that all of Chapter 8 is devoted to them.

Some variable efficiencies

Sometimes you want to concatenate or otherwise combine two variables. Suppose that you want to personalize your program, so you first ask the user to type in his or her name, and then you use that variable along with another variable to create a complete sentence:

```
Dim Msg, Result As String
    Result = InputBox("Please type your first name.")
    Msg = "Thank you, " & Result
    MsgBox(Msg)
```

You have some ways to shorten code. If you're one of those people who is always looking to conserve variable names, you can reuse Result like this, without even needing that second variable Msg:

```
Dim Result As String
    Result = InputBox("Please type your first name.")
    Result = "Thank you, " & Result
    MsgBox(Result)
```

Or if you're one of those people who are really, really conservative and always want to save space and condense code, you can do it like this:

```
Dim Result As String
    Result = InputBox("Please type your first name.")
    Msgbox("Thank you, " & Result)
```

As the preceding code illustrates, a variable can be part of what's assigned to itself. One use for this technique is illustrated in the preceding code: You want to preserve the contents of the variable (Result), but you want to add something to the contents (`"Thank you, "`). To demonstrate this same principle with a numeric variable, perform the following math equation using the variable name:

```
A = 233
A = A + 1
```

Now `A` holds `234`.

Saving time with +=

VB 2005 allows another technique when you are adding a variable's current contents to some new value (as in the example in the previous section). You can avoid repeating the variable's name by combining + with =, for example. Here's how this trick works. Instead of the following code:

```
A = A + 1
```

You can use *plus-equals*, like this:

```
A += 1
```

This condensation has several variations:

- ✔ `A *= 4`: The value currently in variable `A` is multiplied by 4 and assigned to `A`.
- ✔ `A -= 1`: Decrement the value currently in variable `A`.

Here's an example:

```
Dim Brother as String
Brother = "Tom"
Brother &= " and Bob"
```

Now `Brother` contains `Tom and Bob`. This technique avoids repeating the variable name like this `Brother = Brother & " and Bob"` which is the traditional VB approach. It comes in handy to avoid repeating really lengthy variable (or object) names, which are sometimes necessary in VB 2005 Express.

You often can choose from several ways to code, and your personal style will emerge over time. Notice how I always seem to use `Result` or `Response` as the variable names with the `InputBox` command? It's just a little habit of mine; you can use `Reaction`, `Retort`, `Reply`, or `Rejoinder`, just as long as it begins with an *R*. Just kidding! It doesn't have to begin with *R*. You can use `Answer`, `Users_Input`, or whatever. You know the rules for thinking up variable names: You can use pretty much any word or even a nonsense word like `jaaaaakaa`. But it's best to make your variable names descriptive of what the variable holds. And, it's helpful after a while to settle on some consistent way of naming frequently used variables, like those you assign the result of an InputBox user input. This consistency makes your programming easier to read and modify later if necessary. There is a whole set of naming conventions you might want to consider using, such as prepending `txt` whenever naming a TextBox (as in `txtPhoneNumber`), on the Cheat Sheet at the front of this book.

Understanding Data Types for Numeric Variables

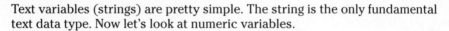

Text variables (strings) are pretty simple. The string is the only fundamental text data type. Now let's look at numeric variables.

There are several fundamental types of numeric variables. The reason for these different numeric data types is to enable you to speed up your applications with some of them and achieve greater precision with others. Table 7-1 lists some important data types. You can find a fuller list of data types and the ranges of values that they can hold on the Cheat Sheet attached to the front of this book.

Table 7-1	Important Numeric Data Types
Type	*How You Use It*
Boolean	The simplest numeric variable type, Boolean can hold only two states: `True` and `False` (it defaults to `False`). Use this when you want a toggle variable (something that switches off and on like a light switch). To create a Boolean variable, use the following code: `Dim MyToggle As Boolean`.
Integer, and its larger sister, the Long type	`Integer` is 32 bits long, and `Long` is 64 bits long (and `Long` is an `Integer` too — no fraction, no decimal point). If your program for some reason needs to use a 16-bit integer, use the type `Short`.
Floating point	The "point" is the decimal point. Floating point, like integer, has small and large versions called `Single` and `Double`, respectively. Use floating point when your program requires the precision that fractions offer: `Dim MyFraction As Single, MyBiggerNumber As Double`.

When creating a program that involves math, you may be surprised at how often the only thing you need is an integer. In most programming, the `Integer` is the most common numeric data type. (No fractions are allowed with an `Integer`.) If your non-fractional number is larger or smaller (a negative) than an integer can hold, make it a `Long` data type.

```
Dim MyLittleNumber As Integer
Dim MyBigNumber As Long
```

In addition to the types listed in Table 7-1, VB has a `Char` type, which is an unsigned (no negatives) 16-bit type that is used to store Unicode characters (a system that codes text characters by giving each a unique number). The `Decimal` type is a 96-bit signed integer scaled by a variable power of 10. If you don't understand what this means, you should at all costs avoid writing a program that involves the `Decimal` type.

Converting Data Types

Sometimes you have to change a variable's data type. When you leave `Option Strict` turned on, as described earlier in this chapter, you often must *coerce* variables to change type: You must explicitly program the change.

VB boasts four ways to change one data type into another:

✔ First, the `.ToString` method is designed to convert any numeric data type into a text string.

✔ The second way to convert data is to use this set of VB functions: `CStr()`, `CBool()`, `CByte()`, `CChar()`, `CShort()`, `CInt()`, `CLng()`, `CDate()`, `CDbl()`, `CSng()`, `CDec()`, and `CObj()`, as in the following example:

```
Dim s As String
Dim i As Integer = 1551
s = CStr(i)
MsgBox(s)
```

✔ The third way is to use the `Convert` method, like this:

```
Dim s As String
Dim i As Integer = 1551
    s = Convert.ToString(i)
    MsgBox(s)
```

✔ The fourth way uses the `CType` function, with this syntax:

```
Dim s As String
Dim i As Integer = 1551
    s = CType(i, String)
    MsgBox(s)
```

Take your pick.

Why division is bizarre

Computers calculate in different ways with different numeric variable types. They can do arithmetic faster with integer types than with floating-point types because floating point suffers from the problem of decimal points and the bothersome fractions to the right of decimal points.

Why are fractions such trouble? The simplest explanation is understandable if you recall that elementary school teachers have to spend much more time teaching *division* than teaching multiplication or other basic arithmetic techniques. Anyone who has written a list for Santa or made a stack of cookies understands addition. Subtraction, too, is clear enough — for example, when an older brother steals some cookies from the stack. Multiplication is pretty easy to get once you understand the idea of addition. Multiplication is just addition repeated over and over.

But division is in a class by itself. Division can cause something to go below unity, below one, into the problematic world of fractions. Suddenly, two simple digits like 3 and 1 can expand into a list of digits bigger than the universe, .3333333333333333333 . . . ; you get an infinitely long result if you try to divide 1 by 3. Infinity is a disturbing result when you're used to getting neat, understandable results from adding and subtracting.

And there are those *remainders*, unsettling things left over after the arithmetic is supposedly finished. Plus, in the real world, if something becomes fractional, it dies. Few creatures, other than worms and some plants, can survive being "in half." All in all, division is a bizarre, dangerous, fantastic maneuver no matter how you slice it.

Computers have exactly the same problems as children when working with division; they have more to consider and more to manipulate. Just like us, the computer must calculate more slowly when working with numeric variable types that can have fractions (the floating-point data types). If you want to speed up your programs, see if you can get away with merely using the integer data type. Integers don't involve fractions. If you don't need the precision that fractions offer — and most of the time you don't — use integers. After all, the IRS lets you round off pennies to the nearest dollar, so be brave and, if possible, just ignore any fractional details in your calculations. (This advice does *not* apply to NASA scientists calculating the Mars Lander trajectory.)

However, the distinctions between numeric data types were more important in the past, when memory was small and expensive, and processing speed was relatively slow. These days, choosing conservative data types may not much matter unless you are writing a program with lots of specialized, heavy-duty number crunching.

If you're interested, there's an actual, physical, *hardware* reason that floating point slows things down in a computer. As Technical Editor John Mueller explained to me (your slap-happy author, who didn't know this), the computer's processor uses an *entirely different* piece of microprocessor hardware when doing math with real (integer) versus floating-point numbers. The floating-point unit within the processor is actually a *state machine,* so it runs slower than the rest of the processor. Integer math, by contrast, is performed within the processor's actual registers, which are very fast.

Table 7-2 shows all the primary VB data types.

Table 7-2	The VB 2005 Express Data Types		
Traditional VB Type	*New 2005 Type*	*Memory Size*	*Range*
Boolean	System.Boolean	2 bytes	True or False
Char	System.Char	2 bytes	0–65535 (unsigned)
Byte	System.Byte	1 byte	0–255 (unsigned)
Object	System.Object	4 bytes	Any Type
Date	System.DateTime	8 bytes	01-Jan-0001 to 31-Dec-9999
Double	System.Double	8 bytes	+/–1.797E308
Decimal	System.Decimal	16 bytes	28 digits
Short	System.Int16	2 bytes	–32,768 to 32,767
Integer	System.Int32	4 bytes	+/–2.147E9
Long	System.Int64	8 bytes	+/–9.223E18
Single	System.Single	4 bytes	+/–3.402E38
String	System.String	CharacterCount * 2 (plus 10 bytes)	2 billion Unicode characters

You can also employ unsigned (non-negative) versions of the Integer, Long, and Short types (named UInteger, ULong, and UShort). By removing the possibility of using a negative number, the size of positive values that can be held in these types doubles. For example, an ordinary (signed) Integer can hold the following range of numbers: –2,147,483,648 to 2,147,483,647. But the unsigned version of Integer, UInteger, can hold these values: 0 through 4,294,967,295. The range of values that can be held is identical for Integer and UInteger, it's just the actual numbers that can be held that differs.

Creating Expressions with Operators

To process data, you can combine variables and other items into an *expression*. As with variables, you can assemble expressions using literal numbers, literal strings, numeric variables, string variables, numeric variables in an array, functions that return numbers or strings, constants, or any combination of these. To create an expression, you need at least two elements separated by an operator. You can use operators to combine, modify, compare, or otherwise manipulate the items in an expression. For example, an expression can be as simple as 2 + 2. The expression "A" > "B" asks whether the literal letter A is greater alphabetically than the letter B, which is untrue, so this expression evaluates to False. The operator here is the greater-than symbol: >.

During run time (while the program executes), VB looks at and evaluates an expression. This evaluation produces a result. It may produce the number 6, the answer True, or some other result, such as with the expression "A" & "sk", which in turn produces the result Ask.

You need to know about the several kinds of operators:

- ✔ **Comparison operators:** These operators compare numbers in various ways (such as greater-than or equals) or compare text in various ways (alphabetically, or find similarity with the Like command). The greater-than symbol (>) is an operator in this example that says n is greater than z: n > z.

- ✔ **Arithmetic operators:** Examples of these operators are * and +. The plus sign (+), for example, is an operator in the following example: 2 + 4.

- ✔ **Logical operators:** These are And, Not, and Or, which you can use to build longer, more complex expressions. For example, many expressions are a combination of programming elements that, taken together, can be evaluated as either *true* or *false,* such as *Mary is older than Sue.* Such true/false expressions are called *Boolean* expressions. Although it's more complex, this, too, is an expression: *Bob is smaller than Stan, but Stan is wealthier than Sondra.* This is also a Boolean expression because it is either true or false.

Even though Boolean expressions can get quite lengthy, if *any* of their assertions are false, the entire expression is evaluated as false. However, some expressions produce results other than simply true or false. The expression 3 + 4, for example, is an *integer expression* because it evaluates to an integer result.

In the following sections, you find out more details about using these different operators, as well as how to use parentheses to specify the order in which the parts of a complex expression are evaluated.

Comparing values

Often, you need to compare two values, and then your program reacts based on the result of the comparison. Say, for example, that the user has typed in his or her age, and you want to respond to the age in your programming:

```
Dim UsersAge As Integer
Dim Msg As String

If UsersAge < 50 Then
    Msg = "You "
    Else
        Msg = "You do not "
End If

Msg &= "qualify for reduced term insurance."

MsgBox(Msg)
```

The *expression* in this code is `UsersAge < 50`. This particular expression uses one of the comparison (also called *relational*) operators: the less-than symbol (<). The line of code means this: If the value in the `UsersAge` variable is less than 50, then show the "You qualify . . ." message. Otherwise (`Else`), show the "You do not qualify . . ." version.

Table 7-3 lists the eight comparison operators used in VB.

Table 7-3	The VB Comparison Operators
Operator	*Description*
<	Less than
<=	Less than or equal to
>	Greater than
>=	Greater than or equal to
<>	Not equal
=	Equal
Is	Two object variables refer to the same object
Like	Pattern matching

Here are some points to keep in mind about the operators listed in Table 7-3:

- ✔ **Remembering the meaning of the < and > symbols is easy.** The large end of the symbol is greater, so A > B means A is greater than B. A < B means A is less than B.

- ✔ **You can use the comparison operators with text as well.** When used with literal text (or text variables), the operators refer to the alphabetic relationship between the strings, with the value of Andy being less than Anne, alphabetically.

✔ **The Is operator is highly specialized.** It tells you whether two object variable names refer to the same object. You can use it with arrays that keep track of controls or forms.

✔ **The Like operator lets you compare a string to a pattern, using wild-cards.** This rarely used operator is similar to the wildcards you can use when using a search utility. The wildcard symbols are * and ?. In the Windows search utility or in Explorer, for example, you can see all files ending with .DOC by typing *.DOC. Check out the nearby sidebar, "Working with the Like operator," for more details.

Working with the Like operator

You employ Like to compare strings, as follows:

```
Dim Msg, A As String
A = "Rudolpho"

If A Like "Ru*" Then Msg = "Close Enough"
MsgBox(Msg)
```

In the preceding example, the message is displayed. The Like operator can be used to forgive user typos. When testing for Pennsylvania, you could accept Like Pen* because no other state starts with those characters, so any misspellings the user makes further on in this word are ignored.

The following example uses the Like operator to compare against a single character in a particular position. (Notice in this next example that the two logical lines are placed on a single physical line, separated by a colon. You can use a separate line for MsgBox(A), but it's so short that I just stuck it onto the end of the other code. If you do put two or more logical lines together, remember that the colon is necessary to separate them.)

```
Dim A As Boolean
A = "Nora" Like "?ora" : MsgBox(A)
```

This results in True.

Recall that many expressions simply evaluate to True or False, and therefore the expression returns a Boolean answer. So, you can declare a Boolean variable to receive that answer, as in the previous example. Here's another example:

```
Dim A As Boolean
A = "Nora" Like "F?ora" : MsgBox(A)
```

This results in False because the first letter in Nora isn't *F*, the third letter isn't *o*, and so on.

You can also use Like to compare when you don't care about a match between a series of characters, like this:

```
If "David" Like "*d" Then
```

This code results in a match. "D*" or "*D*d" or "*i*" all match "David".

Or you can use the following to match a single character in the text against a single character or range of characters in the list enclosed by brackets:

```
If "Empire" Like "??[n-q]*" Then
```

This code results in a match, because the third character in Empire, *p*, falls within the range n-q. You can also use multiple ranges such as "[n-r t-w]".

Or you can use the following to match if a single character in the text is not in the list:

```
If "Empire" Like "??[!n-q]*" Then
```

This code doesn't result in a match (the ! symbol means "not").

Using arithmetic operators

Arithmetic operators work pretty much as you expect them to. They do some math and provide a result. Table 7-4 lists the arithmetic operators used in VB.

Table 7-4	The VB Arithmetic Operators
Operator	*Description*
^	Exponentiation — the number multiplied by itself (for example, 5 ^ 2 is 25 and 5 ^ 3 is 125)
–	Subtraction Negation — negative numbers (such as –25)
*	Multiplication
/	Division
\	Integer division — division with no remainder, no fraction, no decimal point (for example 8 \ 6 results in 1). Use this if you don't need the remainder.
Mod	Modulo arithmetic (explained in the text following this table)
+	Addition
&	String concatenation (This & is still supported in VB 2005 Express, but is no longer necessary. It was used in previous versions of VB with variant variable types. VB 2005 Express has no variants, so you can use + for numeric addition as well as concatenation. This isn't really an arithmetic operator at all, but Microsoft lists it as one.)

Use the arithmetic operators like this:

```
If B + A > 12 Then
```

The modulo (Mod) operator gives you any remainder after a division, but not the results of the division itself. You just get the remainder. This is useful when you want to know if some number divides evenly into another number. That way, you can do things *at intervals*, or as they say: *periodically*. One use for periodicity (don't *I* talk fancy!) is if you want to print the page number in bold on every fifth page. Here's how you could program that:

```
If PageNumber Mod 5 = 0 Then
    FontBold = True
Else
    FontBold = False
End If
```

Here are some more Mod examples:

- ✔ 15 Mod 5 results in 0.
- ✔ 16 Mod 5 results in 1.
- ✔ 17 Mod 5 results in 2.
- ✔ 20 Mod 5 results in 0.

The logical operators

The logical operators are sometimes called *Boolean* operators because technically they operate on individual *bits* (and a bit can be only in one of two states: true or false, on or off). But whatever you call them — and I like *logical* — these operators are most often used to create a compound expression. They chain expressions together just as they chain phrases together in ordinary English.

The logical operators that you'll use frequently are And, Or, and Not. They allow you to construct expressions like this:

```
If BettysAge > 55 And JohnsAge > 50 Then
```

The And operator means that both comparisons must be true for the entire expression to be true.

Similarly, Or allows you to create an expression in which only one comparison *must* be true (but both of them can be true as well) for the entire expression to be true:

```
If TomsMother = Visiting Or SandysMothersAge > 78 Then
```

The Not operator is good for switching a toggle back and forth, like this:

```
Private Sub Button1_Click(ByVal sender As System.Object, ByVal e As
            System.EventArgs) Handles Button1.Click

Static Toggle As Boolean
    Toggle = Not Toggle

    If Toggle Then MsgBox("See this message every other time you click.")

End Sub
```

The `Static` command preserves the contents of the variable `Toggle` (`Dim` does not). Remember the `Static` command; it comes in very handy when you need to retain a value in a local variable (a variable declared within a procedure, as in the preceding code). Typically it's used with counters or toggles.

The `Boolean` variable type is the simplest one. It has only two states: `True` and `False`. It can be flipped back and forth like a light switch. The line, `Toggle = Not Toggle`, means this: If Toggle's value is False, make it now True. If it's True, make it False. You'll be surprised at how often you use this technique in your programming.

Table 7-5 lists all the logical operators, some of which have esoteric uses in cryptography and such.

Table 7-5	The VB Logical Operators
Operator	*Description*
Not	Logical negation
And	And
Or	Inclusive Or
Xor	Either, but not both

Here's an example of a logical operator at work:

```
If 5 + 2 = 4 Or 6 + 6 = 12 Then MsgBox("One of them is true.")
```

One of these expressions is true, so the `MsgBox` comment is displayed. Only one *or* the other needs to be true. Here's another example:

```
If 5 + 2 = 4 And 6 + 6 = 12 Then MsgBox ("Both of them are true.")
```

This is false, so nothing is displayed. *Both* expressions, the first and the second, must be true for the MsgBox to appear.

VB 2005 Express offers two new operators — `AndAlso` and `OrElse` — which differ technically from the way that the `And` and `Or` logical operators work and differ in how expressions using them are evaluated. The purpose of this is to attempt to prevent some esoteric, yet possible, errors. If this is important to you, see the entry titled "AND, OR, XOR, and NOT" in Appendix B on this book's Web site. (See this book's Introduction for details about the Web site.)

Setting operator precedence

When you use more than one operator in an expression, which operator should be evaluated first? This can matter.

Simple expressions are usually unambiguous: 2 + 3 can only result in 5. But sometimes a more complex expression can be solved in more than one way, like this one:

```
3 * 10 + 5
```

Should VB evaluate 3 * 10 and then add 5 to it (resulting in 35), or should it first evaluate 10 + 5 and multiply that result by 3 (resulting in 45)?

Expressions are not necessarily evaluated by the computer from left to right. Left-to-right evaluation in the previous example results in 35, because 3 is multiplied by 10 before the 5 is added to that result. But remember that complex expressions can be evaluated backward sometimes.

Visual Basic enforces an *order of precedence,* a hierarchy by which various relationships are resolved between numbers in an expression. For example, multiplication is always carried out before addition. Fortunately, you don't have to memorize the order of precedence. Instead, to make sure that you get the results you intend when using more than one operator, just enclose the items that you want to be evaluated first in parentheses. Using the previous example, if you want to multiply 3 * 10 and then add 5, write it like this:

```
(3 * 10) + 5
```

By enclosing an operator and its two surrounding values in parentheses, you tell VB that you want the enclosed items to be considered as a single value and to be evaluated before anything else happens.

If you intended to add 10 + 5 and then multiply by 3, move the parentheses like this instead:

```
3 * (10 + 5)
```

In longer expressions, you can even nest parentheses to make clear which items are to be calculated in which order, like this:

```
3 * ((40 / 4) + 5)
```

If you work with these kinds of expressions a great deal, you may want to memorize Table 7-6. But most people just use parentheses and forget about this problem. If you're interested, the table lists the order in which VB evaluates an expression, from first evaluated to last.

Table 7-6   The VB 2005 Express Operators in Order of Precedence

Operator	Description
^	Exponents (6 ^ 2 is 36. The first number is multiplied by itself the second number of times.)
–	Negation (negative numbers such as –33)
* /	Multiplication and division
\	Integer division (division with no remainder, no fraction)
Mod	Modulo arithmetic
+ –	Addition and subtraction
The relational operators	Evaluated left to right
The logical operators	Evaluated left to right

Given that multiplication has precedence over addition, the ambiguous example that started this discussion can be evaluated in the following way:

```
3 * 10 + 5
```

So, the result is 35.

Chapter 8

Superstrings: Managing Arrays

. . . .

In This Chapter

▶ Figuring boundaries

▶ Understanding initialization techniques

▶ Using object arrays

▶ Searching and sorting

▶ Tapping into the `ArrayList` powerhouse

▶ Data binding

▶ Employing enumerators

▶ Hacking hashtables

. . . .

*A*rrays are essential computing tools: They provide a way to efficiently store and retrieve related data. An array is like a little database containing multiple variables — and the data in an array can be manipulated as a group. For example, you can copy the entire array, sort it in different ways, and so on.

But if you think you have some idea about what traditional arrays can do, think again. VB has now taken them to a whole new level of usefulness. You'll find lots of interesting and powerful new ways to manipulate arrays in this chapter.

In VB, arrays can contain objects, they can search and sort themselves, and the `ArrayList` feature is particularly valuable and flexible. In addition, you'll also want to explore the "strong typing" available from the new `HashTable` class. All of these topics are covered in this chapter.

Working in a Zero-Based World

Before exploring the interesting new ways you can use arrays in VB, I first need to point out that arrays are *always* zero-based in the .NET framework upon which VB Express rests. (This framework is a huge collection of procedures, such as `Dim`, that you can use in your programming.)

Zero-based groups are strange to us humans, but some people in the programming community who create languages (such as the .NET languages) don't seem to understand this strangeness and the many bugs it introduces into real-world programs. It's as if you, a wacky mayor, decided that in *your* town, the first house on each street would have the address 0. There would be a family living at 0 Maple Drive, poor things. Imagine the laughter and the pain. Zero-based lists are obviously silly. They're very common in programming languages. (However, until recently, VB sensibly started counting with 1 in its arrays and other such lists. But all that's changed.)

In practical terms, the zero-based array means that you must always be aware that the dimension you declare for your array is not its actual capacity. If you dimension (specify the size of) an array as 10, the array actually can hold 11 items (item 0 through item 10 = 11 items).

Put another way, the index numbers to the items in this array are 0, 1, 2, 3, 4, 5, 6, 7, 8, 9, and 10. The array has 11 index numbers, 11 elements, and these elements can contain 11 values. Just remember that in VB Express, an array can always contain one more value than the number you declare as its dimension.

This has several implications, particularly when you manipulate arrays in loop structures. You can use the `UBound` function of an array (or the `Count` property of an `ArrayList`) to find out the highest element number, like this:

```
UBound(myarray)
```

Or you can use the `Length` property to find out how many *actual* elements (its true capacity) are in the array, like this:

```
myarray.Length
```

In the following example, the `UBound` function returns `10`, but the `Length` property is `11`:

```
Dim MyArray(10) As String

Console.WriteLine("Ubound, the DIMension is: " & UBound(MyArray))
Console.WriteLine("The Length Property is: " & MyArray.Length)
```

Zero-based arrays and other types of zero-based lists have always bedeviled programmers. That's why an `Option Base 1` statement was made available in earlier versions of VB, to force an array to begin its index with 1 rather than zero. Nonetheless, the .NET Common Language Specification requires zero-based arrays "for compatibility with other languages."

The zero-based array is one example of how .NET requires VB to conform to the way the C language and its offspring — C++, C#, Java, and so on — have always done things. In my view, it may have been better to add flexible lower boundaries (base) to the C-type languages than to remove the `Option Base` feature from VB.

Initializing Arrays

In VB Express, you can assign values to variables on the same line that declares them. This same feature is available to arrays. If you want to use this same-line shortcut approach, you must use braces to enclose the array's values, like this:

```
Private Sub Form1_Load(ByVal sender As System.Object, ByVal e As
        System.EventArgs) Handles MyBase.Load

Dim MyArray() As String = {"Clark", "Lois", "Jimmy"}
Dim i As Integer

    For i = 1 To UBound(MyArray)
        Debug.WriteLine(MyArray(i))
    Next

End Sub
```

Notice that you can't specify an upper boundary when initializing values in this fashion. You must leave the `()` after the array's name empty, as this example illustrates. Also notice that when you display the results from 1 to the highest index number, the zeroth item (`Clark`) is ignored. To access all the data, you would need to write your loop like this:

```
    For i = 0 To UBound(MyArray)
```

Creating Arrays of Objects

You can create an array of objects in VB Express that, among other things, allows you to store different data types within a single array. Normal arrays are composed of a single data type — such as a string array that can hold only strings. But with object arrays, you can mix and match different types in the same array. If you're not fond of Object Oriented Programming (OOP), just skip this section.

To create an object array, you first declare an object variable, and then you instantiate (OOP-speak for *create*) each object in the array. This example creates an array holding six book objects. Don't worry that you're creating a *class* here. If you want to explore object-oriented programming, I suggest finding a good book on that topic. Barry Burd's *Java 2 For Dummies,* 2nd Edition (Wiley) offers an introduction to object-oriented programming through Java.

Anyway, OOP fans, here's how to build an object array:

```
Private Sub Form1_Load(ByVal sender As System.Object, ByVal e As
            System.EventArgs) Handles MyBase.Load

Dim arrBook(6) As Book 'create the array object variable
Dim i As Integer

'instantiate each member of the array:
For i = 0 To 6
    arrBook(i) = New Book()
Next

' set the two properties of one of the array members
arrBook(3).Title = "Babu"
arrBook(3).Description = "This book is large."

Dim s As String = arrBook(3).Title
MsgBox(s)

End Sub

End Class
```

Then you type in your Book class *below* the End Class line (see boldface in the preceding code) that concludes the Form1 class:

```
Public Class Book

Private _Title As String
Private _Description As String

Public Property Title() As String
    Get
        Return _Title
    End Get
    Set(ByVal Value As String)
        _Title = Value
    End Set
End Property

Public Property Description() As String
    Get
```

```
        Return _Description
    End Get
    Set(ByVal Value As String)
        _Description = Value
    End Set
End Property

End Class
```

Searching and Sorting Arrays

In VB Express, arrays have the capability to both sort and search themselves. By default, a VB Express array, when asked to sort itself, sorts alphabetically from A to Z. Also note that, when sorted, the array's elements' index numbers change.

Here's an example showing how to use both the sort and the search methods of the array object. The simplest syntax for these two methods is as follows:

```
Array.Sort(myArray)
```

and

```
anIndex = Array.BinarySearch(myArray, "Penni Goetz")
```

To see these features in action, put a TextBox on a form. Then type in this code:

```
Private Sub Form1_Load(ByVal sender As System.Object, ByVal e As
          System.EventArgs) Handles MyBase.Load

Dim myarray(4) As String
Dim cr As String = vbCrLf 'carriage return
Dim show As String
Dim i As Integer
Dim anIndex As Integer
Dim r As String

'fill the array with values:
myarray.SetValue("zero", 0)
myarray.SetValue("one", 1)
myarray.SetValue("two", 2)
myarray.SetValue("three", 3)
myarray.SetValue("four", 4)

For i = 0 To 4
    show = show & myarray(i) & cr
```

```
Next

TextBox1.Text = show & cr & cr & "SORTED:" & cr

Array.Sort(myarray)

show = ""

For i = 0 To 4
    show = show & myarray(i) & cr
Next

anIndex = Array.BinarySearch(myarray, "two")

r = CStr(anIndex)
show &= cr & "The word two was found at index number " & r & " within the array"

TextBox1.Text &= show

show = ""

For i = 0 To 4
    show = show & myarray(i) & cr
Next

TextBox1.Select(0, 0) 'turn off selection

End Sub
```

Note the use of the `SetValue` method in this example. Its syntax enables you to add or replace an item anywhere within an array by specifying the index number. The following line of code sets the third item in `myarray` to the string `one`.

```
myarray.SetValue("one", 2)
```

The `Sort` method has eight variations, including one that sorts only a subset of the array:

```
Array.Sort(myarray, StartIndex, LengthOfSubset)
```

Although this is a rarely used tactic, here's an example that specifies that you want only the fifth through eighth items sorted:

```
Array.Sort(myarray, 4, 7)
```

You might use this approach if, for example, the array had various kinds of data, some of which you didn't want to sort. Perhaps the first three elements of that array don't contain string data; instead they contain Web service data, so you don't want to sort those three elements.

(However, if you are using my suggestion and avoiding the zeroth item, this example sorts the *fourth* through *seventh* items.)

Unfortunately, a bug was introduced into VB several years ago in the earliest .NET version. By default, when you assign some text to a TextBox, as you did in the previous example, it is highlighted (selected, as if the user had dragged the mouse across it to highlight it). This is likely to confuse the user and also looks bad. To deselect the text, you have to add the following line to your programming, as I did previously:

```
TextBox1.Select(0, 0) 'turn off selection
```

Customizing the Sorting Rules

You can even sort one array based on the elements in *another* array. This interesting capability allows you to devise your own, custom sorting rules.

For example, suppose that the entries in a single-dimension array hold first names and last names separated simply by a space character: "Mary Jones," "Bob Smith," and so on.

However, you need to sort them by their *last* names. Using this custom sorting trick, you can solve this problem by creating a second array that holds only the last names and alphabetizing it in sync with the first array (so you're actually also sorting the original array the way you want).

Sorting both, "connected" arrays has the effect of rearranging the original array in parallel with the sorting going on in the new array. Note that the second array is *not* alphabetized. It merely gets sorted in parallel with the first array. The arguments of the Sort method look like this:

```
myarray.Sort(firstarray, secondarray)
```

and only `firstarray` here is alphabetized — `secondarray` merely goes along for the ride in sync.

Here's an example showing how to use this technique:

```
Private Sub Form1_Load(ByVal sender As System.Object, ByVal e As
         System.EventArgs) Handles MyBase.Load

Dim cr As String = vbCrLf 'carriage return

Dim myarray(5) As String
Dim lastnames(5) As String

myarray(0) = "Monica Lewis"
myarray(1) = "Georgio Apples"
```

```
myarray(2) = "Sandy Shores"
myarray(3) = "Dee Lighted"
myarray(4) = "Andy Cane"
myarray(5) = "Darva Slots"

TextBox1.Clear()

'create an array of the last names:

Dim i As Integer
Dim x As Integer
Dim s As String

For i = 0 To UBound(myarray)
    s = myarray(i)
    x = s.IndexOf(" ") 'find blank space
    lastnames(i) = myarray(i).Substring(x) 'get last name
    TextBox1.Text &= lastnames(i) & cr
Next

TextBox1.Text &= cr & "Sorted by last name:" & cr

myarray.Sort(lastnames, myarray)

For i = 0 To UBound(myarray)
    TextBox1.Text &= myarray(i) & cr
Next

TextBox1.Select(0, 0) 'turn off selection

End Sub
```

When using the array `Sort` method in this way, the array that serves as the key (the array to alphabetize by) is the first argument, followed by the array to be sorted. In this example, the arguments are (`lastnames, myarray`), so `myarray` is sorted in sync with the alphabetization that takes place in the `lastnames` array.

Using Many Members

Like most objects in VB Express, the `Array` object has many members. In addition to the properties and methods that most objects have (such as the `ToString` method), several members are unique to the array class (`Reverse`, `GetUpperBound`, and so on).

The simplest syntax for the `Reverse` method reverses all the items in an array, like this:

```
Array.Reverse(myarray)
```

Or you can reverse only a subset of items within the array. In this example, the reversing starts with the item at index number 1 and only reverses two items:

```
Array.Reverse(myarray, 1, 2)
```

To see a list of all the methods you can use with an array, type `Array.` into the code window. As soon as you type the `.`, the list of methods appears.

The ArrayList Powerhouse

The new VB Express `ArrayList` is a powerful tool. You may want to familiarize yourself with it if you expect to ever need to manipulate arrays in your programming. For one thing, it can dynamically resize itself, so you don't have to resort to `ReDim` and other techniques that a traditional array requires when resized. Use an `ArrayList` if you need a dynamic array.

Why use an ArrayList?

Clearly, the `Array` and the `ArrayList` in VB Express include some overlap in their features. Both classes can search, sort, reverse, and manipulate their data in various ways.

An `ArrayList`, however, has more features and is generally more capable than an `Array`. One serious drawback to arrays is that they are a bit like "serial access" storage devices such as a videotape. Removing or inserting items is cumbersome. For example, if you want to remove the fifth item in an array, you must write some programming to loop through the array and move down by one all the values from the fifth element up to the final element. Otherwise there's an empty space where you deleted.

The `ArrayList`, by contrast, is more flexible because it's more like recording on a computer's hard drive or any other "random access" device. The `ArrayList` is designed to be more dynamic: It automatically handles any necessary resizing when you insert or delete elements. (All arrays in VB Express can be resized at any time with the `ReDim` statement or `ReDim Preserve`, but the latter slows the program down.)

To see some of the capabilities of an `ArrayList` in action, start a new VB Express Windows-style project and put a ListBox and a Button on the form. Then type in this code, which illustrates how you can remove an element by using the `RemoveAt` method, specifying an index number. Notice that for this example to work, you want to allow both subs to access your `ArrayList`. To make that happen, you cannot declare the `ArrayList` *inside* one of the subs. Instead, it must be declared outside. To add variables or arrays that are accessible from all the code in a form, you usually put them just above the Form_Load event, like this boldface Public declaration of an `ArrayList`:

```
Public arrList As New ArrayList()

Private Sub Form1_Load(ByVal sender As System.Object, ByVal e As
          System.EventArgs) Handles MyBase.Load

    arrList.Add("ET")
    arrList.Add("Pearl Harbor")
    arrList.Add("Rain")

    ListBox1.Items.AddRange(arrList.ToArray)

End Sub

Private Sub Button1_Click(ByVal sender As System.Object, ByVal e As
          System.EventArgs) Handles Button1.Click

    arrList.RemoveAt(1)

    ListBox1.Items.Clear()
    ListBox1.Items.AddRange(arrList.ToArray)

End Sub
```

Notice that you don't have to use `For...Next` or other loop code to feed the data from an array to a `ListBox`. Instead, you can simply slap it in with the `ListBox`'s `AddRange` method. Alternatively, you can bind the data in an array directly to a `ListBox`. Data binding is illustrated in the section "Data Binding," later in this chapter.

Here's another example of the capabilities of the `ArrayList` class. To see how you can specify an element's *contents* — rather than its index number — as another way of removing it, replace the line in boldface in the previous example with the following line:

```
arrList.Remove("Pearl Harbor")
```

Working with ranges

Among other features, an `ArrayList` can manipulate a range of its elements by adding (to the end of the `ArrayList`), inserting, reading, or removing the range all at once. To see an example that reads a range, replace the code currently in the `Button1_Click` event from the previous example with this:

```
Private Sub Button1_Click(ByVal sender As System.Object, ByVal e As
        System.EventArgs) Handles Button1.Click

    Dim RangeOfArrList As ArrayList = arrList.GetRange(0, 2)

    ListBox1.Items.Clear()
    ListBox1.Items.AddRange(RangeOfArrList.ToArray)

End Sub
```

In this example, the two numbers in the `GetRange` method specify the start index and number of elements in range, respectively. Then that range is copied into a new `ArrayList` named `RangeOfArrList`.

A sometimes useful type of collection, similar to an array, is the `SortedList`. It always automatically maintains its contents in alphabetical order. Whenever you add a new item, that item is inserted into the list in the proper alphabetic location.

Data Binding

VB Express permits you to *bind* ListBoxes, DataGrids, and other list-type controls to an array, hashtable, or other collection. Data binding has been available in VB for several years now, but previously you could bind controls only to a database or a recordset derived from a database.

Binding merely means that the source of the data (such as an array) is linked to the control and provides data to the control — usually so the user can view or manipulate that data. For instance, you can allow the user to select an item in a ListBox by clicking the item.

Using the same ListBox and Button from the previous example in "Working with ranges," replace the Button's Click event with the following code to see how to bind an `ArrayList` to a ListBox:

```
Private Sub Button1_Click(ByVal sender As System.Object, ByVal e As
         System.EventArgs) Handles Button1.Click

Dim Monkey As New ArrayList()

    Monkey.Add("A")
    Monkey.Add("B")
    Monkey.Add("C")
    Monkey.Add("D")
    Monkey.Add("E")
    Monkey.Add("F")

ListBox1.DataSource = Monkey

End Sub
```

Enumerators

Microsoft is encouraging us programmers to use *enumerators* when looping through a collection class (such as an array). If you prefer this approach, here's an example that illustrates how to display the Monkey ArrayList's contents in the Immediate window when you click the button:

```
Dim Monkey As New ArrayList()
Dim MonkeyEnumerator As System.Collections.IEnumerator

Monkey.Add("A")
Monkey.Add("B")
Monkey.Add("C")
Monkey.Add("D")
Monkey.Add("E")
Monkey.Add("F")

MonkeyEnumerator = Monkey.GetEnumerator()

While MonkeyEnumerator.MoveNext()
    Debug.WriteLine(MonkeyEnumerator.Current)
End While
```

This enumeration technique is an alternative to the more traditional VB approach to using a loop to go through a collection, like this:

```
Dim i As Integer
For i = 0 To Monkey.Count - 1
    Debug.WriteLine(Monkey(i))
Next
```

Also, remember that an `ArrayList` is *dynamic* — it reallocates memory as needed when you add items to it. However, you can set the `Capacity` property explicitly if you wish. In fact, you can freely resize an `ArrayList` at any time by changing its `Capacity` property. If you don't expect to add any more new elements to an `ArrayList`, you can free up some memory by using the `TrimToSize` method.

Using Hashtables

The collection class called a *hashtable* is quite similar to the `ArrayList` in both design and features. However, a hashtable permits "strong data typing," as it's called — you can give each element a *name* in addition to its index number.

In some situations, working with a collection of data is easier when each element is labeled with a descriptive name. For example, if you need a collection of data that holds the foods eaten by each animal in a zoo, manipulating the data may be easier — and may make your code more readable — if each element is named after a different animal:

```
Dim Food As New Hashtable()

    Food.Add("Lion", "Meat")
    Food.Add("Bear", "Meat")
    Food.Add("Penguin", "Fish")

    Debug.WriteLine(Food.Item("Bear"))
```

In this example, the names of the animals, rather than their index numbers, are the *keys* you can use to access the elements. Each key must be unique, although the data can be duplicated as much as you wish (`"meat"` and `"meat"` in this example). Hashtables are also used in encryption — to translate a password into a pseudo-random numeric key.

The term *strong typing* is used in several, unfortunately unrelated ways in current computer "science."

Chapter 9

Pretty Printing

*I*n VB Express, you have considerable control over the printer, but there is the usual penalty for this flexibility: additional complexity. To print in VB Express, you have to muster a fair amount of information (such as brush color, the height of each line of text, the margins, and so on), and you have to manage several other aspects of the printing process as well.

Microsoft is working on a simplified way to print using the `My` object, but that welcome feature is not yet available.

I want to thank my friend Evangelos Petroutsos for his valuable suggestions and permission to use some of his code examples in this chapter. He figured out how best to deal with a line cut-off problem in VB .NET printing, an important fix that I've seen nowhere else. The examples in most books, and in some versions of VB Help itself, intermittently cut the last text line on a page in half. Thanks to Evangelos, the programming in this chapter (and thus you) avoids that unhappy bug.

Printing Just the Way You Want with the Printer Objects

In VB Express, you can take charge of how *everything* looks when you send data to the printer. You have great freedom to mix fonts, graphics, and other visual elements. In fact, you can control pretty much everything about the printed page, down to each pixel and its color. Technically, even text is dumped *as a graphic* into a drawing rectangle, as they call it.

The flip side of this freedom is that you have to keep track of what you are printing and where it's going. To put it briefly, when printing text you must ensure that you don't print off the page's right or bottom margins, or that the printer doesn't render only portions of some of the lines of text. Some characters may be cut off on the right side, or a word may be divided awkwardly (*awk* on one line, then *wardly* on the next), or the bottom of the final line on a page may be chopped off (a *g* looks like an *a* and so on). See Figure 9-1.

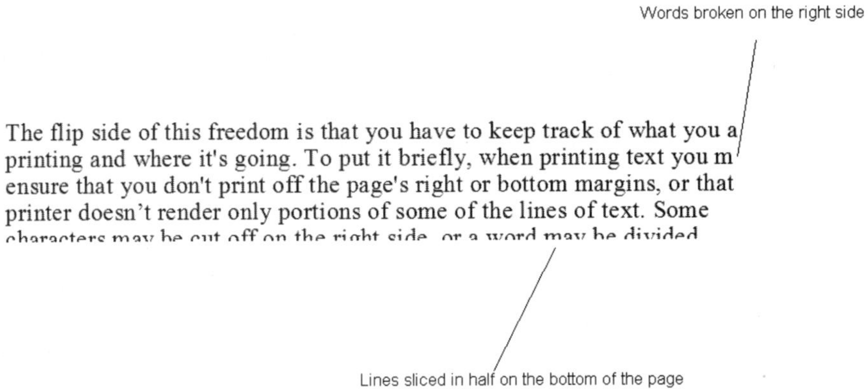

Words broken on the right side

Figure 9-1:
When text is printed, you don't want parts of it to be chopped off on the sides or bottom of the page.

The flip side of this freedom is that you have to keep track of what you a
printing and where it's going. To put it briefly, when printing text you m
ensure that you don't print off the page's right or bottom margins, or that
printer doesn't render only portions of some of the lines of text. Some
characters may be cut off on the right side, or a word may be divided

Lines sliced in half on the bottom of the page

Parsing text for the printer

For most of us, printing text is more common than printing graphics, so tackle this section's text first.

To understand how this all works in VB Express — and to see how to prevent your text from being mangled at the bottom or right margins — follow these steps:

1. **Start a new Windows-style VB Express project by choosing File⇨New Project and then double-clicking the Windows Application icon.**

2. **Double-click the form in the Design window.**

   You now see the Code window.

3. **Before getting started with the actual programming, type the following `Imports` statements at the top of your form.**

   These statements must be entered at the *very top* — above the line `Public Class Form1`. These importations make it possible for VB to use the features available in the code libraries listed.

   ```
   Imports System.Drawing
   Imports System.Drawing.Drawing2D
   Imports System.Drawing.Imaging
   Imports System.IO
   Imports System.Drawing.Text
   Imports System.Drawing.Printing
   ```

4. **Add a TextBox and a Button to your form.**

5. **With the Windows Forms tab selected in the Toolbox, scroll the Toolbox until you see the printer-related controls' icons (they're near the bottom of the Toolbox; see Figure 9-2).**

6. **Add a PrintDocument control to your form by double-clicking its icon in the toolbox.**

7. **Double-click the PrintDocument1 icon in the tray beneath Form1 in design view, as shown in Figure 9-3.**

   A PrintDocument1_PrintPage event is created in the code window.

Figure 9-2:
The printer controls are located at the bottom of the Toolbox, so you have to scroll down to see them.

Figure 9-3:
This control
adds
printing
capabilities
to your
program.

PrintDocument

8. **Move below the End Sub line that concludes the PrintPage event and type in this function (you fill in the programming for the PrintPage event later in this chapter):**

```
Function ParseWord() As String
    'get the next word from the Text, and return it.

'use Static to retain the cursor position value
'between calls to this function
Static CurPos As Integer
Dim Word As String

'Return an empty string if we've reached the end of the Text.
If CurPos >= TextBox1.Text.Length Then Return ""

'find first non-space character
While Not System.Char.IsLetterOrDigit(TextBox1.Text.Chars(CurPos))
    Word = Word & TextBox1.Text.Chars(CurPos)
    CurPos = CurPos + 1
    If CurPos >= TextBox1.Text.Length Then Return Word 'end of Text
End While

'build a word from the characters until you hit a space (IsWhiteSpace)
While Not (System.Char.IsWhiteSpace(TextBox1.Text.Chars(CurPos)))
    Word = Word & TextBox1.Text.Chars(CurPos)
    CurPos = CurPos + 1
    If CurPos >= TextBox1.Text.Length Then Return Word 'end of Text
End While

Return Word

End Function
```

This function looks through all the text in TextBox1, character by character. It keeps track as it moves down through the text by using the variable CurPos (for *cursor position*) which keeps counting up until it is greater than the length of the text:

```
If CurPos >= TextBox1.Text.Length Then
```

This ParseWord function's purpose is to return each word in the TextBox. It simply finds the next word and sends it back. The function knows when it has read a word because it comes upon a space character. The following line means "as long as the current character (CurPos) is not WhiteSpace . . .":

```
While Not System.Char.IsWhiteSpace(TextBox1.Text.Chars(CurPos)))
```

And the following line adds the current character to the word that's being built:

```
Word = Word & TextBox1.Text.Chars(CurPos)
```

The While loop that encloses these two lines ends either when it reaches the end of the Text or when it finds a space character.

Above this While loop is another, similar loop which does its job first each time the function runs. It moves the cursor through white space or other non-printing characters. In other words, it gathers characters that are Not System.Char.IsLetterOrDigit. But as soon as it hits a letter or digit (a text character) this loop is exited and the second loop begins adding characters to build the word that is returned to the caller. The caller is the PrintDocument1_PrintPage event.

Using the PrintPage event

In the previous section you saw how to parse a TextBox's Text property, extracting each word, one at a time, until you reach the end of the text. Now you see how to actually print by setting up the necessary preconditions. You define a rectangle based on the boundaries of the printable space (the paper size minus the margins). You see how to use the important MeasureString method of the Graphics object and how to use DrawString to print each page.

In the PrintDocument1_PrintPage event created in the previous section, type this code:

```
Private Sub PrintDocument1_PrintPage(ByVal sender As System.Object, ByVal e As
        System.Drawing.Printing.PrintPageEventArgs)
        Handles PrintDocument1.PrintPage

Dim printerFont As New Font("Arial", 10)
Dim LeftMargin As Integer = PrintDocument1.DefaultPageSettings.Margins.Left
Dim TopMargin As Integer = PrintDocument1.DefaultPageSettings.Margins.Top

Dim txtHeight As Integer = _
    PrintDocument1.DefaultPageSettings.PaperSize.Height - _
    PrintDocument1.DefaultPageSettings.Margins.Top - _
    PrintDocument1.DefaultPageSettings.Margins.Bottom
Dim txtWidth As Integer = _
    PrintDocument1.DefaultPageSettings.PaperSize.Width - _
    PrintDocument1.DefaultPageSettings.Margins.Left - _
    PrintDocument1.DefaultPageSettings.Margins.Right

Dim linesPerPage As Integer = _
    e.MarginBounds.Height / printerFont.GetHeight(e.Graphics)

Dim R As New RectangleF(LeftMargin, TopMargin, txtWidth, txtHeight)

Static line As String
Dim Words As String
Dim columns, lines As Integer

Words = ParseWord() 'get the first word

' build a single page of text
' if "" then we've reached the end of the TextBox.Text
' if lines > linesPerPage then skip this and use DrawString to print the page

While Words <> "" And lines < linesPerPage
    line = line & Words
    Words = ParseWord()
    e.Graphics.MeasureString(line & Words, printerFont, _
        New SizeF(txtWidth, txtHeight), New StringFormat, columns, lines)
End While
```

```
If Words = "" And Trim(line) <> "" Then 'finished
    'print the last page

    e.Graphics.DrawString(line, printerFont, Brushes.Black, R, _
        New StringFormat)
    e.HasMorePages = False
    Exit Sub 'quit because there are no more pages to print
End If


'print page
e.Graphics.DrawString(line, printerFont, Brushes.Black, R, New StringFormat)
e.HasMorePages = True
line = Words

End Sub
```

This is quite a bit of code to type in, and you're bound to make some errors if you try. It's best to copy and paste all this source code, and it can be downloaded from this book's Web site. (See the book's Introduction for details about the Web site.)

This `PrintPage` source code begins by declaring a few housekeeping variables. The first line merely specifies the font and font size, and the next two lines simply read the margin settings.

Now you need to figure out where on the page you can print, which I cover in the next section.

Determining printable page size

Many printers don't permit you to print all the way to the edges of the paper, and it usually looks pretty bad even if you were allowed to do it. So, there is normally a *printable* area which is smaller that the physical page size.

Sometimes, the user is permitted to adjust the margins in the PageSetupDialog control, for example. After the user has made this choice (or if the user simply leaves the margins set to their default size), your program must work within these measurements (the printable page, as opposed to the physical page).

You can determine the printable space on a page in two ways. Both are illustrated in this chapter's example code. The first way, which I explain in the nearby sidebar "Finding printable space with `DefaultPageSettings`," involves doing a little math with the `PrintDocument` object's `DefaultPageSettings`. The second method, shown in the following code, is simpler. It uses the `e` parameter, `e.MarginBounds.Height`, which holds the vertical measurement

Finding printable space with DefaultPageSettings

To find out the print area, follow these steps:

1. **Find out how much vertical room you have to print by accessing the PaperSize and Margins properties of the `PrintDocument` object's `DefaultPageSettings`:**

```
Dim txtHeight As Integer = _

        PrintDocument1.DefaultPageSe
        ttings.PaperSize.Height - _

        PrintDocument1.DefaultPageSe
        ttings.Margins.Top - _

        PrintDocument1.DefaultPageSe
        ttings.Margins.Bottom
```

By subtracting the top and bottom margins from the physical height of the paper (which is usually 11 inches, but not always), you get the vertical measurement of the printable page. For example, the variable `txtHeight` here is 9 inches if the top and bottom margins are both 1 inch and the paper is 8½ x 11 inches.

Tip: Although you can change it, printer measurements are by default expressed in 100ths of an inch. So you can just use `Integer` variables to manage the printing process. A typical page is 8,500 units wide and 1,100 units high.

2. **Calculate the horizontal free space by subtracting the left and right margins from the paper's width:**

```
Dim txtWidth As Integer = _

        PrintDocument1.DefaultPageSe
        ttings.PaperSize.Width - _

        PrintDocument1.DefaultPageSe
        ttings.Margins.Left - _

        PrintDocument1.DefaultPageSe
        ttings.Margins.Right
```

After you figure out the printable space by using `DefaultPageSettings`, you calculate how many lines of text you can print on this page by dividing the total height (within the margins) by the height of the font being used.

of the printable page (the same value stored in the `txtHeight` variable in the sidebar). This line of code uses the `MarginBounds` object:

```
Dim linesPerPage As Integer = _
    e.MarginBounds.Height / printerFont.GetHeight(e.Graphics)
```

As you see, this project employs the relatively rarely used e parameter, which is passed to all events in VB Express but is usually ignored. In this case, the PrintPage event gets important information from this parameter (`ByVal e As System.Drawing.Printing.PrintPageEventArgs`).

Next in this project, you define a graphic rectangle as your frame, based on the left and top margins and the width and height of the available printable space on the page:

```
Dim R As New RectangleF(LeftMargin, TopMargin, txtWidth, txtHeight)
```

Then you declare a couple of variables to hold the current line and word. You also declare two more variables, `columns` and `lines`. The `MeasureString` method wants a couple of integers at the end of its argument list. And `lines` is also used to prevent the `While` loop from miscounting the lines.

Looping through the text

Now it's time to look at the loop that actually does the work of building each printable page. This `While` loop uses the `ParseWord` function to get each word in the TextBox and add it to the variable `line`. Then it uses `MeasureString` to see if an entire page has been created. When the program exits this loop, the variable `line` holds a full printer-page of text.

```
While Words <> "" And lines < linesPerPage
    line = line & Words
    Words = ParseWord()

    e.Graphics.MeasureString(line & Words, printerFont, New SizeF(txtWidth,
            txtHeight), _
                New StringFormat, columns, lines)

End While
```

Next, an `If...Then` structure tests to see whether the job is done. If the variable `words` contains no text (`""`) and the variable `line` (with leading and trailing spaces removed) isn't empty, that means `line` contains the final page that needs to be printed. So you print the page with the `DrawString` method, set the `HasMorePages` method to `False`, and leave the subroutine:

```
If Words = "" And Trim(line) <> "" Then 'if this is true, then we're finished
    'print the last page
    e.Graphics.DrawString(line, printerFont, Brushes.Black, R, New StringFormat)
    e.HasMorePages = False
    Exit Sub 'quit because there are no more pages to print
End If
```

However, if there are more pages to print, you print the current page and then inform the `PrintPageEventArgs` parameter that there are more pages to print. This causes the `PrintPage` subroutine to begin execution again.

Triggering PrintPage with the Button control

To complete this text-printing utility, follow these steps:

1. **Switch to design view by clicking the Form1.vb(Design) tab at the top of the Code window.**

2. **Double-click the Button on your form to create a Button1_Click event and be returned to the Code window.**

3. **Type this into the Click event to trigger the printing process.**

```
Private Sub Button1_Click(ByVal sender As System.Object, ByVal e As
        System.EventArgs) Handles Button1.Click
    PrintDocument1.Print()

    End

End Sub
```

When the PrintDocument object finishes printing, your program returns to this Click event to `End` the entire project and stop it from running.

4. **Go ahead and press F5 to run this utility.**

5. **Paste a fairly large amount of text into the TextBox so you can see that the right and bottom margins are being correctly calculated and printed.**

Example code in many books, and in VB Express Help itself, lop off part of the final printed line on a page (not on *every* page, but now and then).

This program's PrintDocument1_PrintPage event's source code has some very long lines of code, but each must be preserved as a single long line in the code window. If, when you press F5 to test this code, you see all kinds of error messages in the Task List in the code window (such as "Expected an expression"), you probably have some broken lines. It's hard to fix these in the code window without introducing errors. Instead, try going back and copying the source code from this book's Web site, and this time run Windows Notepad and choose Notepad's Edit➪Word Wrap feature to turn off word wrap. Paste the source code into Notepad and then select all the source code in Notepad (now without line breaks) and copy it (Ctrl+C). Finally, paste this code into the empty VB Express code window. That should eliminate any broken lines.

As you can see, communication with peripherals like a printer is less simple and less direct in VB Express than in previous versions of VB. You write more code, and it's the kind of code in which you have to employ properties and methods in ways that are not always intuitive. Nonetheless, it's not *that* complex, and you can always just copy the code you see in this book, and in Appendix B online, and managing most peripheral jobs should work fine for you.

As you saw earlier by building the preceding project, you use the Print Document control to hold the actual text or graphics that are printed.

The PrintDocument1.PrinterSettings object has many properties you can read, and in many cases change, to manage the printer. They are listed in Table 9-3.

Table 9-3	PrinterSettings Properties
CanDuplex	MaximumPage
Collate	MinimumPage
Copies	PaperSizes
DefaultPageSettings	PaperSources
Duplex	PrinterName
FromPage	PrinterResolutions
IsDefaultPrinter	PrintRange

Table 9-3 (continued)

IsPlotter	PrintToFile
IsValid	SupportsColor
LandscapeAngle	ToPage
MaximumCopies	

Table 9-4 lists the `PrintDocument.PageSettings` properties.

Table 9-4	**PageSettings Properties**
Bounds	PaperSize
Color	PaperSource
Landscape	PrinterResolution
Margins	PrinterSettings

Letting Users Set Print Options

If you want to allow the user to specify such elements as margins, page orientation, paper size, and paper feeder, you can display the PageSetupDialog control (after adding it from the Toolbox to your form):

```
PageSetupDialog1.PageSettings = PrintDocument1.DefaultPageSettings()

If PageSetupDialog1.ShowDialog() = DialogResult.OK Then
    PrintDocument1.DefaultPageSettings = PageSetupDialog1.PageSettings
End If
```

Also, the user can choose the printer, page range, and number of copies by using the PrintDialog control. Neither of these controls is illustrated in the previous example.

Using the PrintPreview Control

Using the `PrintPreview` control isn't difficult, and this new control in VB is sometimes helpful. You can display to users how their output appears when printed (so they don't waste paper printing pages that are not formatted to their liking), and they can click a Print button within the PrintPreviewDialog to initiate printing.

Use this code to display the `PrintPreview`, showing the user a sample of their output:

```
PrintPreviewDialog1.Document = PrintDocument1
PrintPreviewDialog1.ShowDialog()
```

In the example project at the start of this chapter, you put the line `PrintDocument1.Print()` in a Button_Click event so the user can initiate the printing process. If you use `PrintPreviewDialog`, however, be sure *not* to include that line in your program. Why? Because the PrintPreview dialog box itself displays a Print button and a Close button to the user. If the user clicks the Print button, the document printing is initiated from there, automatically, by the PrintPreviewDialog itself.

If the user clicks the Close button without printing, it means the user decided not to print. Perhaps you should display the PrintDialog and PageSetupDialog controls again, to allow the user to make modifications, and then display the PrintPreview dialog box again.

Printing Graphics

You may want to print graphics. It's not difficult, but you probably need to manipulate the graphic to make it look right on the paper in the printer. As is so often the case with graphics, your primary job is to manage size and position. In the following example, you calculate and adjust the position to fit the graphic on the paper.

Start a new VB Express project and put a PictureBox and a Button on the form. Set the PictureBox's `SizeMode` to `AutoSize`. This forces the PictureBox to adjust its size to whatever graphic you assign to it. Use the PictureBox's `Image` property (click its ... button) to find a graphic file on your hard drive to load into the PictureBox.

At the top of the code window, add these `Imports` statements:

```
Imports System.Drawing
Imports System.Drawing.Drawing2D
Imports System.Drawing.Imaging
Imports System.IO
Imports System.Drawing.Text
Imports System.Drawing.Printing
```

Type the following code into the Document1_PrintPage event:

```
Private Sub PrintDocument1_PrintPage(ByVal sender As System.Object, ByVal e As
        System.Drawing.Printing.PrintPageEventArgs) Handles
        PrintDocument1.PrintPage

With PrintDocument1.DefaultPageSettings.PaperSize
    If PictureBox1.Width < .Width Then

        PictureBox1.Left = (.Width - PictureBox1.Width) / 2
    Else
        PictureBox1.Left = 0
    End If
End With

With PrintDocument1.DefaultPageSettings.PaperSize
    If PictureBox1.Height < .Height Then
        PictureBox1.Top = (.Height - PictureBox1.Height) / 2
        Else
            PictureBox1.Top = 0
    End If
End With

Dim r As Rectangle = New Rectangle(PictureBox1.Left, PictureBox1.Top, _
        PictureBox1.Width, PictureBox1.Height)

e.Graphics.DrawImage(PictureBox1.Image, r)

End Sub
```

Type this brief code into the Button's Click event.

```
Private Sub Button1_Click(ByVal sender As System.Object, ByVal e As
          System.EventArgs) Handles Button1.Click

    PrintDocument1.Print()

    End

End Sub
```

When you press F5 to execute this program, you can click the button and send your picture to the printer, as shown in Figure 9-4.

Figure 9-4:
Click this button and the photo goes to the printer.

You could easily make this into a custom personal photo-printing utility by adding an OpenFileDialog control from the Toolbox, then filling the PictureBox with a user-selected graphic with this code (in the Button click event):

```
PictureBox1.Image = Image.FromFile("C:\Graphics\MyDog.jpg")
```

For details about how to use the OpenFileDialog, see this book's online Appendix B (www.dummies.com/go/visualbasic2005express).

Understanding With...End With

The code in the PrintPage event in the preceding section determines the coordinates (the top and left position on the paper) that display the graphic in the center of the page. First you use the `With` structure. Any property or method between `With` and `End With` that begins with a . (period) is assumed to belong to the object defined in the line that begins the `With` structure. This way you can avoid repeating the "full qualification" (the entire object name) each time you refer to one of its properties or methods.

In that previous code example, you start the first `With` structure like this:

```
With PrintDocument1.DefaultPageSettings.PaperSize
```

So all words within this structure that begin with . are part of the `PrintDocument1.DefaultPageSettings.PaperSize` object. (This `With...End With` technique is similar to using the `Imports` statement to add a namespace at the top of a code window. Both techniques save you a little work by relieving you of having to fully qualify in your code all the members of a particular class.)

Notice how these two lines leave out the object qualifier, simply using `.Width` when referring to the `Width` property of the `PrintDocument1.DefaultPageSettings.PaperSize` object:

```
With PrintDocument1.DefaultPageSettings.PaperSize
    If PictureBox1.Width < .Width Then
        PictureBox1.Left = (.Width - PictureBox1.Width) / 2
```

If you decided not to use this `With...End With` structure, you would have to write these lines with fully qualified object references, like this:

```
If PictureBox1.Width < PrintDocument1.DefaultPageSettings.PaperSize.Width Then
    PictureBox1.Left = (PrintDocument1.DefaultPageSettings.PaperSize.Width - _
        PictureBox1.Width) / 2
```

The first line asks: is the PictureBox narrower than the paper? If so, you center the graphic horizontally on the paper by finding out how much narrower it is (subtracting the PictureBox width from the paper width) and then dividing that by 2 (to provide equal left and right margins, thereby centering the graphic.

If the PictureBox is not narrower than the paper, you assign 0 to its position, pushing it as far to the left as possible. Similarly, the second `With...End`

With structure calculates the Top position in order to attempt to center the graphic vertically on the paper.

Then you define a rectangle to hold the graphic and draw the image in the rectangle. The DrawImage method also prints your graphic (because it is in the PrintPage Event):

```
Dim r As Rectangle = New Rectangle(PictureBox1.Left, PictureBox1.Top, _
    PictureBox1.Width, PictureBox1.Height)

e.Graphics.DrawImage(PictureBox1.Image, r)
```

Fine-tuning your graphics print options

To improve the bare-bones printing technique I discuss earlier in this section, you can add code that

✔ Zooms or reduces the graphic.

✔ Allows the user to specify the position on the paper where the graphic should be placed.

✔ Moves the PictureBox's Top and Left position to specify the printer coordinates. (But be warned: Manipulating the coordinates of both the PictureBox and the paper is harder than it at first seems. You have to ensure that the graphic isn't positioned or expanded off the paper's physical size, and you have to avoid distorting the image by changing its aspect ratio — the ratio of height to width — if you stretch or shrink it.)

Chapter 10

Testing and Deployment

. . . .

In This Chapter

▶ Grasping the three types of bugs

▶ Tracking down errors

▶ Breaking in and stepping through

▶ Using the minor debugging techniques

▶ Trapping errors during run time

. . . .

*N*o programming project of any significance simply comes to life error-free. You always have to test your applications and then track down the inevitable problems that are revealed. Then you must fix them.

Bugs usually aren't a result of negligence. Any sizable application is like a large office full of people: With such an enormous number of interacting behaviors, some trouble is unavoidable.

What do you do when you press F5 to test a program you've just written, and VB throws up an error message? You can sit around and mope, or you can take steps. I suggest taking steps. Fortunately, VB offers an unquestionably excellent, powerful suite of debugging tools: the Error List, the Immediate window, watches, breakpoints, single-stepping, and other debugging features.

This chapter explores the more common types of errors you're likely to encounter and the VB Express tools and techniques you can use to fix them.

 VB Express has a feature called *Just My Code* that's turned on by default. It means that the debugging features ignore code you didn't write (that is, code that is automatically written and inserted for you by VB but hidden from you normally). Stepping (described later in this chapter) does walk through such code but won't stop on these lines. The *Just My Code* feature is a very good idea. Don't scare or distract yourself with code you didn't write; so don't go into the Tools⇨Options⇨Debugging⇨General menu system and uncheck the Enable Just My Code option. Leave it as is.

Finding and Fixing Syntax Errors

Debugging starts by finding out where the bug is located — which line or lines of source code are causing the problem. VB's syntax-checking feature watches as you type each line of code. As soon as you finish a line, it checks the line to see whether you mistyped anything or made some other kind of error, such as leaving out something necessary. (VB knows you're finished with a line when you press Enter, use an arrow key to move off the line, or click the mouse pointer on another line.)

To see the syntax checker in action, type the following function in the VB code window in the Form_Load event (just double-click the Form in design view to get to this event):

```
Private Sub Form1_Load(ByVal sender As System.Object, ByVal e As
          System.EventArgs) Handles MyBase.Load

    zum = nara

End Sub
```

As soon as you enter the zum = nara line of code, VB does not like it. To demonstrate its displeasure, it underlines both zum and nara.

Beware the blue sawtooth line. If the syntax checker has a problem with a line of code, it underlines the error or errors with that blue line. In the preceding code example, you typed two variable names, neither of which you declared. VB requires that all variables be declared (unless you add Option Explicit Off to the top of your source code; see Chapter 7 for details). So you get jagged lines under each of the undeclared variable names.

Some people like to make Option Explicit the default for their entire project, so they don't have to specify it in each individual form. To do that, right-click your project's name (it's the one in boldface) in Solution Explorer and then choose Properties from the context menu. Click the Compile tab in the Properties Window and turn Option Explicit on using the drop-down menu next to that option.

To find help fixing syntax errors, you can do the following:

✔ **Move your mouse pointer on top of one of the sawtoothed words in your code,** and VB provides an explanation of the error. Don't click, just slide the arrow onto the bad part, as shown in Figure 10-1.

✔ **Press F5 and you see the errors listed and described in the Error List,** as shown in Figure 10-2.

✔ **Double-click one of the errors in the Error List window** to go to the line in the Code window where the error occurred. The specific command that caused the problem is highlighted. To make the jagged blue lines go away in this example, choose Debug⇨Stop Debugging. Then declare the two variable names by adding these lines just above the existing line of code zum = nara:

```
Dim zum As String
Dim nara As String
```

Figure 10-1:
A brief error message appears when you pause your pointer on top of an error in the code.

Figure 10-2:
The Error List window displays errors in your code.

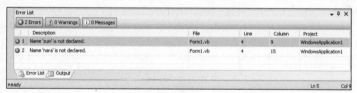

You *still* see a sawtooth line under nara, but now it's relaxed to black, so it's a *warning* — sort of like a scolding — and a rather stupid warning at that:

```
Variable nara is used before it has been assigned a value.
A null reference exception could result at runtime.
```

Don't worry about this nonsense. It's OOP and C-language stuff, and programmers in those languages like to use preposterously fancy-sounding terms. *Exception* is their word for error. I guess it sounds less embarrassing or something.

Press F5 now and you see the warning listed in the Error List. Indeed, the warning is unnecessary — no "exception" happens when you run the project, but in a wild excess of caution, somebody working on VB Express seems to think that *warnings about possible errors* should be sometimes brought to your attention. What's next? Try to ignore this hand-holding behavior.

Tracking Down Logic Errors

Logic errors are usually the most difficult of all to find and correct. VB can't underline logic errors as it can with syntax errors. Some logic errors can be so sinister, so well concealed, that you think you will be driven mad trying to find the source of the problem in your code. VB sensibly devotes the majority of its debugging features and resources to helping you find logic errors.

A logic error occurs even though you have followed all the rules of syntax, made no typos, and otherwise satisfied VB that your commands can be successfully carried out. You and VB think everything is shipshape. When you run the program, however, things go wrong. Perhaps the entire screen turns purple, or every time the user enters $10, your program changes it into $1,000. That's just not right. You know it, even if VB doesn't.

As with almost all programming errors, the key to correcting logic errors is finding out *where* in your program the problem is located. Which line of code (or several lines interacting) causes the problem?

Some computer languages have an elaborate debugging apparatus that can even include the use of two computer monitors: One can show the application just as the user sees it, while the other shows the lines of code that match what the user sees. Using two monitors is a good approach because when you are debugging logic errors, you often want to see the code that's currently causing the effects in the application. Unfortunately, most of us don't have the resources to dual-monitor debug.

It's not that you don't usually notice the symptoms of a logic error: Every time the user enters a number, the results are way, way off, for example. You know that somewhere, your program is mangling these numbers, but until you X-ray the program, you often can't find out where the problem is located. The following sections introduce the tools at your disposal that can help.

The voyeur technique

Many logic errors are best tracked down by watching the contents of a variable (or variables). You want to find out just where the variable's value changes and goes bad.

Four of VB's best debugging tools help you keep an eye on the status of variables. The following examples demonstrate how to watch variables.

You start by adding a breakpoint and going into break mode. Here are the steps:

1. **Replace the lines of code you previously put into the Form_Load Event with this:**

```
Dim a As Double, b As Double

a = 112
b = a / 2
b = b + 6
```

2. **Click the gray margin to the left of the code window to add a red dot (a breakpoint) next to the line `a = 112`.**

3. **Press F5.**

   You are now in break mode; the red dot changes to include a yellow arrow, and the line is highlighted in yellow. These visual effects show you that your breakpoint halted execution at this line. You can now examine your code, though this isn't necessarily the line that's the source of the error. You merely suspect this area of your program, so you added a breakpoint to halt (break) execution here to allow you to take a look around.

While you are in break mode, many debugging features are at your command. Continuing from the preceding steps list, the following steps walk through how you can use these debugging features:

1. **Make four of the debugging windows visible by choosing Debug⇨ Windows and selecting the Locals window. Also select the following two windows: Debug⇨Windows⇨Watch, Debug⇨Windows⇨Immediate.**

2. **Click the Locals tab to look at the Locals window, shown in Figure 10-3.**

   The Locals window displays the variables that have been declared in the currently executing (local) procedure, as well as the parameters passed to this procedure (e and sender, which you can almost always just ignore, though parameters passed to functions or subs that *you* write are very important). You also see the parents of Me (the current object) — the application and form.

3. **Watch the variables in the Locals window change as you press F8 to execute each line in the example code, one by one, step-by-step, as shown in Figure 10-3.**

4. **Also, use the debug windows to query or modify variables or expressions.**

   • *To find out the value in a variable* — b, for example — just type the following in the Immediate window and then press Enter (you must leave a space between the ? and the variable name):

   ```
   ? b
   ```

   The answer — whatever value b currently holds — is displayed (printed) in the Immediate window. (The ? command is shorthand for the Print command.) Maybe you're trying to see where a variable holds a number that's way too large. That's why it sometimes helps to check a variable's value (its contents).

   • *To change the value in a variable during break mode,* double-click the number in the value column in the Locals or Watch window and then type your new value. Changing a variable's value can sometimes affect the program in a way that perhaps points you to the location of a logic error.

   I explain the Watch window shortly.

Using Debug.WriteLine

Some programmers like to insert `Debug.WriteLine` commands at different locations in their code to display the value of a variable. The `Debug.Write Line` command displays its results in the Immediate window and then moves down a line. `Debug.Write` does the same thing but without moving down a line in the Immediate window.

You can insert `Debug.WriteLine` (*MyVariableName*) code here and there in your source code. Run the program and watch the results appear in the Immediate window:

```
Dim a As Double

a = 112
Debug.WriteLine("Variable a now equals: " & a)
```

This displays `Variable a now equals: 112` in the Immediate window.

Using several `Debug.WriteLine` commands is a good idea if you want to quickly see a series of variable values and also write some explanatory messages about these values. You could do the same thing with a series of `MsgBox` commands, but for a group of several variables, it's annoying to have to keep clicking each individual `MsgBox` to close it before you can see the next `MsgBox`. With `Debug.WriteLine`, no clicking is involved; when the program runs, all the messages appear in the Immediate window.

The Immediate window responds

You can type into the Immediate window any executable commands that can be expressed on a single line, and then you can watch their effect. Note that you do this while the VB program is halted during a run; you can test conditions from within the program while it's in break (pause) mode. I've never found this feature too helpful. I suspect I use it about four times a decade.

You can get into break mode in several ways: by inserting a `Stop` command into your code, by setting a breakpoint in the code, by single-stepping (repeatedly pressing F8 to move through the source code line by line), by choosing Break All in the Debug menu (or the Toolbar), or by pressing Ctrl+Break.

The watch technique

The Locals window is fine for local variables, but what about form-wide or project-wide variables that have a larger scope in your source code (*global* variables, as they're sometimes called)? They don't show up in the Locals window. To deal with this, you want to use conditional breakpoints. However, they are not available in VB Express. As the Help entry says: "This feature is found in Visual C++ Express Edition and Visual Studio Professional, Enterprise, and Enterprise Architect Editions only." So we VB users have to do without this most useful debugging tool. You'll have to do the best you can with Watches and ordinary breakpoints.

An alternative way to use the Watch window is to keep an eye on the watches you've defined as you single-step through your code. The Watch window displays the value of all active watches. To add a watch, right-click any line of code and choose Add Watch from the context menu.

Another tool in the Debug menu is the Quick Watch option. If you highlight (select) an expression or variable in the code window and then choose Debug⇨Quick Watch (or press Shift+F9), VB shows you the current contents or status of the highlighted expression or variable. VB also gives you the option of adding the item to the watched items in the Watch window. Quick Watches cannot be specified during design time, only in break mode during execution.

Setting breakpoints

Sometimes you have a strong suspicion about which form or module in your application contains an error. Or you may even think you know the specific procedure (event, function, or sub) where the error can be found. In these cases, breakpoints, which enable you to slow the process down and check what's going on, can be one of the most useful debugging aids.

To stop a running program in its tracks, you can press Ctrl+Break (the Break key is to the right of the function keys on most keyboards). But what if the program is moving too fast to stop just where you want to look and check on things? What if it's rapidly alphabetizing a large list, for example, and you can't see what's happening?

In this case, you want to add breakpoints before the program runs. Then, later, when it's running, the program stops at a breakpoint just as if you had pressed Ctrl+Break. The code window pops up, showing you where the break occurred, so you can see or change the code, single-step, or look at the Locals or Watch windows to see the values in variables.

To add breakpoints before a program runs, follow these steps:

1. **Either click the gray area to the left of the line where you want the breakpoint or click the line to select it and then press F9.**

   The red dot appears to the left of the line.

   You can set as many breakpoints as you want.

2. **With the breakpoints in place, press F5 to execute the program at normal speed.**

   VB stops when execution enters the form or procedure that is marked with a breakpoint.

3. **After halting the program in a suspect region, press F8 to single-step through the next lines while you watch the values of suspect variables in the Local window.**

4. **Click the red dot a second time to turn off a breakpoint.**

Another use for breakpoints is when you suspect that the program is never even executing some lines of code. Sometimes a logic error is caused because you think a subroutine, function, or event is getting executed when, in fact, the program for some reason never reaches that procedure. Whatever condition is supposed to activate that area of the program never occurs.

To find out whether a particular event is executing, set a breakpoint on the first line of code in that procedure. Then, when you run your program, if the breakpoint never halts execution, you have proven that the procedure is never called.

Fixing Errors with the Minor Debugging Tools

The following three tools are used infrequently in ordinary programming, but perhaps you'd like to try them.

Step Over (Shift+F8)

Step Over is the same as single-stepping (pressing F8), except that if you are about to single-step into a procedure, Step Over executes the procedure all at once, rather than step by step. No procedure calls are carried out, but all other commands are executed. So, if you are single-stepping (pressing F8 repeatedly) and you come upon a procedure that you know is not the location of the bug, press Shift+F8 to step over the entire procedure. This option gets you past areas in your program that you know are free of bugs and can take a lot of single-stepping to get through.

Step Out (Ctrl+Shift+F8)

This feature appears on the Debug menu only during break mode. It quickly executes the remaining lines of the procedure you're currently in but stops on the next line in the program (following the current procedure). Use this to quickly get to the end of the current procedure that you don't want to single-step through if you don't want to press F5 to restart execution either. When you use Step Out, you remain in step mode, just not through this particular procedure.

Run to Cursor (right-click in Break mode)

To use the Run to Cursor option, click somewhere else in your code (thereby moving the insertion cursor). VB remembers the original and new locations of the insertion cursor. Right-click in your code window and choose Run to Cursor from the context menu. The code between the original and new locations is executed.

This is a useful trick when you come upon a large For...Next loop. You want to get past the loop quickly rather than waste time completing the loop by pressing F8 over and over. Just click a program line past the loop and then choose Run to Cursor. VB executes the loop at normal execution speed and then halts at the code following the loop. You can resume stepping from there.

Set Next Statement (right-click in Break mode)

You must be in break mode to use Set Next Statement. With this feature, you can move anywhere in the current procedure and restart execution from there (it's the inverse of the Run To Cursor feature). While the program is in Break mode, go to the new location from which you want to start execution and then click the new line of code where you want to resume execution. Now, pressing F8 single-steps from that new location forward in the program.

This is a way to skip over a line or lines of code. Suppose that you know that things are fine for several lines, but you suspect other lines farther down. Move down using Set Next Statement and start single-stepping again.

Show Next Statement (right-click in Break mode)

If you've been moving around in your program, looking in various events, you may have forgotten where in the program the next single-step takes place. Pressing F8 shows you quickly enough, but you may want to get back there without executing the next line. Show Next Statement moves you in the code window to the next line in the program that is to be executed, but halts and doesn't execute it. You can look at the code before proceeding.

The Call Stack

The Call Stack feature is in the Debug⇨Windows menu. The Call Stack provides a list of still-active procedures if the running VB program went into Break mode while it was in a procedure that had been called (invoked) by another procedure. Procedures can be nested (one can call on the services of another, which in turn calls yet another). The Call Stack option shows you the name of the procedure that called the current procedure. And if that calling procedure was itself called by yet another procedure, the Call Stack shows you the complete history of what is calling what.

Adding Structured Error Handling

Some errors occur only during run time. Your programming is valid, but something unexpected happens while the *user* is running the program. You've tested it, but users' environments and behaviors might differ from yours. You can't predict *everything*. So, you use *error-handling* techniques to deal with errors that confront your users — after all, something has to be built into your code to deal with problems when you're not there.

Runtime errors are often related to a peripheral, such as a hard drive. For example, suppose that the user has no file named `myfile.doc` on drive `C:\`, and your program executes this code trying to open that file:

```
Private Sub Form1_Load(ByVal sender As System.Object, ByVal e As
        System.EventArgs) Handles MyBase.Load

Try

    Dim sr As New System.IO.StreamReader("c:\myfile.doc")
```

```
        Catch er As System.IO.FileNotFoundException
        MsgBox(er.ToString)

    End Try

    End Sub
```

The hair-raising error message shown in Figure 10-4 is displayed, which you definitely don't want your users to see. You need to prevent, or at least gracefully handle, runtime errors. It's no good having a smoothly running program that suddenly halts if the user, say, forgets to put a disk in drive A: or fails to close the drive door. In the following sections, I explain what you need to know about runtime errors and how to add exception handling so that your users don't see such nasty error messages.

Figure 10-4:
This
message is
likely to
terrify, or
at least
depress, a
user. It sure
depresses
me.

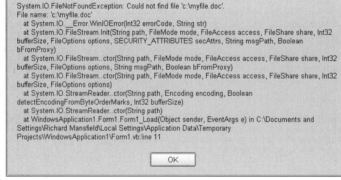

If you read the all the drivel displayed on the error message shown in Figure 10-4, you'll understand why so many of us experienced programmers have nothing but contempt for the code bloat and sheer foolishness of so much of object-oriented programming. The first line of the error message is sufficient.

How runtime errors occur

Runtime errors include unexpected situations that can come up when the program is running. While you're writing a program, you can't know a number of things about the user's system — for example, how much disk space is available on the hard drive. Is it already so full that when your program tries to save a file, enough room won't be available? Are you creating an array so large that it exceeds the computer's available memory? Is the printer turned off, but the user tries to print anyway? And what wacky mistake might some users type when you ask them to provide a telephone number?

Whenever your program is attempting to interact with an entity outside the program — such as the user's input, disk drives, Clipboard, and RAM — you need to take precautions by using the `Try...End Try` structure, which I explain later in this chapter. This structure enables your program to deal effectively with the unexpected while it runs.

Unfortunately, your program can't correct many runtime errors. For instance, it can let the user know only that his or her disk is nearly full. The user will have to remedy this kind of problem; you can't correct it with your code.

Runtime errors can also occur because of such unexpected problems as numeric overflow (a variable grows too large for its variable type) or array boundary violations (an attempt is made to access an item from an array index outside the range of the array). Other runtime errors result from attempts to use remote objects' methods or properties incorrectly (such as when accessing a database, an API, or a Web service). Remote objects return error messages, error codes (numbers that you must then look up in an error code list), or a combination of the two. Some runtime errors are the result of numina from parallel worlds.

Error messages can also sometimes be returned from within an object or directly by a function. When you use a function that is supposed to provide you with the length of some text, but it returns –1, that's an error flag. In all these cases, you must read the documentation that describes both how error messages are returned to your project and what those messages mean. Often, however, VB intercepts incoming error messages from remote classes and signals them to your project as a VB-style runtime error.

Understanding Try

If you suspect that a particular location in your source code may trigger a runtime error, use the `Try` command to trap the error. Attempting to set things right by first handling the error if possible within your project is always better than shifting an unnecessary burden to the user.

If you don't use `Try` and solve the problem in your VB source code, Visual Basic displays an error message to the user. You should usually provide your *own* runtime error messages (you'll see how in a moment). VB error messages, like the one shown in Figure 10-4, are generally intended for you, the programmer, not for ordinary users.

Instead of displaying a system message, you substitute your own, custom, user-friendly error message, like this:

```
Private Sub Form1_Load(ByVal sender As System.Object, ByVal e As
          System.EventArgs) Handles MyBase.Load

Try

   Dim sr As New System.IO.StreamReader("c:\myfile.doc")

   Catch er As system.IO.FileNotFoundException

   MsgBox("No file named myfile.doc was found on Drive C:")

End Try

End Sub
```

Notice that you put the `Try...End Try` structure around possible error-triggering code. In fact, in some situations, you surround *all* the code in a procedure with the `Try...End Try` envelope. Here's how the `Try...End Try` structure works:

```
Try

'watch the line(s) of code here for any problems
Catch a type of error
' insert line(s) of code here to handle that particular error

Catch another type of error
' insert line(s) of code here to handle that second error

Finally

'insert optional line(s) of code here that you want executed
'within the Try structure

End Try
```

The purpose of that `Finally` zone in the `Try...End Try` block is mysterious at first glance. Why do you need it? Couldn't you just put the code *after* the `End Try`? I'll explain the `Finally` command soon.

It's pretty easy to understand the relationship between `Try` and `Catch`. The relationship is similar to the following:

```
' Start of Try structure
If there was an error Then 'Catch
React in some way to this error
End If 'End of Catch code block
If there was a different error Then 'Catch
React in some way to this error
End If 'End of Catch code block
' End of Try structure
```

The term *exception* is used in C-like languages (and now by the VB officials) to mean *error*. Code between the `Try` and `End Try` commands is watched for errors. You can use the generic `exception` or merely trap a specific exception such as the following:

```
Catch er As DivideByZeroException
```

You can include in your `Try...End Try` structure as many `Catch` phrases as you want, and you can respond individually to each of them. You can respond by notifying the user (as in the preceding example) or by quietly correcting the error in the source code following the `Catch`. You can also provide a brief error message:

```
er.Message
```

Or, as you did in the preceding example, you can provide a "fully qualified" (meaning "all the adjectives") error message:

```
er.ToString
```

The official syntax for Try...Catch...Finally

Here's the full, official `Try...Catch...Finally` structure's syntax:

```
Try
    tryStatements
[Catch₁ [exception [As type]] [When expression]
    catchStatements₁
[Exit Try]
Catch₂ [exception [As type]] [When expression]
    catchStatements₂
[Exit Try]
...
Catchₙ [exception [As type]] [When expression]
    catchStatementsₙ]
[Exit Try]
[Finally
    finallyStatements]
End Try
```

Following the `Try` block, you list one or more `Catch` statements. A `Catch` statement requires a variable name and an `As` clause defining the type of exception (`er As Exception`). One Exception type is generic and therefore traps all exceptions, not just a specific one such as `FileNotFound`.

For example, here's how to trap *all* exceptions:

```
Try

    Dim sr As New System.IO.StreamReader("c:\xxxxx")

Catch er As Exception

    'Respond to any kind of error.

End Try
```

An optional `Exit Try` statement causes program flow to leap out of the `Try` structure and continue execution with whatever follows the `End Try` statement. If code is in the `Finally` block, however, it is executed.

Understanding Finally

The `Finally` statement contains any code that you want to be executed after error processing has been completed. Any code in `Finally` is *always* executed, whether or not any `Catch` blocks were executed. You would use the `Finally` block primarily because the source code that follows the `End Try` line may never execute, depending on how things go in the `Try` structure.

How does this work in the real world? Suppose that a major disaster occurs, and your `Catch` block includes an `Exit Sub` or `Exit Function` command to leap out of your procedure in response to the disaster. In either case, any code in that procedure that follows `End Try` is not executed. By contrast, code in the `Finally` block executes no matter what. The most common use for the `Finally` section is to free up resources that were acquired in the `Try` block, to close opened files, and the like.

Note that if you use the `Exit Try` command to get out of a `Try` block prematurely (before executing other `Catch` blocks or other nested `Try` blocks), the code in the `Finally` block will nonetheless execute.

For example, if you were to acquire a Mutex lock (don't ask!) in your `Try` block, you would want to release that lock when you were finished with it, regardless of whether the `Try` block exited with a successful completion or an exception (error). You typically use the following type of code in the `Finally` block:

```
objMainKey.Close()
objFileRead.Close()
objFilename.Close()
```

Throwing exceptions

You can use a `Throw` command to generate your own error flags and attach error messages. This is how you inform outside code (some other program using your program) that is using one of your methods or procedures that an error occurred.

Both of these syntaxes work:

```
Dim e As Exception
e = New Exception("F problem")
Throw e
```

Or, more simply:

```
Throw New Exception("Problem in the Addition function")
```

I repeat: When you `Throw` an exception, you're telling an outsider (source code that tried to execute your procedure, also called a *client*) that a problem occurred. When you write a Web service or create a custom control, you are building an object that can be used by a client.

Here's an example. Suppose that you write a function that wants to always get the name *Bob* sent to it. If the client tries to send some other name, you throw back an exception. The Form_Load event in this example is the outsider that calls the `IsItBob` procedure:

```
Private Sub Form1_Load(ByVal sender As System.Object, ByVal e As
          System.EventArgs) Handles MyBase.Load

    Try
        IsItBob("Chris") 'call the procedure
    Catch er As Exception 'find out if there was an error thrown back at us
        MsgBox(er.ToString) 'if there was an error thrown, display it
    End Try

End Sub

Sub IsItBob(ByVal s As String)

Dim er As Exception

If s <> "Bob" Then 'they sent the wrong name!
    er = New Exception("This Function needs the name Bob")
        'create an exception variable
    Throw er 'throw it back to the caller
End If

End Sub
```

Tips for using Try...End Try

Here are a few additional points to remember about VB's `Try...End Try` approach to error handling:

- ✔ If you want, you can nest `Try...End Try` blocks in other `Try...End Try` blocks.

- ✔ The `Try...End Try` technique was written from scratch with .NET in mind. As a happy result, the `Catch` command can catch all errors that can happen in the .NET framework (in any method or property of all the zillions of objects in that framework).

- ✔ Some programmers might be tempted to enclose their entire project in a huge `Try...End Try` block, thereby ensuring that any and every possible runtime error will be caught. This slows execution somewhat, but it sure would catch everything. It's rather clumsy, though, and you will likely want to trap errors in specific areas where you think they might actually occur, rather than enveloping the entire code.

Part III
Dealing with Databases

The 5th Wave   By Rich Tennant

"We're here to clean the code."

In this part . . .

Part III focuses on databases — the heart of the majority of computer programs. Computing is, after all, data processing, so the data has to be collected somewhere and preferably organized into some kind of sensible structure. In this part, you see how tables, rows, and columns form a structure wherein data can be efficiently stored, making it easier to search and sort. You also find out how to manage the important Dataset technology, a way of detaching a table (or several) from a database to avoid the overhead of having to maintain a continual connection to the central database itself. When you finish this part, you're ready to begin managing the data part of data processing.

Chapter 11

The Basics of Databases

*E*xperts estimate that 80 percent of all computer programming involves databases. In this chapter, you survey the elements of today's most popular type of database, the *relational* database. When you're done, you'll understand not only the theory behind contemporary database management, you'll understand the practical implications of that theory.

Contemporary computing is divided into three primary areas of study. Traditional Windows programming is the primary area, so I spend most of the chapters in this book discussing it. However, two sub-categories are quite important as well — they expand on the classic programming techniques and provide you with additional features and capabilities. One special category is database management, the subject of this and the following two chapters. (Programming for Internet Web sites is the final category, and it differs in some significant ways from traditional programming. It's the topic of Chapters 14 and 15.)

Processing Data

Computers are sometimes called *data processors*, meaning that they take raw information such as

  ✔ A shirt costs $12

  ✔ Local sales tax is 7%

From this data, a computer can create some new information by *processing* the data (carrying out some steps that manipulate the information). For example, a computer program might multiply price by sales tax and then add that result to the original cost. This way, the program calculates the final cost. Processing, or computation, takes the form of steps, actions carried out on data:

1. Multiply the cost of the shirt times the local sales tax percent.

2. Add the shirt cost to the result of Step 1.

   So the total cost is $(.07 \times 12) = .84$. Then, Step 2 gives the final answer: $12 + .84$ results in $12.84.

Think of data as a list of raw materials, just as sugar, flour, eggs, salt, and butter are the raw materials that can be processed into a cake by following a series of steps that manipulate these raw materials.

A typical database organizes a collection of raw data so that you can process that data more efficiently. For example, you could put information about your business into a database by dividing your business into major categories and then creating a table (a collection of related data) for each category: customer information, inventory, employee information, and so on. With your raw data organized in this way, you can then process it easily in all sorts of ways.

Fortunately, Visual Basic Express has many tools to help you create, revise, manage, and otherwise deal with databases efficiently. This section of the book shows you how easy it is to use some of those tools.

But first, you need to come to grips with the major concepts by which databases are organized: tables, fields, and records. If you're not familiar with databases, I explain all these concepts in the next section. When you understand how databases are organized, you're ready to start using them to process data, which I explain later in this chapter.

Understanding Tables, Columns, Rows, and All the Rest

Of the various types of databases, I focus on the type of database that is currently by far the most popular: the relational database. A *relational database* has three primary qualities:

> ✔ **Data is stored in tables (which are subdivided into *fields* or, as they are sometimes called, *columns*).** For example, your personal address book could be a table with fields such as LastName, FirstName, Street, City, State, ZipCode, and PhoneNumber. The fields are the categories into which the data is subdivided.

✔ **You can *join* tables (in a *relationship*) so that you can later extract data from more than one table at a time.** Both joined tables must include a field that uniquely identifies each record in the table for this *joining* to work. For example, a unique ID field (made up of a series of non-repeating numbers) can enable the database to determine how to match up the data in the two tables because this field contains no duplicated data. The term *relational database* derives from the relationships you can create by joining tables. If this seems hard to understand, don't worry. It will come to you if you decide you need to relate two tables. Many small database projects use only *one* table — so you never have to bother with joining.

✔ **You can query tables, getting back DataSets (subsets of a table or tables).** A *DataSet* is a query (or request) for a list of, for example, all the customers in Texas who are more than 30 days past due paying their bills . . . the slackers.

In the following sections, I elaborate on what you need to know about each of these features of a database, so you can begin to work with databases effectively.

Tables, fields, and rows

Relational databases have three main building blocks: tables, fields, and records. You define the structure of a database when you create it. You determine how many tables it has and the fields in each table.

Tables

Suppose that a small talent agency creates a database to computerize the information about each actor they represent. This small, simple database has only one table, which in your database you name `Addresses`. (Tables are relatively large-scale collections of data, but a database can be even larger because it can contain multiple tables, representing, say, all the information about the employees, products, sales, and other data for a corporation.) Figure 11-1 illustrates the structure of a table a talent agency might create to keep track of its actors.

Fields

The top line on each page in the talent agency's table is a group of titles describing characteristics such as Name, Age, and so on. You can see where the term *fields* comes from. Reading down a field tells you the same category of information about all the different entries in the table, as shown in Figure 11-2.

Table

Figure 11-1:
A table is a
relatively
large-scale
set of data;
it includes
multiple
records and
fields.

FIRST NAME	LAST NAME	AGE	DESCRIPTION OF FACE
Lois	Lane	44	Ovoid, vacant expression
Don	Cantelopi	88	Square jaw, shock of white hair, eyebrows, frowns
Delores	Goets	22	Quite striking, happy lips
Sandy	Fastpass	29	Looks like Jon Bon Jovi
Joe	Normals	35	Bulging eyes, fishy look
Saundra	Doubleclick	12	Too soon to tell. Chubby.
Noah	Roah	24	Borderline personality look
Gary	Cheesefoot	72	Suspiciously smooth, tight skin for his age. Permanent smile.

Each field has its own name, such as `DescriptionOfFace`, that labels the field, identifying the nature of its contents. Some databases allow you to use more than one word for field names, such as `Description of Face`. However, other database styles require you to enclose multiple-word names in brackets or single quotes: `[Description of Face]` or `'Description of Face'`. And yet other databases simply forbid multiple words (by not allowing the use of spaces).

Column

Figure 11-2:
A field is a
vertical
category
of data,
described
by a
category
name.

FIRST NAME	LAST NAME	AGE	DESCRIPTION OF FACE
Lois	Lane	44	Ovoid, vacant expression
Don	Cantelopi	88	Square jaw, shock of white hair, eyebrows, frowns
Delores	Goets	22	Quite striking, happy lips
Sandy	Fastpass	29	Looks like Jon Bon Jovi
Joe	Normals	35	Bulging eyes, fishy look
Saundra	Doubleclick	12	Too soon to tell. Chubby.
Noah	Roah	24	Borderline personality look
Gary	Cheesefoot	72	Suspiciously smooth, tight skin for his age. Permanent smile.

TIP

If you're having trouble with a two-word field name when programming, try enclosing the name in brackets or single quotes. Although Microsoft Access–style databases permit spaces in field names, most relational databases do not permit spaces. If the database does not permit you to use spaces, you must resort to using an underscore character to separate words (such as `Description_of_Face`) or slamming the words together (such as `DescriptionOfFace`.) My advice is to just go for the common denominator and use single-word field names — that way *any* database will accept the names with no problem.

Records

A *record* (also called a *row*) contains the actual information that fills the fields, such as `Quite striking, happy lips`. Rows do not have label names.

Each record reads horizontally in the table and the data in a record usually fills several fields. In the talent agency example (see Figure 11-3), each record has four fields: `FirstName`, `LastName`, `Age`, and `DescriptionOfFace`.

Row

FIRST NAME	LAST NAME	AGE	DESCRIPTION OF FACE
Lois	Lane	44	Ovoid, vacant expression
Don	Cantelopi	88	Square jaw, shock of white hair eyebrows, frowns
Delores	Goets	22	Quite striking, happy lips
Sandy	Fastpass	29	Looks like Jon Bon Jovi
Joe	Normals	35	Bulging eyes, fishy look
Saundra	Doubleclick	12	Too soon to tell. Chubby.
Noah	Roah	24	Borderline personality look
Gary	Cheesefoot	72	Suspiciously smooth, tight skin for his age. Permanent smile.

Figure 11-3: A record is a *horizontal* set of data describing a single person or thing.

Joining and querying tables

If you're not interested in the concept of joining tables, skip this section. Here's an example that illustrates *relational* tables, related via joining. Say that you create an Address Book table with all the first and last names and addresses of your friends and relatives. Now you want to put their birthdays, which you have on your calendar, into a second table in your database. You name the table Gifts and define five fields for it: LastName, Birthday, FavoriteColor, ShoeSize, and Comments.

Records and fields: A scoreboard analogy

One way to think of the relationship between records and fields is to think of a baseball scoreboard. Picture a scoreboard with three labels across the top: Runs, Hits, Errors. These are the *field names*, and they describe the meaning of the columns of data below them.

The records contain the data about the two individual teams. Remember that a record contains a set of information about an individual entity. A scoreboard has two records: *Guest* and *Violent Toads* (or whatever fauna or warrior the local team is named after).

The data for the Guest record might be 4, 6, 3, and for the Toads, 74, 63, 1. With 74 runs, you know this is either high school baseball or a ballgame on Mars.

Notice that both your Addresses table and your Gifts table have a LastName field in common. These two LastName fields contain the same data in both tables. This common field enables you to *join* the tables. You can then *query* (ask for information from) both of these tables at once. Here's how it works:

1. You can use a query such as, "What is Normals's address and birthday?"

   His address information is held only in the Addresses table, and his birthday is listed in the Gifts table.

2. Because both tables contain `Normals` in a LastName field, they can provide their respective additional information about Mr. Normals: his address from the Addresses table and his birthday from the Gifts table.

   (Although I use LastName here as an example, this usually isn't the best way to join the tables; for details see "Tangled relationships: Using unique data to tie tables together," later in this chapter.)

3. The *result* of this query (the information you get back) is made available in what's called a *DataSet*. It contains only the data that you need for a particular purpose — in this example, mailing a birthday gift.

If you are particularly sharp right now, you may say, "What happens if *two* people share the same last name, *Normals*?" Very good point. Now sit down! That is a problem, because at least *one* field must contain unique data for each record. This problem is solved with keys and indexes, which I cover later in this chapter, in the section whimsically titled "Indexes — a Key to Success."

Why use multiple tables?

Why even introduce the complexity of more than one table — Addresses and Gifts? Why not just put all the data into one big table? Unfortunately, bulging, single-table databases are less flexible and less efficient than multiple, smaller tables, both when used by average people and when manipulated by a programmer.

You separate data into tables and then you separate it further into fields for the same reason that most people use labeled folders in their filing cabinets. Storing, retrieving, and managing the contents of an organized filing cabinet with many, thin, alphabetized folders is much easier than using a few huge folders bursting with papers.

If the database is small, however, its organization doesn't matter much. You don't have to worry about dividing your little address book database into several tables because it doesn't have that many entries. You're not *that* popular, are you?

But if you're designing a multiuser database with 250,000 records, every little efficiency matters when searching and sorting such a large amount of data. By creating several tables, you can improve the organization of the database, write programming code for it more easily, and generally retrieve records faster when querying. Why? Primarily because putting everything into one big database can result in dreadful redundancies.

To understand how and why this redundancy occurs, and why it's good to use several tables rather than one great big one, consider a database that lists 100 book publishers and 8,000 books. The database is divided into four tables: Authors, Publishers, TitleAuthor, and Titles. If all this information were stored in a single table, data would be duplicated all over the place.

Why? You would have to repeat the publishers' names, addresses, and phone numbers many times for each of the 8,000 books. It would be better to store each Publisher and their data (name, address, and phone number) *only once*.

When you look up a title in the Titles table, the publisher's name is part of each title's record (so you do have to provide the publisher's *name* 8,000 times). But if you want the publisher's address, phone number, and other details, no problem — because the Publisher's table and the Titles table both contain a PublishersName field. That way, you can get the other details about a publisher by matching the PublishersName field in the two tables. You store each publisher's address and phone number only once because you have separate tables. What's more, if you need to change the publisher's phone number later because they move to new offices, a single change in the Publishers table is the only change you have to make in the entire database.

Tangled relationships: Using unique data to tie tables together

When you specify a relationship between tables while designing a database, you're saying, "I may need additional information about this fellow, and if I do, it can be found in this other table using a field that is identical in both tables — the *primary key.*"

Suppose that you have several tables in a database, and every table has a field named ID. In each of these tables, John Jones has an ID number of 242522. The database may have several people named John Jones, so name fields are not going to provide you with a unique key to a unique record about a particular Mr. Jones. To be specific about which Mr. Jones, I look up the ID number in the second table.

A *key* is a field in a table that guarantees each entry in the field is unique to the record it resides in. Sometimes called the *primary key,* a key field prevents confusion. You can't use the FirstName field as a key because you may have six or more Joes in your organization. You can't use the LastName field because you could have more than one person named Smith. Phone numbers *seem* good, but no. You can't use the home phone number field because your office may suffer from raging nepotism and all four of the boss's offspring work for Daddy. What's a puzzled database designer to do? Well, don't sit there wringing your hands and moaning. Figure out a field that must always be unique. A SocialSecurityNumber field, for example, makes a good key field. Or, as I explain in the next section of this chapter, you can generate a series of unique ID numbers within a table automatically. You can let the computer assign serial numbers, like the sequential, never-repeated numbers on a roll of movie tickets.

Let the database do it for you: AutoNumber fields

You can let the database generate a unique ID number for each record. These serial numbers start with 1 when you add the first record and go up by 1 for each new record entered into the database. (Some database programmers insist that every table should have a field with a unique serial number so that you can ensure that every record is unique.)

Such database-generated serial numbers are put into an *AutoNumber* field. The AutoNumber field acts as a unique key, and its main function is to permit tables to be linked. How? When designing the database, you specify that the AutoNumber field be included in more than one table as a way of joining those tables.

Indexes — a Key to Success

Information in a relational database is not automatically stored alphabetically (or by numeric order, if the field is numeric). In a Name field, *Anderware* can follow *Zimbare*. Or maybe not. Whatever. At first, this seems surprising because you certainly don't expect a "filing system" to permit folders to be stored in any order.

However, records in a relational database aren't sorted. When someone adds a record to a database, it's just put at the end of a table. No attempt is made to place it in some particular position, such as alphabetical order. When a record is deleted, who cares? A relational database has a real "la-ti-dah" attitude about alphabetization. When designing a database, however, you should specify one or more of its fields as *indexes*. That's the key to the organization of a relational database.

Imagine nonalphabetic yellow pages

Many fields are not indexed (sorted). If you want to search for a particular record in a field that's not indexed, the database software must search down through every record until it finds the right one. How would you like it if the Yellow Pages were not alphabetized? You'd be turning pages all night looking for a plumber, hoping to stumble on the right page.

An index in a relational database is the one exception to the blithe, uncaring order I've just described. An indexed field solves the problem of finding a particular record in the jumble of data. The database software can quickly locate a specific record if a field is indexed.

So, when you're designing a database, you need to decide which field or fields should be indexed. (Unindexed data *can* be searched; it just takes longer.) Indexing doesn't, of course, speed things up in some kinds of queries. If the query is, "Give me a list of all people over 50," and the Age field isn't indexed, each record still must be searched.

Here's the general rule: You should index any fields that are likely to be searched. In the example address book database (remember it had two tables, one for Gifts), you are far more likely to search some fields than others. You'd probably search the Name and Birthday fields, but you would not likely search the [Favorite Color], [Shoe Size], or Comments fields. The purpose of the Gift table is to help you buy gifts for people, so it's unlikely that you'd ever query it like this: "Give me a list of everyone whose favorite color is green." But it's quite likely that you would query like this: "List everyone who has a birthday in August."

So, for the Gift table, you may specify that the Name and Birthday fields should be indexed and that the others should be left unindexed. But what happens if you later buy some size 8 blue shoes on sale and want to search the database to see whether any of your friends or relatives wears that size and likes blue? No problemo. Remember, you can always still conduct searches on unindexed fields; finding the information you need just takes longer. You are simply optimizing the average execution speed of your database when you decide which fields to index.

The database software automatically creates and maintains the indexes you specify. You need to do nothing more than specify which fields should be indexed.

Hey, let's index every field!

Some of you are probably thinking, "Why not index all the fields? That would be super-efficient." Wrong. Chill. When publishers create an index for a book, they don't index *all* the words in the book, do they? They include only the words likely to be searched for, not words such as *the* or *twelve*.

An index of all the words would suffer from several drawbacks. First of all, it would be bigger than the book. Second, most of the index would be of little use to anyone; it would be inefficient precisely because it was so big. A quick scan of the book itself would be faster than slogging through a massively bloated, highly repetitive index.

You don't index every field in a table for a similar reason: Too much of a good thing is a bad thing. Efficiencies start to degrade, storage space gets tight, multiuser traffic jams can occur, and other bugaboos arise.

Chapter 12

Quick Database User-Interface Techniques

*I*n this chapter, you get further into database management and see how to manipulate both datasets (tables that have been detached from their databases) and databases. You also explore the important DataGridView control.

The first consideration when presenting a database to the world is this: What's the easiest way for the user to view and manipulate data? Read on to find the answer.

Organizing the Entry Fields

Sometimes data needs to be edited or deleted, or new records must to be entered. In fact, your user interface should have provisions for massive initial data entry — somebody might have to sit down and type an entire cookbook's worth of recipes, for example.

To make data entry easier, your best approach is to try entering a few records yourself. That way you see what your user is up against, and can perhaps make the job of data entry more pleasant and more efficient. The easiest way for a good typist to enter the various fields in a record is if you ensure that those fields are in the proper order. For example, in Chapter 11, I explain how to create a table with two fields: Title and Instructions. The proper order for these fields is identical to the order in which they appear in the data source — cookbooks in this case.

So, you want the Title field on top, and the Instructions field below. And you want the typist to be able to easily visualize the size of these fields — so allow the typist to enter the Title data into a single-line TextBox but provide a larger TextBox for the greater amount of typing necessary to provide instructions.

By using this design, your data entry screen resembles the structure of the data being entered. Also, you should add labels describing each field, so it ends up looking something like Figure 12-1.

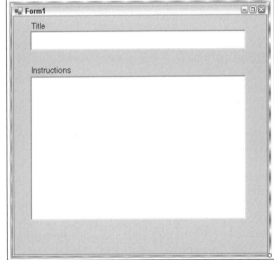

Figure 12-1:
Design data entry forms to reflect the size and position of the original data fields.

Navigating through Fields with the Tab Key

Perhaps even more important than getting the size and position of the fields correct is providing typists with a good way to navigate the fields *without having to use the mouse*. Nothing slows down a typist more than having to take his hands off the keyboard and reach for the mouse. (Well, perhaps a big kiss from a stranger or the cat spilling a glass of milk on the keyboard.)

You want to allow the typist to go to the next field by pressing the Tab key. Visual Basic uses a *tab order* for the various components on a form. You should change the `TabIndex` property to reflect each TextBox's position in the desired tab order. To set the tab order in the example shown in Figure 12-1, do the following:

1. **Click the Title TextBox to select it.**

2. **In the Properties window (press F4 if it's not visible), enter 0 for the TextBox's `TabIndex` property.**

3. **Click the second, larger textbox and set its `TabIndex` to 1.**

4. **If there are other controls on the form, like the "Title" and "Instructions" Labels in this example, set their `TabStop` property to `False` (so tabbing will skip them).**

5. **Finally, if you add a button or other control to save the current record and display a new blank record ready for a new entry, set that button's `TabIndex` to 3.**

Using this system, the typist can quickly move from one field to the next and from a filled-in record to a new, blank entry form.

Binding to Data

One of the greatest things about Visual Basic's design system (or IDE, integrated design environment) is how easy it is to do things that used to take days to accomplish via pure programming alone.

In this next example, you see how to connect a VB program to a database (or *data store* as they're now calling a source of data) and, after the connection is established, how to connect individual fields (columns) in the database's tables to VB controls, such as TextBoxes.

Loading a sample database

To follow the upcoming example, you must first have a database to work with. For years, Microsoft has provided some sample databases for people to play around with. One of them is called the Northwind database, and it comes with Microsoft Office, specifically Access, the database program in Office. If you have Office, see if you can find `Northwind.mdb` in this location on your hard drive:

```
C:\Program Files\Microsoft Office\Office11\Samples\Northwind.mdb
```

Note that `Office11` here might be `Office10` or some earlier version — choose whichever one you see on your computer.

If you can't find it, download `Northwind.exe` from:

```
www.microsoft.com/downloads/details.aspx?FamilyID=C6661372-8DBE-422B-
    8676-C632D66C529C&displaylang=EN
```

After you download it to your hard drive, double-click `Northwind.exe` in Windows Explorer to extract the `.mdb` (database) file. Save it in the folder of your choice, but remember its location.

Don't download Northwind from this SQL Server 2005 Express location:

```
www.microsoft.com/downloads/details.aspx?FamilyId=06616212-0356-
    46A0-8DA2-EEBC53A68034&displaylang=en
```

This is the download link listed with SQL Server 2005 Express, but extracting and installing this `.msi` file is impossibly complicated. And even after jumping through hoops, I couldn't get it to work on the command line (don't ask!). So just download the `.exe` version recommended earlier in this section.

Connecting to a database

To see how to make a connection between a database and a VB program, follow these steps:

1. **Choose File⇨New Project.**

2. **Double-click the Windows Application icon in the dialog box.**

   A new project template appears, ready for you to add a user interface.

3. **Drag and drop a TextBox from the Toolbox onto Form1. Drag the TextBox to make it a bit wider and to position it near the top of the form.**

4. **Click the TextBox to select it and then, in the Properties window, change its `FontSize` to 11.**

5. **Click the TextBox to select it and then press Ctrl+C.**

   A copy of the TextBox, including its new font size, is saved to the clipboard.

6. **Press Ctrl+V three times.**

   Three new TextBox clones appear on your form.

TIP

This copy-paste technique is a quick way to set the properties of multiple controls. You can also drag your mouse around a group of controls already on the form. This selects them as a set; when you change one of the properties they have in common (such as font size) in the Properties window, all of them are changed at once.

7. **Add a BindingNavigator control from the Toolbox.**

   If you can't see it, scroll down in the Toolbox until you see the section titled Data, followed by the data-related controls.

8. **Choose Data⇨Add New Data Source.**

   The DataSource Configuration Wizard opens.

9. **Click Next.**

   You can now choose the source of the data, as shown in Figure 12-2.

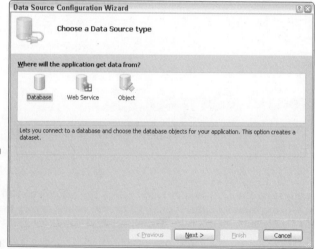

Figure 12-2:
You can choose from three data sources.

10. **Click Database to select it as your data source, as shown in Figure 12-2.**

11. **Click Next.**

12. **Click the New Connection button.**

   The Add Connection dialog box opens.

13. **Click the Change button and double-click Microsoft Access Database File.**

14. **Click the Browse button and locate and select** `Northwind.mdb` **or** `Nwind.mdb` **on your hard drive; then click OK.**

   The Add Existing Item dialog box closes.

15. Click Next in the Data Source Configuration Wizard.

A dialog box tells you that the data file you've chosen isn't yet in the current project.

16. Click Yes to add the data file to your project.

17. Click Next.

The Wizard opens, analyzes the database, and shows you the schema (structure) of the data, as shown in Figure 12-3.

Figure 12-3:
Choose which tables and fields (columns) you want to attach to your project.

18. Locate and open the Employees table (click the + next to Tables, and then click the + next to Employees). Click the check boxes next to the fields LastName, FirstName, Title, and BirthDate, as shown in Figure 12-3.

The Wizard will create a dataset (a set of records that is extracted from, and separate from, the database itself). You discover lots more about datasets in Chapter 13.

By default, the Wizard has named the dataset it's about to create either `NwindDataSet` or `NorthwindDataSet`. Leave this default name as-is for this example. You can always rename it later. When creating a project in the real world, you might want to change the name here in the Wizard, using a name more descriptive of what the dataset does in the program.

19. Click Finish.

A new dataset has been added to your program. You can see it listed in the Solution Explorer as `NwindDataSet.xsd` or `Northwind`. Now the real fun begins.

Binding controls to a dataset

In VB Express, you can "bind" (attach) any control to any field in a dataset. (What's more, you can even bind most of the control's properties if you wish.)

Automatic responses

When a control is bound, if your user or program moves to a different record, the bound control automatically responds, displaying the new record's data or otherwise reacting in some other way. All this happens automatically, behind the scenes, so you don't have to do any programming to make it work.

To bind controls to your dataset, follow these steps:

1. **Click the Data Sources tab at the bottom of the Solution Explorer.**

2. **Click the + next to the Employees table to open the fields you speci-fied for this dataset (in Step 18 in the previous section).**

   You see the `NorthwindDataSet`, as shown in Figure 12-4.

Figure 12-4:
You can drag a dataset's table (like Employees here) onto a Form, thereby making it bindable to all the form's controls.

3. **Drag the LastName field from the Employees table and drop it onto the top TextBox on Form1.**

   A check button appears next to LastName in the DataSources list, and TextBox1 is bound to this field. Also, three new icons appear on the tray beneath the Form, next to the existing BindingNavigator icon, as shown in Figure 12-5.

Figure 12-5:
When you drop a table or one of its fields onto a Form or control, VB automatically adds Dataset, BindingSource, and TableAdapter controls to your Form.

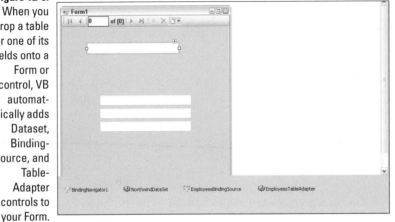

4. **Repeat Step 3 to drop the FirstName, Title, and BirthDate fields into the respective remaining TextBoxes.**

   You're now ready to give it a try.

5. **Press F5 to execute your new data-entry program.**

   You should see the results shown in Figure 12-6.

Figure 12-6:
You didn't do *any* actual programming, and here you have a fully functional database management system.

Try it out. Use the data navigator bar to move to the next, first, previous, or last record in the dataset. Also try adding a new record, editing an existing one, or deleting a record. However, any modifications you make are not saved permanently to the dataset — so you won't see your changes the next time you run the application. To actually save modifications, delete records, or add new records, you do need to do a little programming . . . but just a little. See the next chapter, Chapter 13, for details.

Viewing the automatic code

Before seeing how to use the powerful DataGridView control, first take a quick peek at a little bit of programming that VB automatically wrote for you. It was added to the code window when the Wizard created your dataset. Choose Debug➪Stop Debugging to halt the program (which you started by pressing F5 in Step 5 in the previous section) and return to normal VB design mode. Double-click the Form to open the code window to see the following code in the Form_Load event:

```
Private Sub Form1_Load(ByVal sender As System.Object, ByVal e As
          System.EventArgs) Handles MyBase.Load

    'TODO: This line of code loads data into the 'NorthwindDataSet.Employees'
    'table. You can move or remove it, as needed.
    Me.EmployeesTableAdapter.Fill(Me.NorthwindDataSet.Employees)

End Sub
```

This line of code fills the TableAdapter with the Employees table's data, making it available to the various controls to which it is bound.

Using the DataGridView

If you want to present a large amount of data at once, in tabular format, the DataGridView is an excellent choice. You can create this component by simply dropping a table onto a Form.

To see how this works, follow these steps:

1. **Start a new VB project by choosing File➪New Project and then double-clicking the Windows Application icon.**

   A new project is ready for you to work with.

2. **Choose Data➪Add New Data Source.**

   The DataSource Configuration Wizard opens.

3. **Click the database icon and then click Next.**

4. **Click the New Connection button.**

   The Add Connection dialog box opens.

5. **Click the Change button and double-click Microsoft Access Database File.**

6. **Click the Browse button, locate and select Northwind.mdb or Nwind. mdb on your hard drive, and then click OK.**

   The Add Existing Item dialog box closes.

7. **Click Next in the Data Source Configuration Wizard.**

   A dialog box tells you that the data file you've chosen isn't yet in the current project. Click Yes to add it.

8. **Click Next.**

   The Wizard opens, analyzes the database, and shows you the schema (structure) of the data.

9. **Click the + next to the Tables entry.**

   All the tables in the database are displayed.

10. **Locate the Customers table and click the check box next to Customers.**

    All the fields in the Customer table are simultaneously selected and will be made available to your project as a dataset.

11. **Click Finish.**

    The new Northwind dataset has been added to your program and is listed in the Solution Explorer as NorthwindDataSet.xsd.

12. **Click the Data Sources tab at the bottom of the Solution Explorer.**

    You see the dataset listed with the Customers table beneath it.

13. **Drag the Customers table and drop it onto the form.**

    Several exciting things happen: Four controls are added to the tray beneath the form — the DataSet, a BindingSource, a TableAdapter, and a BindingNavigator. You also see that the BindingNavigator control (the toolbar with navigation buttons) appears on the form, along with the DataGridView control, with a title bar showing some of the table's fields listed across the top, as shown in Figure 12-7.

14. **Take a quick look at how the DataGridView looks when filled with the records from the Customers table.**

    Notice the small black right-arrow at the top right of the DataGridView — it's up next to the Region field's title in Figure 12-7. Microsoft calls this new feature a *smart tag*. It indicates that something is behind the scenes — a context menu or some other feature you can use to manipulate the object. Just click the smart tag to reveal the hidden features.

15. **Click the smart tag on the DataGridView.**

    A special Tasks menu opens, as shown in Figure 12-8.

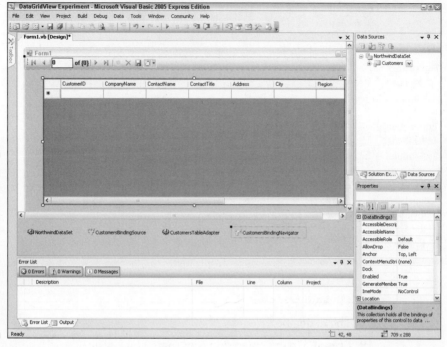

Figure 12-7:
Simply
dropping
a table onto
a form
creates a
functional
data display
and
navigation
system.

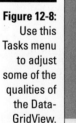
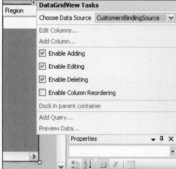

Figure 12-8:
Use this
Tasks menu
to adjust
some of the
qualities of
the Data-
GridView.

16. **Click Preview Data.**

    A Data Preview dialog box opens.

17. **Click the Preview button in the dialog box.**

    You now see the grid fill with actual records, as shown in Figure 12-9.

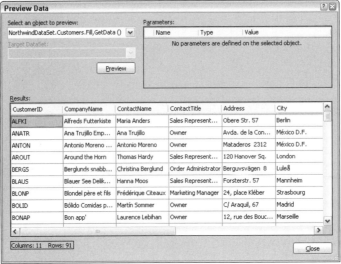

Figure 12-9:
You can
check your
data
connection
and see the
actual
records
while still in
design view
by using
this Data
Preview.

18. **Click Close.**

The dialog box closes.

19. **Press F5 to execute your program.**

The DataGridView appears, ready for use, as shown in Figure 12-10.

Figure 12-10 illustrates what happens if the user modifies a record. A small pencil icon appears on the left side (see where the mouse pointer is located in Figure 12-10).

If the user wants to save any changes (technically this is called *committing the edit*), he can simply click the disk drive icon (the *Save Data* button) on the BindingNavigator control at the top.

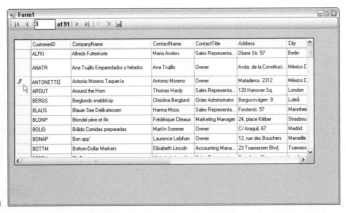

Figure 12-10:
Notice that
the user has
dragged
some of the
cells to
make the
cells taller
and wider,
so all the
data is
viewable.

However, to allow this to happen — to actually let the user update the dataset — you probably want to add a little program that goes "under" (or, as some people prefer to say, behind) that Save Data button on the BindingNavigator.

Saving Data to a DataSet

When you use a DataGridView or otherwise bind a data source to a data control, some programming code that allows the user to save changes to the data (editing, deleting, adding records, and so on) is automatically created.

To see how to modify the code that updates the dataset, follow these steps:

1. **Go through the process described in the previous section to create a DataGridView filled with the Customers table data.**

2. **Click the Save Data (disk icon) button on the BindingNavigator control to select it.**

   Look in the Properties Window and you see that the BindingNavigatorSaveItem's properties are now listed.

3. **Double-click the Enabled property in the Properties window until it reads True.**

4. **Double-click the Save Data (disk icon) button on the BindingNavigator control.**

   The code window opens and you see the Sub BindingNavigatorSaveItem_ Click event, in which you enter code that reacts when the user clicks that disk icon.

5. **Type the following line of boldface code just above the ELSE in the existing code that VB already entered for you:**

```
Private Sub bindingNavigatorSaveItem_Click(ByVal sender As
         System.Object, ByVal e As System.EventArgs) Handles
         bindingNavigatorSaveItem.Click

If Me.Validate Then
    Me.CustomersBindingSource.EndEdit()
    Me.CustomersTableAdapter.Update(Me.NorthwindDataSet.Customers)
    MsgBox("Your changes were saved.")

    Else
        System.Windows.Forms.MessageBox.Show(Me, _
            "Validation errors occurred.", "Save", _
            System.Windows.Forms.MessageBoxButtons.OK, _
            System.Windows.Forms.MessageBoxIcon.Warning)
End If

End Sub
```

6. **Press F5.**

   Your program runs and the data form appears.

7. **Change some of the data. Rename some people or give one of them the Contact Title *Aggressive Nerd*.**

8. **Click the Save Data icon (the diskette symbol) on the BindingNavigator.**

   The dataset is updated with your changes, and a message box appears, confirming the update.

9. **Exit the program.**

   It stops running.

10. **Press F5 again to start it running.**

    Look for your changes to appear in the DataGridView, proving to yourself that in fact the update did occur. Your changes are now saved to the dataset, *but they're not saved to the actual database.*

Saving Data to a Database

Remember, a dataset is a detached group of data. Datasets may or may not be merged back into the database from which they came. It's up to you, the programmer, whether and how such merging takes place.

Do you want to first check the data to ensure it's valid and not some crazy error, like someone's age being stored as 2,344? Some validation code is automatically entered by VB, as shown in Step 5 in the previous section, but you wouldn't want to leave that code in a finished program. The error message displayed would make even brave people faint. You want to replace it with a message that's much more meaningful and less frightening. Do you want to request clarification from the data entry person? Do you need to compare this dataset to another dataset that someone else is trying to merge back into the database? Remember, the database itself is a semi-sacred repository — you don't lightly permit changes to it by every Tom, Dick, and Harry.

Everything is stored together

To make life easier for the programmer, Microsoft has lately been copying almost everything that a project needs — graphics, binary files, your programming in the source files, datasets, whatever — *into the same folder*. Data, for example, may reside in the main folder or in a sub-folder under that main folder. But, when you copy the main folder, you automatically copy all the "dependencies" (other files) needed to make the application work. In the case of mdb files, *this includes the database.*

Decoding the code

The bizarre importation OOP code in the "Saving edited records" example breaks down like this:

```
Dim DataChanges As NwindDataSet.CustomersDataTable
```

This line of code creates a `CustomersDataTable` object you can use to reference a table in the dataset.

```
DataChanges = CType(NwindDataSet.Customers.GetChanges(DataRowState.Modified),
    NwindDataSet.CustomersDataTable)
```

This line assigns the customers table (the new, edited version) to the object you created in the previous line. Simultaneously the `GetChanges` and `Modified` methods ensure that any modifications the user made to the dataset are assigned to the `DataChanges` object.

```
Try
    If Not DataChanges Is Nothing Then
        CustomersTableAdapter.Update(DataChanges)
        MsgBox("Change to database.")
    End If
```

This clumsy, double-negative, *not nothing* means that if the `DataChanges` object has something in it (if it was transformed by the `GetChanges` method above), then use the `Update` method (of the `TableAdapter` component) to revise the contents of the dataset.

```
Catch ex As Exception
    MsgBox("Error attempting to save your changes to the database: " & ex.ToString)
Finally
    If Not DataChanges Is Nothing Then
        DataChanges.Dispose()
    End If
End Try
```

At the end, you can "dispose" (delete) the object when you're finished using it. The idea is that objects can hang around, taking up memory and slowing things down, unless you dispose of them. My understanding is that using this `Dispose` tactic is entirely unnecessary in VB Express, so you can safely ignore that part of the code if you wish. C programmers are likely to feel compelled to use it, so I include it.

Therefore, if you look for the project you've been working on in this chapter, you'll notice that it has a copy of the `Nwind.mdb` database in the /BIN folder (along with the compiled, executable version of the program — the `.exe` file). *This* `.mdb` database file is updated when you use the following techniques to save changes to the dataset. The original `Nwind.mdb` file — wherever you put it on your hard drive — is not updated. So you now have two databases.

In a real-world database management project, you would likely have your program rename the original, unmodified database file Nwind.BAK or something similar — to keep it as a backup file, and to avoid confusing it with the current database.

Saving edited records

To see how to commit (save) any *edited* records back to the database, follow these steps. Notice that this does not save any new records *added* to the recordset by the user, nor does it delete any records. You see how to do those jobs shortly.

1. **Double-click the Save Data (disk icon) button on the BindingNavigator control in the project you built in the previous sections in this chapter.**

   The code window opens, and you see the Sub BindingNavigatorSaveItem_ Click event, where you added the MsgBox code in the previous section.

2. **Delete all the code in the event.**

3. **Replace the code with the boldface lines in the following:**

```
Private Sub BindingNavigatorSaveItem_Click(ByVal sender As
          System.Object, ByVal e As System.EventArgs) Handles
          BindingNavigatorSaveItem.Click

Dim DataChanges As NwindDataSet.CustomersDataTable

DataChanges = _
    CType(NwindDataSet.Customers.GetChanges(DataRowState.Modified), _
    NwindDataSet.CustomersDataTable)

Try
    If Not DataChanges Is Nothing Then
        CustomersTableAdapter.Update(DataChanges)
        MsgBox("Change to database.")
    End If
Catch ex As Exception
    MsgBox("Error attempting to save your changes to the database: " & _
        ex.ToString)
Finally
    If Not DataChanges Is Nothing Then
        DataChanges.Dispose()
    End If
End Try

End Sub
```

Ignore the squiggly underline that VB displays under `DataRowState`.

The line that begins with `DataChanges` = must be typed on a single, long line. Don't press the Enter key after typing the =.

4. **At the very top of the editing window, on the first line, type this necessary "importation" of the database-related function library:**

```
Imports System.Data
```

Without this `Imports` statement, some of the commands in your code won't work.

You don't need to get into the dreary details about why this job uses so much code, or indeed to try to memorize what it all means. Just use it as-is and hope that reason will prevail and simplicity will return to Basic. If you're nonetheless interested in what's going on in all that bloated code, I explain it in the nearby sidebar, "Decoding the code."

5. **Press F5.**

The program executes.

6. **Make some changes to a record — such as changing the name *Anton* to *Blutz*.**

7. **Click the Save Data icon on the BindingNavigator control.**

This data is saved to the *copy* of the `Northwind.mdb` database residing in the /BIN folder of your project.

You can see that the change was made by double-clicking the `Northwind.mdb` database. It opens in Microsoft Access, and the name *Blutz* is now in it. Or write a new VB Express project that uses the *copy* of the `Northwind.mdb` database and look for the Blutz change.

Chapter 13

Managing DataSets

● ●

In This Chapter

▶ Understanding the DataSet

▶ Creating a DataSet via programming

▶ Using global object variables

▶ Defining a schema

▶ Managing collections

▶ Opening DataSets

▶ Adding and removing records

▶ Maneuvering through a DataSet

● ●

*T*he key to understanding the database technology in VB Express is understanding the DataSet. In this chapter, you focus on how to create, save,
and load a DataSet. To better understand the DataSet concept — and to give
yourself maximum flexibility — you go through these various tasks *programmatically.* That means you write the code rather than leave those tasks up to
a wizard or a component such as the DataView or some other helper.

Managing DataSets in your programming isn't difficult, and you'll likely appreciate having power over the process. The DataSet is a central feature of VB
Express, just as databases are central to computing in general.

Delving into DataSets

The kind of DataSet that you work with in this chapter is a copy of some data
(at least one table, but containing as many tables as you want) that is held in
memory or stored as two XML files on a hard drive. To simplify the contents

of each XML file, the structure (the names of the tables, columns, and other features) of the DataSet is stored in one file, while the actual *data* (the specific records — or rows — of information) is stored in a separate file. This is a typical XML tactic.

To work with a DataSet, you don't need a continuously active connection to a database. A DataSet object is fairly self-sufficient — it can execute a variety of commands (methods) and properties to manage its data.

Typically, you connect to a large database, like the `Nwind.mdb` sample database (see Chapter 12), and then extract a DataSet from that database. This way, you need not maintain a constant connection between your computer and the database (which might be on the Internet somewhere else in the world). Instead, you can work all you want with the DataSet in your local machine and then return the DataSet for merging with the big database on its server computer.

This kind of *disconnectedness* (also known as *distributed applications* or *distributed programming*) is perhaps the primary distinction between traditional programming and programming designed to work on the Internet. On the Internet, this disconnectedness means that each visitor receives his or her own DataSet (requiring only a brief connection to the database to extract the DataSet), which has important advantages:

- ✔ **More people can view your data** — such as your catalog of current products — by having a DataSet sent to their machines. If everyone maintained a connection to your database, fewer people could access it. (Access, for example, begins to fume and groan after 10 or 20 simultaneous connections.)

- ✔ **More people can update your data.** For example, visitors can update a customer database with, say, a new phone number or e-mail address. Then they can click a Submit button on your Web page and their revised DataSet is sent back to your server and merged with the database (requiring only a brief reconnection for the update).

- ✔ **Your server has a lighter load to manage.** If 2,000 people simultaneously remain connected to your company's database, your little server computer will probably start *smoldering*! To take the load off, each person can have his or her own disconnected portion of information from the catalog.

Consider this: At the annual family reunion picnic, all 457 cousins don't converge on the big stew pot and push and shove to stick in their forks. No. Everyone gets their own bowl and goes off to eat on their own tree stump or perhaps on a rock down by the river. That way, nobody starts one a-them feuds. Good manners make for good reunions; that's my belief.

Building a DataSet Programmatically

DataSets are stored in XML files, so they are especially useful for transmitting data over networks, such as the Internet. You can extract DataSets from existing databases, or you can just create a brand new DataSet that isn't derived from a larger database.

In this chapter, you see how to create an independent DataSet that isn't extracted from some larger database. And you work within a Windows-style application, not an Internet Web site–style application. The programming techniques illustrated in this chapter can, nonetheless, serve you well if you want to use a DataSet with Internet programming or with an existing database. For details about attaching a database to a Web site, see Part IV of this book.

Actually, given the fairly powerful set of built-in commands, you can use a DataSet for some smaller database jobs, rather than resorting to a full database management system.

Try creating a little DataSet that mimics a cookbook. It will have one table (named `recipes`). This table will be the equivalent of an entire cookbook. The table will have two fields (or columns) named `title` and `description`.

Each record — or row (think of a record as a single recipe in your cookbook) — will therefore be divided into two sections: the `title` section holding the recipe's title and the `description` section holding the recipe itself. Let's get cooking.

Importing namespaces

First off, as usual, you want to import some namespaces (to make referring to database objects and their members easier).

This importation requirement, though mind-numbing, is currently required in VB Express.

To begin creating your programmatic DataSet by importing namespaces, follow these steps:

1. **Start a new VB Express project (File⇨New Project).**

2. **Name the project Ds, for DataSet.**

3. **Double-click the Windows Application icon in the New Project dialog box.**

4. **Double-click the form in the Design window to get to the Code window.**

An alternative to importing namespaces?

Perhaps a better system will appear down the road in the next version, and by *better* I mean simply avoiding this useless exercise. There's no good reason why you should have to *import* what should be automatically available always in the language. Namely: the code libraries should simply be *there* ready to use, rather than requiring you to remember to add `system.text` when you plan to work with text, and so on.

Using `Imports` doesn't lighten the load for the programmer — it makes life more difficult because some errors result from not importing the correct library. And the error messages don't make this clear to you, so you can waste time puzzling over it. What's more, `Imports` doesn't make programs smaller or faster. Only the code necessary for program execution is compiled; entire libraries that you "import" are not loaded in as part of the finished application.

No, the only load that's lightened is for the people at Microsoft who have a clerical problem to solve (now that they're juggling tens of thousands of functions in their huge collection of libraries). So the buck gets passed to us. They should collect all the common libraries — database, security, text management, and so on — into a default, built-in library that you need not import. If absolutely necessary — and I think it isn't — they can leave out some rarely used libraries, such as deployment or historical database functions.

Right now, some of the most frequently used libraries, such as `IO` (input output) and `text`, are *not* by default in the References section of the Solution Explorer (click the Show All Files button on the explorer's title bar to see the default libraries, or *namespaces* as they now insist on calling them). This means you have to explicitly use `Imports` to use their features. But, in a bizarre twist of events, the rarely used (by us programmers) `System.Drawing` library *is* a default library! Nobody can explain these strange choices, but one can imagine a better future, and the victory of common sense over OOP. Evidently not too much thought went into the selection of default libraries, given that frequently needed functions are left out, and rarely used functions (like drawing circles) are included.

To make matters even more painful, sometimes it's not enough to just use an `Imports` statement. You get error messages in some cases even after you `Imports` some libraries; you have to go a step further and *also* employ Project⇨Add Reference and then include a `.dll` (dynamic link library) or other library. There is no discernible pattern to which libraries are added to your project in which ways, so don't try to figure it out. Just remember that sometimes you have to use `Imports` and other times you must also add a reference. Messy, and it's not really our job as programmers to sort all this stuff out anyway. It's as if the postman dumped the entire town's letters in your driveway and said, "Find yours."

5. **Go to the very top of the Code window and enter the following `Imports` statements at the very top of the code window (and I mean up above *all code*, including `Public Class Form1`):**

```
Imports System.Data
Imports System.XML
Imports System.Xml.XmlDataDocument
```

See the squiggly lines under these `Imports` statements? That's VB Express telling you that these commonly used libraries can't even be imported, much less be expected as default libraries.

6. **Choose Project➪Add Reference.**

7. **With the .NET tab selected, Ctrl+click the System.Data.dll and System.XML.dll entries to select both of them and then click OK to close the dialog box and add these libraries to your project.**

Now you can use their functions in your programming.

The following imports may or may not be required, depending on your version of VB. If these namespaces are not recognized (VB draws a wavy line under your `Imports` code because it cannot "find" the namespace), just delete that `Imports` line of code.

```
Imports System.Data.OleDb
Imports System.Data.SqlTypes
Imports System.Data.SqlDbType
Imports System.Data.SqlClient
```

You might want to always attach *all* these `Imports` when working with data in VB Express. For now, just go ahead and add them as listed.

Declaring the global variables

Okay, after you import the namespaces, you can do some of your own programming now.

You want to declare some global variables. In VB Express, you can place global variables in a module (Project➪Add Module) and thus make the variables available to the entire project (all the forms and other containers in the project). Working from the example in the preceding section, you just need to make the variables global to an individual form.

To do so, just below `Public Class Form1`, type the lines that appear here in boldface:

```
Public Class Form1

    Dim ds As New DataSet(), dr As DataRow, dt As DataTable

    'holds a deleted record
    Dim titlehold As String, descriptionhold As String

    'holds the current filenames
    Dim schemafilepath As String, datafilepath As String

    'holds the total records and current record number
```

```
Dim TotalRows As Integer, CurrentRow As Integer

Private Sub Form1_Load(ByVal sender As System.Object, ByVal e As
        System.EventArgs) Handles MyBase.Load
```

You've just created your global variables. These variables will be used by more than one procedure (subroutine) in your project, so you want them to be *global* — to retain their contents even when the program isn't executing within the procedure where they were declared (with the `Dim` command). Solution? Declare them *outside* any particular procedure (as I've done here) in what's called the *General Declarations* section of the class (the form).

Building a DataSet in code

After you declare the global variables, it's time to create the DataSet.

Although you can create a DataSet by using database controls or from the Data menu in VB Express — as you can see in Chapter 12 — sometimes you want to let the user create his or her own DataSet files from scratch. In that case, you have to create the DataSet programmatically. (How, for example, would you know while programming what the user wanted to call the tables and columns?)

The structure of the DataSet has to be built while the program executes, based on the user's input. To do that, you need to create the DataSet not with controls during program design, but within your source code during program execution.

Type this within the Form_Load event:

```
Private Sub Form1_Load(ByVal sender As System.Object, ByVal e As
        System.EventArgs) Handles MyBase.Load

'Create a new table named Recipes with title and description
'(the description of the actual recipe) columns.

dt = New DataTable("Recipes")
dt.Columns.Add("title", GetType(String))
dt.Columns.Add("description", GetType(String))
ds.Tables.Add(dt)

' stick some data into the first record's two columns
dr = dt.NewRow()
dr!title = "First Test Recipe"
dr!description = "Instructions on making popular pies..."
dt.Rows.Add(dr)

'save the structure (schema) of this DataSet
ds.WriteXmlSchema("c:\Recipesdataset.xml")
```

```
'save the actual data that's currently in this DataSet
ds.WriteXml("c:\RecipesData.xml")

Debug.WriteLine("DataSet Loaded. ")
Debug.WriteLine("Number of Tables: " & ds.Tables.Count)

Dim s As String

s = ds.Tables(0).Columns.Count.ToString

Debug.WriteLine("Table 1 has " & s & " columns")

s = ds.Tables(0).Rows.Count.ToString()

Debug.WriteLine("Table 1 currently has " & s & " rows" & "(" & s & _
    " records of data)")

dt = ds.Tables(0)
For Each dr In dt.Rows

    Debug.WriteLine("ColumnName: " & dt.Columns(0).ColumnName & "  Data: " & _
        dr(0).ToString)
    'Debug.WriteLine(" ")

    Debug.WriteLine("ColumnName: " & dt.Columns(1).ColumnName & "  Data: " & _
        dr(1).ToString)
Next

End Sub
```

Press F5. To see the results of your experiment, open the VB Express Immediate window by choosing View⇨Other Windows⇨Immediate. You should see the following results at the bottom of the Immediate window — you may have to scroll down to see it:

```
DataSet Loaded.
Number of Tables: 1
Table 1 has 2 columns
Table 1 currently has 1 rows(1 records of data)
ColumnName: title  Data: First Test Recipe
ColumnName: description  Data: Instructions on making popular pies...
```

When you're working on a program in VB, you often want to get some feedback — to see the contents of a variable or the status of some other object. If you need to see only one or two things, a MsgBox works okay:

```
MsgBox ("Number of Tables: " & ds.Tables.Count)
```

But if you need to see several items, the MsgBox approach can be a pain; each MsgBox halts execution, and you have to keep clicking OK to close each box. Instead, use the `Debug.Write` or `Debug.WriteLine` technique illustrated in the example. That way, you get your report all neat and listed in the

Immediate window without having to click OK to shut a bunch of message boxes. (`Debug.WriteLine` causes VB to move down a line in the Immediate window.) Another advantage is that you can study the results in the Immediate window — all sitting there together for your perusal. And the results remain until you erase them — future writing to the Immediate window is simply appended.

For in-depth coverage of debugging techniques, see Chapter 10.

Analyzing the code

In the recipe example I've been building on throughout this section, you've seen how to create a new DataSet and define a table and columns within it. Also included is the code necessary to read information from — and store information in — a DataSet's records. For each task accomplished in this code, comments within the code describe what the code does. However, consider some of the highlights.

As you read through these explanations and find unfamiliar terminology, flip to Chapter 11, where I offer details on database basics.

Creating global object variables

The code example began with a statement that declared a few global variables:

```
Dim ds As New DataSet(), dr As DataRow, dt As DataTable
```

With this line, you created global object variables for a DataSet object (`ds`), a DataRow object (`dr`), and a DataTable object (`dt`). The DataRow object will contain a collection of all the individual rows (often called *records*) of data, however many there may be. The number of rows can grow or shrink depending on whether new data units (rows) are added or deleted from the DataSet.

Creating the table object

The code proper began by creating a table named `Recipes` (so far, this is just a table object; it hasn't been made part of the DataSet yet):

```
dt = New DataTable("Recipes")
```

Note that you can create as many tables as you want, but you're going to use only one in this DataSet.

Then you created two columns (also known as *fields*). These are named `title` and `description`, but you could have named them anything you wanted to. At the same time you created them, you added them to the Columns collection of the `Recipes` table object:

```
dt.Columns.Add("title", GetType(String))
dt.Columns.Add("description", GetType(String))
```

You can add as many columns as you want to your table, but you use only two categories in your recipe DataSet: the title of each recipe and the description (the recipe itself). So, given that you have two categories of information in this table, you should use just two columns.

Then, pleased with yourself, you added the `Recipes` table to the Tables collection of the DataSet named `ds`:

```
ds.Tables.Add(dt)
```

Defining a schema

You specified the tables and columns in your DataSet. In other words, you've defined the structure of the DataSet. It's as if you had a book full of blank pages, wrote RECIPES on the cover, and on each page drew a line from top to bottom, dividing each page into two zones. Then you labeled the two zones *Title* and *Description*. A DataSet's structure is called its *schema*.

Adding some records (the actual data)

With the DataSet's schema in place, you stored an actual row in the DataSet. A DataSet contains both categories (tables, and within tables, columns) as well as rows (records of data). You created a new row:

```
dr = dt.NewRow()
```

Then you added some data to each of the two columns:

```
dr!title = "First Test Recipe"
dr!description = "Instructions on making pies..."
```

And finally, you added the new row to the `Rows` collection of the table (which already resides in the DataSet, so this row becomes part of the DataSet):

```
dt.Rows.Add(dr)
```

Saving the data

Then you used the `WriteXMLSchema` command to save the structure into one file:

```
ds.WriteXmlSchema("c:\Recipesdataset.xml")
```

and used the `WriteXML` command to save the data (the rows) in a separate file:

```
ds.WriteXml("c:\RecipesData.xml")
```

Note that a DataSet need not be saved to the hard drive as files. Indeed, it's more common to simply keep the DataSet in the computer's memory while the user reads it or modifies it. Then, when the user is through, any changes can be merged back into the original database and the DataSet itself is simply left to die, to evaporate from RAM memory. This approach has a security benefit — none of your data remains on disk unless buffered.

However, to give you a good idea how you can manipulate independent DataSets, in this example, you store them to disk. I chose the location and filenames simply for convenience. You can change `c:\RecipesData.xml`, for example, to whatever path and filename you wish. There is no special place that you must store a DataSet, nor is there a special filename that you must give it.

Extracting the data to display it somewhere

To extract all the data in a table, you first have to find out *how many* columns and rows that tables has. The following code does the trick:

```
Dim s As String

s = ds.Tables(0).Columns.Count.ToString
s = ds.Tables(0).Rows.Count.ToString()
```

Finally, you used a technique that extracts all the data in your table:

```
For Each dr In dt.Rows

    Debug.Write("ColumnName: " & dt.Columns(0).ColumnName & "  Data: " &
            dr(0).ToString)
    Debug.WriteLine(" ")

    Debug.Write("ColumnName: " & dt.Columns(1).ColumnName & "  Data: " &
            dr(1).ToString)
    Debug.WriteLine(" ")
Next
```

This is the kind of code you could use to fill a ListBox with all the titles — `dr (0)` — in the DataSet. Then the user can click one of those titles to choose that particular row, and you could display both the title and the description in a pair of TextBoxes, for example.

By the way, to add more rows, just repeat the code that created the first record, changing only the actual data that you're putting into the new rows:

```
dr = dt.NewRow()

dr!title = "2nd Test Recipe"
dr!description = "All about fish"

dt.Rows.Add(dr)
```

Playing around

Perhaps you feel like playing around with this example a little (try adding a second table, if you wish) and working with the `Debug.WriteLine` command to find out how to generate mass quantities of debugging information. You can always see the results in the Immediate window.

After you understand the basics of the DataSet, you're ready to explore some additional ways to manage DataSets in your programs. In the following sections, you can find more details.

Understanding Collections

Note that many objects contain collections. *Collections* are similar to arrays. A DataSet contains a `Tables` collection, and, in turn, each table has a `Columns` collection, which tells you how that table is subdivided (its structure, the names of its fields), and a `Rows` collection, which contains the actual items of data in the collection.

You can usually query or edit individual elements in a collection in two ways. You can refer to each element by its index number (starting with zero) or by its name. For example:

```
dt = ds.Tables!Recipes 'by name
dt = ds.Tables("Recipes") 'same, but an alternative punctuation
dt = ds.Tables(0) 'same, but here we use the table's index number
                  'rather than its name.
```

Whichever of these options you use, when this code executes, the global dt variable points to the particular DataSet.

For an introduction to indexed tables, see Chapter 11.

Opening an Existing DataSet

What if you want to allow the user to save and open a DataSet using his hard drive for storage? In the first example in this chapter, you created a DataSet and saved it to two files on the hard drive, using this code:

```
'save the structure (schema) of this DataSet
ds.WriteXmlSchema("c:\Recipesdataset.xml")

'save the actual data that's currently in this DataSet
ds.WriteXml("c:\RecipesData.xml")
```

Let's flesh out the previous example to illustrate additional DataSet manipulation techniques:

1. **Use the Toolbox to add two TextBoxes to your form, one above the other, and also add a Button. Enter `Open DataSet` as the button's `Text` property.**

2. **Change the `Name` property of the lower TextBox to `txtDescription` and the `Name` property of the upper TextBox to `txtTitle`.**

3. **Double-click the button to get to the Code window and then edit the following lines in boldface, just below the `Public Class`:**

```
Public Class Form1

Dim ds As New DataSet(), dr As DataRow, dt As DataTable
    'holds a deleted record

Dim titlehold As String, descriptionhold As String

Dim schemafilepath As String = "C:\recipesdataset.xml"
Dim datafilepath As String = "C:\recipesdata.xml"
```

4. **Locate the Button1_Click event in the code window and type in this code that opens existing DataSet files:**

```
Private Sub Button1_Click(ByVal sender As System.Object, ByVal e As
            System.EventArgs) Handles Button1.Click

Try

    'get the structure file
    ds.ReadXmlSchema(schemafilepath)
```

```
        'get the data file
        ds.ReadXml(datafilepath)

Catch er As Exception 'if there was a problem opening this file

    Throw (er)

Finally
    dt = ds.Tables!Recipes ' set dt to point to this table

End Try

TotalRows = dt.Rows.Count
CurrentRow = 0

txtTitle.Text = dt.Rows(CurrentRow).Item(0)
txtDescription.Text = dt.Rows(CurrentRow).Item(1)

End Sub
```

5. **Press F5 to test the project and then click the Button to activate the code in its event.**

The recipe should appear in the TextBoxes. You pointed the DataTable variable (`dt`) to your newly opened DataSet with this line of code:

```
dt = ds.Tables!Recipes ' set dt to point to this table
```

Then you put the total number of records into the global variable `TotalRows`, set the `CurrentRow` pointer to 0 (the first record),

```
TotalRows = dt.Rows.Count
CurrentRow = 0
```

and displayed the current record in your two TextBoxes:

```
txtTitle.Text = dt.Rows(CurrentRow).Item(0)
txtDescription.Text = dt.Rows(CurrentRow).Item(1)
```

Adding and Removing Data

You've finished code that opens a DataSet, so now you can experiment with adding and removing records from a DataSet.

Adding data to a DataSet

To make it possible for the user to add records to your DataSet, follow these steps:

1. **Use the Toolbox to put a new Button on the form.**

2. **Change the Button's Name property to btnAdd and its Text property to Add Record.**

3. **Double-click this new Button to get to its Click event and change it to look like the following:**

```
Private Sub btnAdd_Click(ByVal sender As System.Object, ByVal e As
         System.EventArgs) Handles btnAdd.Click

'if they have no active DataSet, refuse to allow a new record:
If ds.Tables.Count = 0 Then

    MsgBox("Please Open a DataSet, or create one using the New " & _
        "option in the File menu before attempting to add a " & _
        "new record.")
    Exit Sub
End If

'if they have an incomplete record, refuse:
If txtTitle Is "" Or txtDescription Is "" Then MsgBox("One of your " & _
        "TextBoxes has no data. You must enter something for the " & _
        "title and something for the description.") : Exit Sub

' stick the new data into the first row's two columns
dr = dt.NewRow()
dr!title = txtTitle.Text
dr!description = txtDescription.Text
dt.Rows.Add(dr)

Me.Text = "Record Added..."

End Sub
```

4. **Press F5 and then click the Open DataSet button. Change both the Title and Description TextBoxes and then click the Add Record button.**

The first line in this code tests whether the user has a currently active DataSet. If not, you post a message and exit this subroutine without executing any additional code. Users who haven't yet created or opened a DataSet shouldn't be trying to add a record to this non-existent data. Also, you don't want an incomplete record.

However, if the user does have a new record (text in the TextBoxes) that he wants to save to the DataSet (*committing it*, as the saying goes), you let him.

You use the `NewRow` method to notify your DataSet that a new row of data is coming. Then you fill the new row's two columns (`title` and `description`) with the data in the TextBoxes. Then the `Add` method commits the data to the DataSet. Finally, you increment your total records counter and your current row pointer.

Because users don't like to click a button and see *nothing* happen — it worries them — you might want to place a reassuring message in the form's title bar, telling them that the record has been added.

Removing data from a DataSet

Users must be able to delete records from your DataSet. Here's code that can be used to remove the "current" record:

```
dt.Rows.Remove(dt.Rows(CurrentRow))
```

If you look in VB Express's Help, you might think that there are two methods for deleting a row in a DataSet: `Delete` and `Remove`. However, the `Delete` method doesn't actually get rid of a row; it simply marks the row for later deletion when (or if) the programmer uses the `AcceptChanges` method. (Technically, the database management system itself, not your program, does the actual deleting.) Marking a row in this fashion is useful for such jobs as permitting an Undo option, thus restoring the row. In this example, however, you use the `Remove` method, which gets rid of the row completely right then and there.

Moving through the DataSet

Users often want to scroll up or down through a set of data. It's up to you, the programmer, to organize and navigate the data "rows" inside the DataSet (or you can bind your data to a DataNavigator control, as described in Chapter 12).

To allow the user to maneuver, you created `TotalRows` and `CurrentRow` global variables. These variables keep track of where the user is located in the set of rows. (Technically, `TotalRows` isn't necessary; the DataSet knows that information and you can ask for it at any time with `ds.Tables(0).Rows.Count`.)

Code that moves *down* the rows in a DataSet looks like this:

```
CurrentRow = CurrentRow - 1

txtTitle.Text = dt.Rows(CurrentRow).Item(0)
txtDescription.Text = dt.Rows(CurrentRow).Item(1)
```

Or, to go *up*:

```
CurrentRow = CurrentRow + 1

txtTitle.Text = dt.Rows(CurrentRow).Item(0)
txtDescription.Text = dt.Rows(CurrentRow).Item(1)
```

Look for a variety of additional DataSet members (properties and methods you can employ) in VB Express Help. Use the Index to search for "DataSet class."

Part IV

Programming for the Web

The 5th Wave   By Rich Tennant

"Look into my Web site, Ms. Carruthers.
Look deep into its rotating, nicely
animated spiral, spinning, spinning, pulling
you in, deeper... deeper..."

In this part . . .

You cannot ignore the Web for long if you're involved in selling something, even if it's just selling your talents. Internet programming — building and maintaining a Web site — has become a major aspect of programming. Part IV shows you how to use the new Visual Web Developer, along with VB Express, to move Web pages up onto the Internet for all the world to see. You explore the powerful ASP.NET technology that allows you to write "code behind" the visuals of a Web page, building intelligence into your Web site programs, making them compelling and responsive to visitors. You also experiment with other important Internet programming techniques, such as how to store variables, connect a Web page to a database, deal with cookies, and communicate back and forth between your site's server and the computers used by visitors to your site.

Chapter 14

Painless Internet Programming

Creating an Internet site presents the programmer with some challenges not faced when writing a Windows program. First, there's the communication back and forth between two parts of the program: the *client* part that the user loads and sees in the browser, and the *server* part that sits on your Web site machine. What happens when the user clicks a button on your Web page asking to see more of your catalog? A message is sent back to your server, and it must respond. This separation of client and server creates communication and security problems that you just don't have with ordinary Windows programming, where the communication is pretty much limited to messages between your keyboard, mouse, and hard drive.

Second, a Windows program generally involves just one user interacting with it. But if you're lucky and your Web site becomes popular, why, bless me, you could have dozens or even thousands of simultaneous users interacting with your quivering little server! The ability to adapt effectively from managing a few users to ramping up and handling many users is known as *scalability* — being able to shift the scale or size of your program's behaviors.

So, because Internet programming differs in a few profound ways from Windows programming, VB Express offers a separate, specialized tool for Internet programming: Visual Web Developer 2005 Express (VWD).

If you haven't yet downloaded it, go to Microsoft's Web site and install VWD on your computer:

```
http://lab.msdn.microsoft.com/express/vwd
```

Creating the Simplest Web Program

Just as the DVD Collection example program included with VB Express is *way* more complicated than it should be, so, too, is the Personal Web Site Starter Kit included with VWD. I can't imagine who at Microsoft thought those sophisticated, lengthy programs were good places for beginners to get their feet wet programming.

Setting up the program

Instead of the "sample," let's try the ASP.NET template. For this example, you want to put a TextBox on your Web page in which the user types the total dollar amount of his purchase. You also include a button that, when clicked, adds 7 percent sales tax to the user's order and displays the total cost back to the user. This would be pretty simple in a Windows program — but remember, the Internet is all about sending messages between computers, so what's simple in Windows becomes more complicated in Web site programming. To better understand the security issues, see the nearby sidebar, "Why viruses distort Internet programming." Now, on with the example:

1. **With VWD running, choose File⇨New⇨Web Site.**

2. **Double-click the ASP.NET Web Site icon in the New Web Site dialog box.**

   You now see a `Default.aspx` file. (I explain ASPX in greater detail shortly.) For now, you just want to create and test a simple Web page to see how the process of designing interactive Internet pages actually works.

3. **Click the Design tab at the bottom of the Code window.**

   You see a blank Web page with a Toolbox tab to the left and, on the right, the familiar Solution Explorer and Properties window. In fact, everything looks strangely like the normal VB Express Windows programming editor — but *just a little different*, as you can see in Figure 14-1. For example, notice the <div> button in the Properties window. This is an HTML element tag. You can always tell tags because they're enclosed in greater-than and less-than symbols (< . . . >). But don't bother your pretty head about HTML — a real mess of a language, believe me. Happily, you can stay up above HTML and just drag and drop objects from the Toolbox, and the Web Developer automatically writes all that nasty HTML code for you. It's like when Mae West turned to her maid and said, "Beulah, peel me a grape." You've got somebody else to do the tedious, messy HTML drudgery.

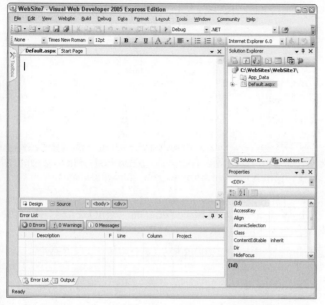

Figure 14-1:
The
Web pro-
gramming
editor is
very similar
to the
standard
Windows
program-
ming VB
Express
editor.

4. **Double-click the TextBox in the Toolbox to place a TextBox on your Web page.**

5. **Double-click a Button in the Toolbox as well.**

6. **Now, to get to the code area where you can write some programming, double-click the Button on the Web page.**

   A new file named `Default.aspx.vb` is created when you start a new Web project. This is called a *code-behind* file, and it's useful because it separates the programming (which remains on your server) from the HTML page on which you design the buttons, background, and other visual elements that get sent to your user's browser.

   Although you can also mix code into the HTML page by using a `<SCRIPT>` zone in the HTML (and programmers often do this), I think it's far cleaner and simpler to keep your programming code in an entirely different file from the HTML code. For one thing, the person talented at designing a Web page visually is often not the same person who is talented at pro-gramming. If people have their own separate files, they avoid stepping on each other's toes and, worse, messing up each other's code.

7. **In the button's Click event, type the programming code that adds sales tax:**

```
Sub Button1_Click(ByVal sender As Object, ByVal e As System.EventArgs)

    Dim result As Single
```

```
    result = CSng(TextBox1.Text) * 1.07
    TextBox1.Text = result.ToString

End Sub
```

This is pretty much the same process — and the same VB Express language commands— that you use when writing Windows programs.

Ignore any of those annoying warning messages about "implicit conversion" and so on. You know what you're doing, so you don't care that a numeric variable type is being substituted, or that VB Express is all atwitter that you might be losing some precision in your math. That's what the "implicit conversion" warning is all about.

You do need the decimal point so that cents show up, not just dollars. That's why you use the Single (floating point) data type rather than the usual Integer type (which has no decimal point).

Anyway, because you're going from a TextBox's text (which is a string variable) to a Single (CSng converts text to Single), .NET wants you to specifically make variable-type conversions. You can us the .ToString method to go the other way and change the Single *result* back into text for the TextBox. Nearly everything in .NET has a ToString method. Few outside Microsoft know why all this fuss is necessary, but those in charge of .NET seem to think it is.

The next step is to test this program to see how it works.

Testing your program

Now for the testing part. This is pretty cool, and those at Microsoft who designed it are to be praised — it works smoothly and effectively. Here's how it's done:

1. **Press F5 as usual to run your new program.**

   After some behind-the-scenes grinding and fussing, your Web page — complete with TextBox and button — appears in your default browser.

2. **If you see the warning message displayed in Figure 14-2, click OK to add a Web.config file and debugging (as the Visual Web Developer should automatically do for you).**

   If you don't see the message, fine. It's not necessary and, for beginners, it's just one more source of confusion. Perhaps by the time VWD is finished, the message won't appear, and the sensible default (debugging) will simply take effect without asking your permission. Then when your program is finally tested and finished and ready to be sent off into the world for everyone to enjoy — you disable the debugging feature to achieve maximum program execution speed.

Why viruses distort Internet programming

A user visiting your Web site might live in Des Moines (of all places) and might be up late at night wearing nothing more than a fetching nightgown. With lace trim, perhaps. But I stray. My point is this: Web site programming is not limited to a single computer or a single hard drive. Your program (code "behind" on the server) is *interacting* with the user's Web browser, using the Web form you designed in design view.

In our example program, a click on the Button in the user's browser in Des Moines causes the contents of the user's TextBox to be *sent back* over the Internet to your server, where the tax is calculated. Then the result of that calculation is *sent back* to the user.

Why not just calculate the tax on the user's end, with some programming built into the Web page that was sent from your site to the user's browser? The answer, my friend, is blowing in the wind: It's those brainless virus spreaders who make all this complexity necessary. (Lots of them don't *write* the virus code; they're too dumb — they just get it off the Internet and spread the virus around to cause trouble).

Executable code is, in theory, not supposed to be embedded within your Web form and is not supposed to be downloaded — because there's no effective way for the user's browser to distinguish between your harmless little tax calculation code and a virus. So, like many of modern life's annoyances, *security* is the reason you can't send executable code to a user's browser. However, that's just theory because Web sites do in practice frequently rely on scripting for such jobs as client-side validation (checking to make sure they entered all the necessary information in a form, for instance).

In the example Web site you've created in this chapter, no scripting *is* sent. Because the active tax calculation takes place on your server, the user is not endangered. What gets sent back to the user is merely the text result of the calculation: the total cost expressed by visual symbols — some digits. No *programming code* gets sent, just HTML for TextBox, button, the digits inside the TextBox, and any other *visual* elements, such as color, that you've specified as part of your page design. *Programming code* doesn't get sent. Many users' browsers — and other security measures — are set to reject scripting or other kinds of executable code. This is an ideal approach because new visitors to your site don't have to agree to "trust" this site before their browsers' security features will permit your Web pages to be loaded and displayed.

However, to be technically accurate, small client-side scripts are often necessary, if only to store a cookie or perform some other minor job. Either the users trust your Web site or they don't. If they do, they can add you to their trusted-site lists and allow your scripts to run. Many users turn scripting off for everyone except these trusted sites. Indeed, the code that Visual Web Developer generates automatically and sends to the client sometimes contains client-side scripts. True, you the programmer, don't add those scripts, but an ASPX page sometimes generates them automatically. So in practice, most Web pages you create using VWD will probably contain at least some scripting. My advice is to stick to writing code-behind programming, and at least in the first page of your Web site avoid scripting if at all possible. And if you find your customers or your site's visitors refusing to interact with your site, find out which controls or other elements of your VWD page are creating security issues in users' browser and consider eliminating those controls or programming.

Figure 14-2:
This
message
may or may
not appear
the first time
you try to
test a
Web page.

3. **Interact with your Web program just like the user would.**

That's how you test your Web pages. Your local computer mimics the communication between a user's browser and your Web site's server machine.

Type `123` into the TextBox as the purchase price, click the button. The result is calculated on the virtual "server" and "sent" back to the browser — in imitation of a real-life Internet communication between that lovely user in Des Moines and your server computer. The resulting total cost including tax is shown in Figure 14-3.

Congrats! You've just written your first Web page programming in the new VWD Express editor.

Figure 14-3:
The tax
calculation
has been
successfully
sent back to
the user's
browser.

Positioning objects with the Style Builder

Web pages by default simply stack objects one on top of another against the left side of the form. Notice in the preceding example that you cannot just drag the button or TextBox wherever you want to position them on the form (Web page). One way to freely position objects is to use the "absolute" positioning feature of CSS (cascading style sheets). Fortunately, you don't have to get into CSS yourself because the Visual Web Developer has a built-in Style Builder utility that creates CSS code for you. To try it out, follow these steps:

1. **Right-click the button on the Web form (from the previous example).**

   A context menu pops out.

2. **Choose Style from the context menu.**

   The Style Builder dialog box opens.

3. **Click the Position option in the left pane of the dialog box.**

   The position features are displayed.

4. **Click the down-arrow icon to drop the list of *position mode* options and select Absolutely Position.**

   Now your button can be dragged wherever you wish on the Web form.

5. **Click OK.**

   The dialog box closes.

6. **Drag the button and drop it anywhere on the form.**

   It stays wherever you position it.

If you look at the HTML source code — by clicking the Source tab on the bottom of the design window — you see that the following CSS code has been added to this button:

```
Style="left: 352px; position: absolute; top: 200px
```

The 352 and 200 coordinates will differ in your example. They specify precisely where (left, top) on the form your button has been dragged, and 352, 200 are the coordinates specifying where *I* dragged *my* button.

Even more useful would be the ability to specify globally that the entire Web form — all controls on it — should be permitted absolute positioning. In other words, in previous versions of the Web form editor, each form had a PageLayout property you could set to what was called GridLayout. This had the effect of applying the absolute positioning style to all controls — current or added later — to that form. It was a handy feature, and perhaps it will be reinstated in the Visual Web Developer. But *not yet . . .* and maybe never. Microsoft has shown an increasing tendency over the past few years to remove useful features from VB, add useless complexity, and otherwise behave in ways that puzzle me to no end.

Coming to Grips with ASP.NET

ASP.NET is the technology built into the .NET framework that you use to create Web pages. How about an overview of the ASP.NET features that you may find useful as you expand your programming skills beyond the Windows (local hard drive) platform and move into the brave new world of Internet programming? Well . . . how about it?

ASP.NET involves two interacting elements: Visible Web-page forms or <div> sections (similar to Windows forms) display user-interface controls in a browser; the second technology, called *code behind,* which lives in a separate file, contains the Visual Basic to handle any necessary programming.

Programming Web sites to interact with users was extremely complex before ASP.NET came along. Back then, it was a nasty, brutish business at best, using clumsy tools and messy, buggy technologies. Thank your lucky stars for ASP.NET.

ASP.NET is a rather complex topic, and I can cover it only briefly in this book. If you're interested in finding out more about it, take a look at my book *Visual Basic .NET All-in-One Desk Reference For Dummies* (Wiley).

The purpose of ASP

The main idea of Active Server Pages (ASP) is that, instead of seeing a simple Web page, people surfing the Internet who arrive at a page on your Web site want to see *dynamic,* interactive content. A dynamic site is attractive, up-to-date, varying, and thus potentially more interesting to the visitor.

HTML's limitations

Web pages are programmed in Hypertext Markup Language (HTML), which all Web browsers understand and respond to. Pure HTML merely describes how text and graphics should *look* — size, location, color, and so on. You can do no actual *computing* with HTML. It can't even add 2 + 2.

HTML merely specifies, say, that a headline is large, that some body text on the Web page is blue and is not as large as the headline, that one graphic is lower on the page than another graphic, and so on. HTML also includes a few, simple objects such as tables and list boxes. However, even the tables and list boxes are static, essentially lifeless display objects.

To expand the capabilities of HTML, the idea of an *active server* was developed. All programming, all *computation,* takes place on the server. When the server's programming finishes its job, the results of that computation are composed into a page of HTML (just as the sales tax result in the previous example was put into the HTML TextBox). The HTML page is then sent to the visitor's computer for viewing in a browser. This capability brings Web pages alive and gives them the ability to execute programs without sending executable code to the *client* — the user's browser — where it would be rejected as a potential virus.

With ASP technology, therefore, you can do lots of useful things on your server that you could never do with HTML alone. You can access a database, insert prewritten components, and revise your Web pages (include news about your company, today's date, and so on) so that visitors don't get bored seeing the same content each time they visit. The visitor sees the most recent product announcements, late-breaking information, and anything else you want to provide. Perhaps more important, your Web pages are interactive and can respond to requests for information or other actions by the user.

Firewalls and other necessary evils

Recall that ASP sends standard, harmless HTML to the user's browser. Firewalls — designed to keep hackers, whackers, crackers, viruses, worms, and other invaders out of your computer — permit HTML to pass unchallenged. Innocent, merely descriptive visual HTML can do no damage to your computer, any more than a picture of a gun can fire bullets.

You *can* insert some scripting code into an HTML page and, therefore, let the visitor's computer do some limited computing. This is called *client-side* scripting. It works fine if you're sure that all your visitors have the necessary language components installed on their machines, that their security settings permit scripting (many people block scripts), and that they're all using the same browser (and that the browser supports scripting). So, if you're running a site that is intended merely for use in-house on an intranet, and everybody in your company uses Internet Explorer, and you're sure they all have the right components on their hard drives, go ahead and try some client-side computing. Intranets often permit scripting. However, for Internet pages, there are many reasons to prefer ASP's solution: server-side computing that sends harmless HTML results to clients. But see the sidebar earlier in this chapter titled "Why viruses distort Internet programming" for additional details about why scripting is, alas, sometimes a necessary evil.

Getting to Know WebControls

When you use Web forms in the Visual Web Developer, you also have a full set of controls in the Toolbox that you can put onto those forms. This is a very quick way to build a cool-looking Web site. I assume that you're familiar with the classic Windows controls — such as the TextBox. Here, I explain special behaviors of various useful controls for Web page programming.

Displaying images

Use the Image control to show graphics (.GIF, .JPG, .JPEG, .BMP, .WMF, and .PNG files; .PNG is Adobe's effort to replace .GIF). You can assign the graphics file during either design time or run time by providing a URL to the ImageURL property or by binding the Image control's ImageURL property to a database containing graphics. Put a copy of the graphics you use into the folder where your project is located. You'll find your projects at C:\WebSites\.

The Image control is unusual among WebControls in that it has no events. You can't respond if the user clicks the image, for example. If you want to display a map of Europe and let the user click one of the countries in the map to, say, ask for a list of olive oil brands from that country, you can use the ImageMap control. It not only has a Click event, but it also includes a HotSpots property, which you use to specify how to respond to clicks on various locations within the image.

Containing with the Panel container

The Panel WebControl is a container for other controls. The Panel's borders create a zone — a subdivision of the Web page — within which you can define a look (change the Panel's BackColor, for example), add controls dynamically, or manipulate a group of controls simultaneously (such as a set of RadioButtons that work together; for example, when the user clicks one button, the previously clicked button is unselected automatically).

For example, you can set the Panel's Visible property to False, and *all* controls contained within the Panel also become invisible. You can also type text into a Panel.

The Panel must be selected for you to add other controls to it by double-clicking them in the Toolbox. Add a Panel control from the Toolbox and then click the Panel to select it in the design window. Now, in the Toolbox, double-click other controls that you want to place within the Panel.

You can also add controls to a Panel by dragging the controls on the form in Design view onto the Panel.

The Table control

You can build a typical HTML table with the WebForm Table control by following these instructions:

1. **Add a Table control to the design window and then click the Rows collection in the Properties window.**

   The TableRow Collection Editor appears. Use the TableRow Collection Editor to add new rows, as shown in Figure 14-4.

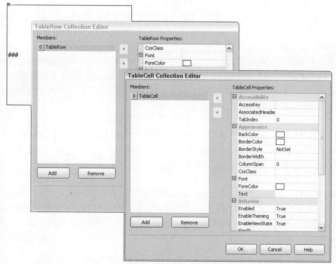

Figure 14-4: Use these dialog boxes to manually add rows and columns to your table control.

2. **Click the Cells collection ellipsis button inside the TableRow Collection Editor dialog box to bring up the TableCell Collection Editor.**

3. **In the TableCell Collection editor, you can**
   - Add columns by clicking the Add button.
   - Type in data.
   - Otherwise manipulate the columns (fields).

The rich Calendar

Taking HTML to its limits, the clever Calendar control provides a valuable addition to your bag of Web-programming tricks.

The Calendar control is based on a nice set of date/time functions built into VB. It has many members, such as GetDayOfYear, GetDaysInMonth, GetDaysInYear, GetEra, and so on.

The Calendar control permits users to view and navigate between dates, as well as to send (postback) their choice of day or days back to your server for processing. This would be an improvement over some hotel reservation Web pages, which require that you search through four ListBoxes (arrival day and month, departure day and month). With the calendar control, visitors could simply select the days they will be staying.

The calendar is rendered as an HTML table, of course, but plenty of script is in there as well. You can't see much of the actual HTML source code by clicking the Source tab in the Design window. Instead, press F5 and then use the browser's View↝Source option. You might be startled at the massive redundancy so typical of HTML. A <TD> element is included for each day in the entire calendar, including JavaScript postback events that trigger when the user clicks any of the days.

If you're programming for a company's personal intranet, you could also use the Calendar control to display scheduled meetings, appointments, tasks, or other information related to scheduling.

Users can move between months by clicking the arrows at the top corners of the Calendar, or you can provide them with additional navigation methods (such as a TextBox in which they type a date, Buttons, ListBoxes, and so on). Then you can change the month displayed programmatically, like this:

```
Sub Calendar1_SelectionChanged(ByVal sender As Object, ByVal e As
            System.EventArgs)

    Calendar1.VisibleDate = CDate("12/16/2005")

End Sub
```

Press F5, click any date within the calendar, and December 2005 is displayed, thanks to this programming. This example illustrates merely how to use code to manipulate the calendar and change the displayed month programmatically. You most likely don't want to display December 2005 regardless of which date the user clicks.

The AdRotator

The AdRotator WebControl displays an advertisement on your WebForm. It requires an XML file whose URL you specify in the AdRotator's `AdvertisementFile` property.

AdRotator has some restrictions: The XML file must be stored with "the application's domain," as they say. In plain English, just save it to the hard drive in your application's folder (the same folder with the `.aspx`, `.vsdisco`, and other support files for your project). Also, save the advertisement graphic file in that same folder.

Follow these steps to use the AdRotator:

1. **Right-click your project's name (it's the one in boldface) in the Solution Explorer.**

   A context menu opens.

2. **Choose Add New Item from the context menu.**

   The Add New Item dialog box opens.

3. **Double-click the XML File icon in the Add New Item dialog box.**

   The dialog box closes, and the new XML file is now part of your project. It's ready for you to type in the necessary XML code.

4. **Type in (or better yet, copy and paste from this book's Web site) the following XML code:**

   ```
   <Advertisements>
      <Ad>
         <ImageUrl>button.gif</ImageUrl>
         <NavigateUrl>http://dell.</NavigateUrl>
         <AlternateText>Cannot display</AlternateText>
         <Keyword>Take 1</Keyword>
         <Impressions>100</Impressions>
      </Ad>
   </Advertisements>
   ```

   Substitute the name of your graphics file for button.gif. Also, instead of dell., use the name of your computer. (XP users can find the name of their computers by choosing Start⇨Control Panel⇨Performance and Maintenance⇨See Basic Information about Your Computer⇨Computer Name.) Note that the NavigateUrl property points to the URL of the page to be displayed if the user clicks your AdRotator.

   This little project requires care: make a single mistake in your XML file and it may not work. Also ensure that the graphics file has the same name in the folder as in the XML code, and that your computer name is correct, and that the graphics file is stored in your project's folder.

5. **Put an AdRotator control on your WebForm and select it.**

6. **In the Properties window, change the AdvertisementFile property to MyAd.XML.**

7. **Press F5 and you see your ad displayed . . . unless the browser is set to block such ads.**

Your XML file must be well formed. So, if you're in the habit of writing *badly formed* XML, get with the program! The XML file must conform to this format:

```
<Advertisements>
<Ad>
    <ImageUrl>Filename of the graphic to display</ImageUrl>
    <NavigateUrl>URL of the path to the page the used sees if the user clicks
                your ad</NavigateUrl>
    <AlternateText>Text to display if image can't be displayed </AlternateText>
    <Keyword>Keyword to filter ads</Keyword>
    <Impressions>relative weight of ad<Impressions>
</Ad>
</Advertisements>
```

However, of all these properties, only the `ImageURL` is absolutely required. The `AlternativeText` property is displayed as a ToolTip in Internet Explorer if the graphic is not successfully displayed. You can also use the `Impressions` property to define how often the ad is displayed. You can fill the XML file with as many <Ad> sections as you want. Give them relative weight by setting the <Impressions> property. If one of the <Ad> sections has `1000` as its weight, and the only other <Ad> section has a weight of `100`, the second <Ad> is displayed one tenth as often as the first ad.

Using style objects with WebControls

As you saw in the preceding section, you can either define the properties of an AdRotator in an event named `AdCreated` when the control first comes into existence, or you can reference a separate XML file to define those properties. This is how ASP.NET segregates the work of designers who manipulate the appearance of a Web page (HTML) from the work of a programmer who manipulates the behavior of that page (using VB). They can both work on different files. Similarly, cascading style sheets (`.css` files) and other techniques permit two files to define one object.

Adding abstraction

You can employ a level of abstraction with WebControls. Some ASP.NET WebControls let you use *style objects* to specify properties. The DataList WebControl, for example, has a `BorderStyle` property, and `SelectedDayStyle` is part of the Calendar control. The Button control has a `ControlStyle` property that works in much the same way.

You can, of course, use the Property window to specify styles, or do it programmatically in an event (or by modifying the HTML). A third way is to use a style object.

To see how this works, put a Button control on your WebForm and then double-click that Button to get to the code-behind code window (the

VB Code window). You see the empty Button1_Click event. Type this into the event:

```
Sub Button1_Click(ByVal sender As Object, ByVal e As System.EventArgs)

    Dim stl As New Style()

    stl.BackColor = System.Drawing.Color.Blue
    stl.BorderColor = System.Drawing.Color.Red

    Button1.ControlStyle.CopyFrom(stl)

End Sub
```

When you employ the CopyFrom method, as illustrated in the preceding code, *all* the style object's settings are applied to the Button (or whatever WebControl is being used). This includes nulls (empty values). Try a different tactic using the MergeWith method. Replace the CopyFrom method in the previous code with this:

```
Button1.ControlStyle.MergeWith(stl)
```

MergeWith sets only the properties already defined in the style object and does not change any properties undefined in the style object.

Inheritance and precedence in style objects

In some sophisticated WebControls, style objects can inherit properties from other style objects. The Calendar WebControl, for example, bases its SelectedDayStyle property on its DayStyle object. If you don't specify properties for SelectedDayStyle, it inherits its properties from the DayStyle object. Put another way, if you do specify one of these properties, your choice wins (has precedence).

WebControls offer two properties that let you manipulate CSS styles: CSSStyle and CSSClass. If you set the CSSStyle property, you can set a string of style attributes to be applied to the control. The CSSStyle property specifies style attributes that are not exposed through other properties; it allows you to assign a style-sheet class to the control.

Attaching a Database to Your Web Page

Displaying data from a database is pretty easy in Visual Web Developer. To see how to do it, follow these steps:

1. Choose File⇨New Web Site.

You see the New Web Site dialog box.

2. **Double-click the ASP.NET Web Site icon.**

   A new, blank site template opens.

3. **Locate your copy of the sample database `Nwind.mdb` (or `Northwind.mdb`) on your hard drive (see Chapter 12 for information on downloading or locating it).**

4. **Copy `Nwind.mdb` to the folder where your new ASP.NET project is located (in boldface in Solution Explorer).**

   It will be something like `C:\WebSites\WebSite5\`.

5. **Click the Design tab at the bottom of the design/code window in VWD.**

   The design window opens.

6. **Double-click the GridView icon in the Toolbox. You may have to click the Data header (in boldface) in the Toolbox to reveal the data-related controls such as the GridView.**

   A GridView is placed on your Web page, and a Common GridView Tasks dialog box (from a "smart tag") appears, as shown in Figure 14-5.

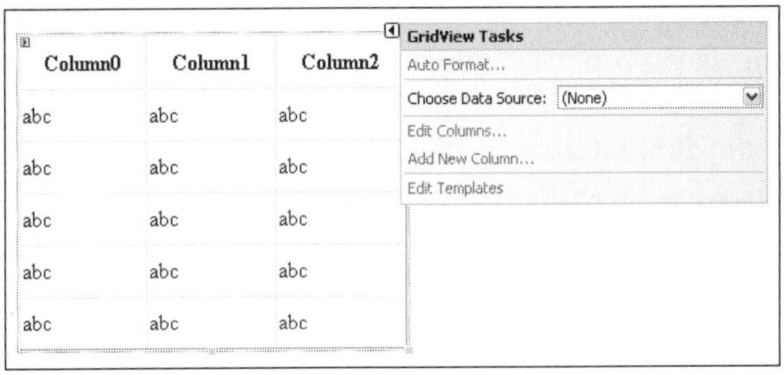

Figure 14-5:
Here's
where you
can define a
source of
data for
your Web
page.

7. **Click the down arrow next to Choose Data Source.**

   A list drops.

8. **Click New Data Source.**

   The Data Source Configuration dialog box opens.

9. **Click Access Database.**

10. **Click OK.**

    A new dialog box opens in which you can specify the location of the database.

11. **Click the Browse button to locate your** `Nwind.mdb` **or** `Northwind.mdb` **sample database in the project's folder or type the path, which is something similar to** `c:\WebSites\WebSite5\Nwind.mdb`, **into the dialog box.**

12. **Double-click** `Nwind.mdb`.

13. **Click Next.**

    You see the dialog box where you can specify the table and fields (columns) that you want to display on your Web page, as shown in Figure 14-6.

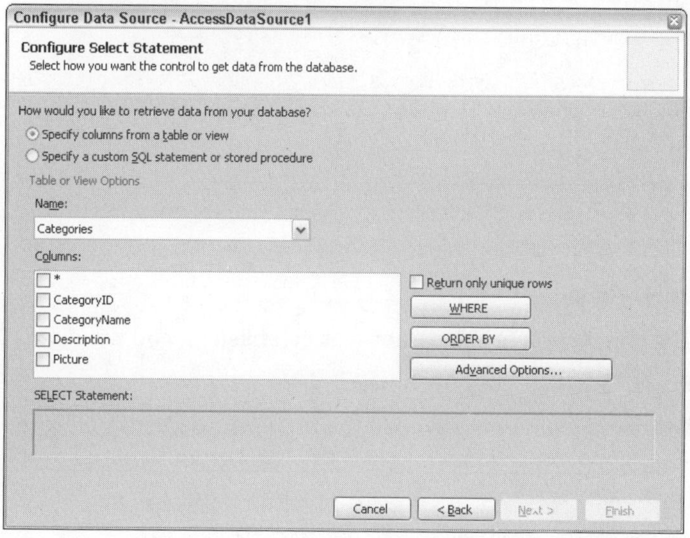

Figure 14-6:
Specify a
table and a
subset of
data (an
SQL query)
from that
table
using this
dialog box.

14. **Click the down arrow next to the Name (table) list.**

    The list of tables in the sample database is displayed.

15. **Click Employees.**

    The list of fields (columns) in the Employees table is shown.

16. **Select LastName, FirstName, and BirthDate.**

17. **Click Next.**

    You can now test your SQL query results.

18. **Click the Test Query button.**

    You see the data fill the columns, as shown in Figure 14-7.

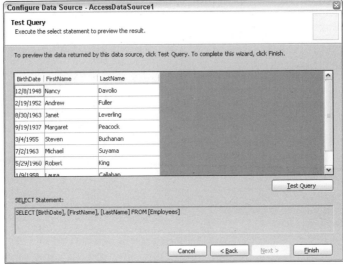

Figure 14-7:
Test your
SQL query
here to see
whether the
data con-
nection
works and
whether
you're
getting
back the
information
you want
displayed on
the Web
page.

19. Click Finish.

The connection to the database is established, and the dialog box closes.

20. Press F5 to test your Web page.

You see the data displayed in the browser, as shown in Figure 14-8.

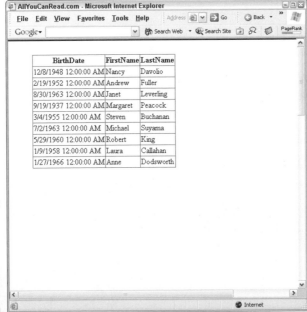

Figure 14-8:
Success!
You've
connected a
database to
a Web page.

Chapter 15

Everything's Eventual: Web Page Management

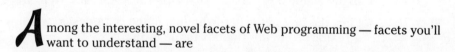

mong the interesting, novel facets of Web programming — facets you'll want to understand — are

✔ **How to manage splitting your application's code between server and client** (all the actual *programming* is done on your server; then you just send the results to the user's browser).

✔ **How to preserve the state of your variables.** By *preserving the state of variables,* I mean ensuring that data survives Internet interactions. This is called persistence and it's the topic of the following section.

✔ **Why you might want to avoid using cookies.**

This chapter explores these and other issues unique to Web page programming. Be prepared, that's my motto.

Before you can explore the concepts in this chapter, you need a special program designed to help you create Web sites. So, if you haven't already downloaded the Visual Web Developer 2005 Express (VWD) program, go to Microsoft's Web site and install VWD on your computer:

```
http://lab.msdn.microsoft.com/express/vwd
```

Understanding Server-Side Controls in ASP.NET

One of the great features of the VWD is how easy it can be to create a Web page that interacts effectively with the user. Not only do you get to use many controls — like the TextBox — that are familiar to you from traditional Windows programming, you also get to work with design and code windows that are familiar as well.

Enough theory, it's time to plunge in and get a feel for ASP.NET Web page development. In the following example, you built a pretty sophisticated interactive Web page — mostly using tools you've already mastered if you've already done much of the classic Windows programming I discuss earlier in this book:

1. **Start Visual Web Developer Express.**

2. **Choose File⇨New⇨Web Site.**

3. **In the dialog box that opens, double-click ASP.NET Web Site.**

4. **Click the Design tab at the bottom of the code/design window and add a TextBox from the Toolbox to the form.**

5. **Click the Source tab at the bottom of the design window.**

With the Source tab open, notice that when you added the TextBox, VB enclosed it within an HTML form:

```
<form id="form1" runat="server">
    <div>
        <asp:TextBox ID="TextBox1"
            runat="server"></asp:TextBox>

    </div>
    </form>
```

Note that `runat="server"` attribute. ASP.NET sees this command and automatically forces the value of server-side controls to be POSTed (sent) back to the server if the user makes a change or enters some information into the TextBox. Each control within the HTML form includes the `runat="server"` command.

Having server-side controls is a great feature. It preserves the state of the controls (their values and properties) and lets the server know the values that the user entered. ASP.NET handles this communication between the client (browser) and your server automatically.

The problem of persistence

When users fill in a textbox or perhaps a more complicated form on your Web site, they don't like it at all if they come back to that form later and have to fill it in a second time! They expect stability and efficiency. They expect data to be *durable*, not to evaporate in their browser window just because they click a button or press F5 to redraw the browser screen. This durability is a quality known to programmers as *persistence*. Data or variables that survive various changes are said to *persist*.

How does ASP.NET manage to preserve *state* (the current status of something, such as its size) and any values it holds (such as text in a TextBox)? ASP.NET makes some changes to your source code when you use server-side controls.

Fleshing out your ASP.NET project

To see a bit more behind the scenes in an ASP.NET Web page, follow these steps to create an interactive Web page.

1. **In Visual Web Developer, use the Toolbox to add a Label, two TextBoxes (just add one if you're using the project you started earlier in this chapter that already has a TextBox on it), and a Button to your form.**

2. **Double-click the Button.**

   You see the Code window. This is the *code-behind* file, so called because it works behind the scenes to provide computing power to an associated HTML page. This is *not* the same as the simple HTML code you see if you click the Source button on the bottom of the design window. The code-behind file contains whatever Visual Basic language programming your project needs. You add some VB programming in the next step.

You are simply going to provide some source code in the button's Click event that adds together the numbers that the user enters into the two TextBoxes. Just for fun, you also display the current time. Repeatedly clicking the button updates the time, illustrating the ASP.NET cycle: The user's browser sends a Click message to the server, the page is dynamically refreshed (a whole HTML page is rebuilt) at your server, and then the page is sent back to the browser where it's repainted for the user to see the results.

3. **Type this into the Button_Click event:**

```
Sub Button1_Click(ByVal sender As Object, ByVal e As System.EventArgs)

Dim firstnum, secondnum, totalnum As Integer

    firstnum = CInt(TextBox1.Text)
    secondnum = CInt(TextBox2.Text)

    totalnum = firstnum + secondnum

    Label1.Text = "The sum is: " & totalnum & "<br/>" & _
    "The current time is: " & Format(Now, "h:mm")

End Sub
```

4. **Press F5.**

It takes a little while for the communication to be set up between the "server" and your browser, but pretty soon Internet Explorer appears with the page loaded into it. (You may see a message box warning you that debugging isn't enabled. Click OK to enable it and the message box closes.)

The VWD makes use of a special built-in Web "server" that behaves like a real server — communicating between your VWD project and Internet Explorer. Thanks to the jerks who like to bother the rest of us with their viruses, special security measures have to be taken all the time. In this situation, the built-in Web server uses a non-standard "port address." Instead of port 80, it uses a random port associated with each particular VWD project. Also, Microsoft has made this special "server" inaccessible from the Internet, so it helps prevent one of the virus kiddies from gaining access to your computer.

5. **Type 12 in the first TextBox and 23 in the second TextBox; then click the Button.**

You see the response from the server, as shown in Figure 15-1.

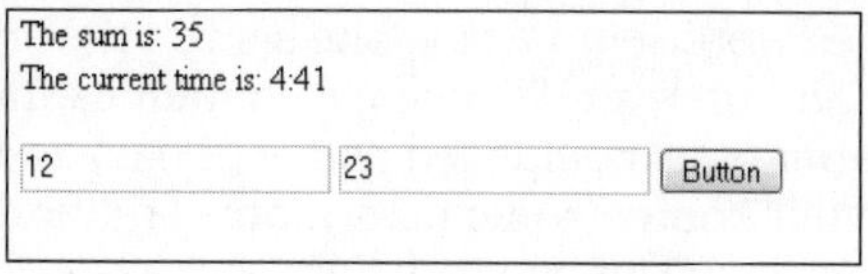

Figure 15-1:
Communica-
tion between
the server
and client
browser.

```
The sum is: 35
The current time is: 4:41

12                    23                    Button
```

Viewing the code

After you Press F5 to run the program in Internet Explorer, take a look at the
changes to your original source code by choosing View⇨Source in IE. Here's
what you'll see:

```
<!DOCTYPE html PUBLIC "-//W3C//DTD XHTML 1.1//EN"
          "http://www.w3.org/TR/xhtml11/DTD/xhtml11.dtd">

<html xmlns="http://www.w3.org/1999/xhtml" >
<head><title>
    Untitled Page
</title></head>
<body>
    <form name="form1" method="post" action="Default.aspx" id="form1">
<div>

<input type="hidden" name="__VIEWSTATE" value=
          "/wEPDwULLTEwNjExNzk5MjgPZBYCAgMPZBYCAgEPDxYCHgRUZXh0BSxUaGUgc3VtIG
          lzOiAzNTxici8+VGhlIGN1cnJlbnQgdGltZSBpczogNDo0MWRkZBxTN/DOPXF4lA8+K
          Xg2H3o+Ocym" />
</div>

    <div>
        <span id="Label1" style="height:19px;width:142px;">The sum is:
          35<br/>The current time is: 4:41</span>
        <br />
        <br />
        <input name="TextBox1" type="text" value="12" id="TextBox1" />
        <input name="TextBox2" type="text" value="23" id="TextBox2" />
        <input type="submit" name="Button1" value="Button" id="Button1" />

    </div>
    </form>
</body>
</html>
```

You see some surprises; ASP.NET has been a busy little bunny. This source code is the HTML, which ASP.NET composed in response to you (or the user) clicking the Button. The values were sent back to the server, the addition was accomplished on the server, and then an HTML page containing the results of the addition and the current time was composed and sent back to the user's browser. ASP.NET looked at your source code, made some additions and adjustments, and then created the HTML you see here.

The `Value` elements in the TextBoxes in browser HTML source code contain the numbers that you typed in before clicking the Button. These values have *persisted* during the round trip from browser to server and back to browser.

None of your VB source code (the code-behind programming in the Click event of the Button) appears in the browser's source HTML code. The VB *code-behind* sits "behind" the HTML and does any computing that's required *on the server.* The only reference to the VB code in the browser's HTML page is `action="Default. aspx"`. The VB code runs on the server and is never sent to the user's browser; only pure HTML is sent to the user. Well, you *can* also send DHTML and scripting mixed in with the HTML if you wish, but it might well be refused by a firewall or by the browser's security system. But the point is that your VB programming is certainly never sent to the user's browser.

If you do try to send DHTML or executable objects, most firewalls scream bloody murder and do everything they can to block the transmitted page. As I explain in Chapter 14, security concerns (concerns that executables may be viruses) are the primary reason that code execution must take place server-side rather than in the visitor's computer.

ASP.NET retained your form's and controls' `Name` properties (such as `Label1`) and used those names for the HTML ID attributes as well. Every server control is given a unique ID (and if you don't supply one yourself, ASP.NET supplies it). Unique IDs allow you to write programming for every server control (identifying a control by its ID).

This entire page in the browser is, in an abstract sense, an *object*, containing input and output features, behaviors (adding numbers), properties (values), and events (click). However, unlike an ordinary (encapsulated) control, the "pure" HTML looks like ordinary, passive, descriptive HTML to a firewall, so it is permitted to pass over the firewall into a visitor's browser. In this way, computation becomes possible on a Web page — as long as the computing is done on the server and only the displayable results are sent to the browser.

Adding Simple Validation

With ASP.NET, the entire VB Express language is available to you for programming that executes on your server. (You could also use other languages, such as C#, but why would you?) You can also do all kinds of computing with VB. For example, you can implement validation safeguards on the server. *Validation* is the process of checking data to see if it's appropriate or not, such as ensuring that users enter at least five digits for their zip code. Fewer digits would be invalid data.

Here's an example showing how to add some validation code to the example you constructed in the previous section. This validator reacts if the user enters a larger number than you want in TextBox1 (the new source code you should type in is in boldface):

```
Sub Button1_Click(ByVal sender As Object, ByVal e As System.EventArgs)

    If CInt(TextBox1.Text) > 999 Then
        Label1.Text = "You must provide a number lower than 1000."
        Exit Sub
    End If

    Dim firstnum, secondnum, totalnum As Integer

    firstnum = CInt(TextBox1.Text)
    secondnum = CInt(TextBox2.Text)

    totalnum = firstnum + secondnum

    Label1.Text = "The sum is: " & totalnum & "<br/>" & _
    "The current time is: " & Format(Now, "h:mm")

End Sub
```

Just as in Windows applications, you can refer in your code-behind module to the various properties of controls on your form. In this example, you check to see what users have typed into their browsers in the first TextBox by looking at its `Text` property. Then, if necessary, you put a message into the `Text` property of the label to warn the user. Also, you refuse to add the numbers together (instead, you leave the procedure via `Exit Sub`). The user can try again, and with each Button click, the code checks to see if valid data was entered according to your rules.

Notice, too, that `<br/>` (the HTML tag for a line break) is embedded in the string for `Label1.Text`:

```
Label1.Text = "The sum is: " & totalnum & "<br/>" & _
"The current time is: " & Format(Now, "h:mm")
```

`<br/>` is HTML, not VB, but when you're writing for a Web page, special characters like that are necessary. In a Windows-style VB program, you can use the carriage-return linefeed constant `vbCrLf` to force the text display to move down one line in the label, as in the following code:

```
Label1.Text = "The sum is: " & totalnum & vbCrLf & _
"The current time is: " & Format(Now, "h:mm")
```

However, when your text is being displayed in the HTML of a WebForm, you must use the HTML tag for line break: `<br/>`. This is just one of those oddities of programming for the Web.

Managing State with Server-Side Controls

Now that you're creating Web sites, you need to understand new, tricky ways of *managing state,* or preserving variables' values. Why all this concern over what would have simply been global `Public` variables in earlier versions of Visual Basic?

The answer is that Web programming is necessarily different from traditional Windows programming in several important ways. Put simply: When you write traditional VB Windows applications, you're working within a limited, stable, one-on-one environment. There's just the application's user communicating with his or her hard drive. That's a *predictable* relationship, simplifying everything from security to communications.

But if you expose your server hard drive to the Internet when you create a Web page, the relationship becomes unpredictable in a number of ways:

- ✔ **You're permitting perhaps thousands of people to access your Web page at the same time, and that number can change at any time.** If your site is really popular, it may be hosting more than 10,000 simultaneous visitors, especially if your name gets in the papers after another incident like that time in Tijuana back when you were in college.

  Managing state enables your source code to better handle interactions with one person but then suddenly expand to manage 10,000 people. Your Web application's source code, database system, server hardware, and other elements of your Web site need to be flexible. (The term *scalability* describes your code's capability to handle large numbers of visitors.)

- ✔ **Your programming becomes more open to security risks.** Out of 10,000 people, a small minority (at least 7) are either crazy or evil. Suddenly, what was a private, relatively safe Windows application environment becomes a public nightmare, with seven nut cases jumping around. With a Web site, you've now got some of the problems facing celebrities: creepers, stalkers, peepers, trash talkers, and other inconvenient folk.

- ✔ **The potential for memory problems increases dramatically.** If you managed state for a Web site in the same way you do for Windows programs, how could your server store 10,000 separate pages simultaneously to preserve the variables for each visitor to your site? The answer is that your server — even a monster server farm — would struggle to store this much constantly changing data.

Given the back-and-forth, client-server-client, divided nature of ASP.NET applications, you may well be wondering just what you, the programmer, can do to manage and preserve variables and to know what is going on at any given time? Working in partnership with ASP.NET, you must use various strategies to preserve *state* (the properties of controls, the values in variables, and so on). For example, can you find out if this is the first time a visitor is seeing your Web page? Or have they been interacting with it for several minutes and have made several round trips between their browser and your server? Perhaps they've clicked a button several times. How can you know? It would be *useful* to know.

In the following sections, you find out a variety of techniques for managing state as visitors come and go from your Web site.

Identifying a user's first visit

You must be able to tell whether a form is about to make its first trip to the visitor's browser or whether it has been posted back (meaning that previous requests have occurred from this particular client — this visitor — at this particular time). You can use an `If...Then` construct in your ASP.NET source code to determine whether this is the first trip.

Why must you know? Let's say that you need to fill a ListBox with the names of all the books you sell. It would be inefficient to fill this ListBox over and over each time the visitor sends another request back to your server to view the page (by clicking a Submit button or whatever). Just fill it the *first time,* and subsequently the server doesn't waste its time repeating the job.

Here's how to detect whether this is the first time a visitor has viewed your Web page:

```
Private Sub Page_Load(ByVal sender As Object, ByVal e As
          System.EventArgs) Handles Me.Load

'Put user code to initialize the page here

    If Not Page.IsPostBack Then
    'make a connection to the database and fill a ListBox with book title info.

        Response.Write("First Time")

        Else

    Response.Write("Not the first time...")
    'make a connection to the database and fill a ListBox with book title info.

    End If

End Sub
```

You don't need to access your book database every time the user sends a post back. That's unnecessary and wastes time. Worse, it also destroys information you may need from the user. For example, suppose that the user clicked one of the items in your ListBox. You need to know (for processing on the server in your VB code) which item the visitor selected. If you refill the ListBox during the postback, you *destroy* the user's selection. You can no longer query the SelectedItem.Text property of the ListBox if you refill it.

The WebForm's Page_Load event is triggered every time the page is loaded into your server, so you can use the event to react to the first request and then use the event to react differently to subsequent requests. Query the IsPostBack property of the Page object to decide how your code should react.

Every time a Web page is first requested or posted back, the server processes its events. First, the Page_Load event is triggered, causing the page and any controls' ViewStates to be automatically restored. Any other triggered events on the page are processed next (although they are not triggered in any particular order that the server can detect). You can respond to these events in your code.

After all the controls' events have triggered, the Page_Unload event triggers. In that event, you can write code to terminate database connections, discard objects, and otherwise gracefully close down the page. You can also employ similar Session_OnStart and Session_OnEnd events.

You locate the Page Load or other events in the code-behind window in the Visual Web Developer just as you do in ordinary Windows VB Express: Drop the list boxes at the top of the code window, as shown in Figure 15-2.

Figure 15-2:
Find events in the two drop-down lists at the top of the code-behind window.

Preserving values within a single page

You also sometimes need to preserve the contents of variables in Web programming. In the wonderful world of the Web, objects blink in and out of existence faster than bubbles at a car wash. You, the programmer, must know how to make some information durable and persistent in this flickering, transitory world of Internet communication.

How do you force information to persist between round trips from the user's browser and your server?

Recall that given the high traffic possible on the Internet (many people potentially communicating all at once with your server), it is impossible to preserve controls, variables, and other information in the same way that this data is held in RAM memory when one person is using one machine, as is the case with traditional Windows applications.

Remember that in ASP.NET, the server composes a new HTML page each time it replies to the user's browser, and then it sends that page off to the browser and *throws away* its copy of what it just sent off. But perhaps you need data to persist. For example, what if you want to permit the user to click a button, and you want to increment a counter each time the button is clicked?

Although ASP.NET doesn't keep Web pages in memory on the server after it sends them off, you can tell it to preserve most states on a page between round trips from user to server. It preserves controls and their properties, for example, in the `ViewState` object (and you can also use the `ViewState` object to store your data). use the `ViewState` object — a "bag" that you can dump information into — and trust that the information will survive the round trip from the user to the server and back to the user.

The `ViewState` object is a bit like VB's traditional `Static` command, forcing data persistence within a procedure. The `ViewState` object:

✔ Is useful for storing an individual visitor's information. (To preserve data needed by *all* visitors to your site, use the `Application` object, described later in this section.)

✔ Can store more complex data than simple data types can.

✔ Can also hold hash tables, arraylists, and dataset objects.

Here's how STET`ViewState` works: Double-click the button in the example program you've been using in this chapter. You now see its `Click` event. Replace the current programming in the Click event with this:

```
Sub Button1_Click(ByVal sender As Object, ByVal e As System.EventArgs)

    Dim counter As Integer
    counter = CInt(ViewState("counter"))
    counter += 1
    ViewState("counter") = counter   'save the value of counter
    Response.Write(counter.ToString())

End Sub
```

Press F5 to run this Web application and then notice that each time you click the button, the variable `counter` increments and displays the new count in the browser. Remember that each click triggers a round trip to the server, and that the Web page HTML is *discarded* by the server each time it sends that page back to the browser. Nonetheless, given that you dumped the counter's value into the `ViewState` "bag," the value of `counter` is saved between those round trips.

Preserving values across pages

You can choose from a couple of good ways to pass data *between* pages in a Web site. The first one, which I explain in this section, is relatively straightforward but not secure, so don't pass sensitive data using this technique. (You find out how to pass data securely in the section later in this chapter titled, "Storing data with the Session property.")

Follow these steps to slyly add some data to the HTML that describes a hyperlink and then pass the data using that hyperlink. First, you add a second Web page, and a hyperlink control to your project:

1. **Click the Design tab at the bottom of the WebForm1.aspx design window.**

   You see the design mode for this form.

2. **Click the boldface Standard entry at the top of the Toolbox.**

   You see all the primary Web controls.

3. **Double-click the HyperLink control icon.**

   A hyperlink is added to your `Default.aspx` page.

4. **Choose Website➪Add New Item.**

   You see the Add New Item dialog box.

5. **Double-click the WebForm icon in the Add New Item dialog box.**

   A second Web page (named `Default2.aspx`) is added to this project.

6. **Go back to `Default.aspx` (click its tab) and, if it's not selected, click the hyperlink control on WebForm1 to select it.**

7. **In the properties window, click the `NavigateUrl` property of the `HyperLink` control to select it.**

8. **Click the ... (ellipsis) button in the `NavigateUrl` property.**

   The Select URL dialog box appears, as shown in Figure 15-3.

Figure 15-3:
Use this
dialog box
to direct a
hyperlink on
one Web
page
(WebForm)
to target
another
Web page in
your project.

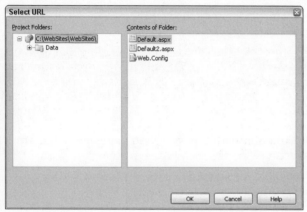

9. **Double-click your new Web page, `Default2.aspx`, in the Select URL dialog box.**

   `Default2` now becomes the target of the Hyperlink control, and the dialog box closes.

10. **Change the HyperLink1 control's `Text` property to `Go to page 2 in My Site`.**

Now you're ready to take the steps that actually pass data from WebPage1 to WebPage2. Follow these steps:

1. **Click the Source tab on the bottom of the Default.aspx design window.**

   You see the HTML view.

2. **Locate the Hyperlink control's HTML code and modify its `URL` property by adding `?MyString=3` to the code, like this (shown in boldface):**

   ```
   <asp:HyperLink ID="HyperLink1" Runat="server" NavigateUrl=
         "~/Default2.aspx?MyString=3">HyperLink</asp:HyperLink><br />
   ```

3. **Click the Default2.aspx tab at the top of the code/design window and then click the Design tab at the bottom of the code/design window.**

   The design window displays the Default2 Web page.

4. **Double-click the Button control icon in the Toolbox.**

   A Button is added to Default2.

5. **Double-click the Button on Default2.**

   You are taken to the Code window and the Button's Click event.

6. **Type the following code. It retrieves the value of MyString and makes it available to WebForm2's VB code:**

```
Private Sub Button1_Click(ByVal sender As System.Object, ByVal e As
        System.EventArgs) Handles Button1.Click

    Dim MyString As String

    MyString = CStr(Request.QueryString("MyString"))

    Response.Write("The data was passed and it is: " & MyString)

End Sub
```

7. **Click the Default.aspx tab to switch to page one. Then press F5 to test your project.**

   You see Default1, the startup page, in Internet Explorer.

8. **Click the hyperlink.**

   The browser switches to the Default2 page.

9. **Click the Button control on Default2.**

   You see that the value of the variable MyString, which was 3, has been passed to Default2 from the Default page.

Using a URL to store data is highly unsecure. Not only is it easy for others to view the URL, but they can also make changes to it and send it back to your server with modified, possibly poisoned data. A better way to store data — if security is an issue — is to use the Session property, as I explain in the following section.

Storing data with the Session property

When you need a secure and elegant way to save information between round trips to the server, employ the Session property of the Page object. Session variables use up memory on the server (as opposed to client-side cookies, which are maintained on the visitors' individual hard drives), but, well, memory is cheap these days.

Because the ViewState object described earlier in this chapter works only within a single Web page, you can't use that to move data between Web pages. But the session state (or "session property") has wide enough scope to embrace all the Web pages in a Web site. So you can use session state to pass data between a Web site's pages.

To see how this works, follow these steps:

1. **Start a new ASP.NET project in the Visual Web Developer and then click the Default.aspx tab in the design window.**

   WebForm1 is displayed in the design window.

2. **Double-click the Button control in the Toolbox twice.**

   You add two Button controls to WebForm1.

3. **Double-click Button1.**

   You are taken to the Code window and the Button's Click event.

4. **Type the following code that adds two items of data to the `Session` property:**

   ```
   Sub Button1_Click(ByVal sender As Object, ByVal e As System.EventArgs)


           Session("Message") = "This information"
           Session("SecondMessage") = "comes from the session property "


   End Sub
   ```

   Note that the name within the parentheses is equivalent to a variable name, and the data following the = sign is equivalent to a variable's value.

5. **Click the Default.aspx tab in the design window.**

   The page named Default is displayed in the design window.

6. **Double-click Button2.**

   You are taken to the Code window, where you see Button2's Click event.

7. **Type this into Button2's Click event:**

   ```
   Sub Button2_Click(ByVal sender As Object, ByVal e As System.EventArgs)

       Dim firstinfo As String = Session("Message").ToString
       Dim secondinfo As String = Session("SecondMessage").ToString

       Response.Write(firstinfo & " " & secondinfo)

   End Sub
   ```

8. **Press F5 to run the project and then click Button1.**

   The data and its associated "variable names" are stored in the session property.

9. **Click Button2.**

   The browser displays the information that's been retrieved from the `Session` property.

Session state by default expires (its data evaporates) after not being used for 20 minutes. You can, however, extend the session state's lifetime by adjusting its `Timeout` property. You specify its lifetime in minutes, so to force it to wait for an hour of inactivity before disappearing, use this code:

```
Session.Timeout = 60
```

Exploring the Application object (an alternative to Session)

The `Session` property is one of several clever ways that you can store values in ASP.NET. The `Application` object is best used to store values that your entire application needs, such as your company's current sale items or a database connection string. In addition, use this technique only for values that don't frequently change after your Web project has been instantiated (brought to life, started running); otherwise, you can slow things down. The `Application` object works similarly to the `Session` property, except you must lock and unlock `Application` objects, as shown here:

```
'add a variable and provide a value to it:
    Application.Lock()
    Application.Add("namehold", "Rita Jones")
    Application.UnLock()
```

Why Not Use Cookies?

You've heard of cookies, right? They're little files that Web sites store on your hard drive — then later, when you revisit that site, information can be retrieved from the cookie about your preferences, your logon ID, what pages you've visited, and whatever damaging personal quirks were revealed by your Web surfing habits.

So, as a site programmer, why wouldn't you use cookies to save data? That would shift the burden of maintaining state from your server to each user's hard drive. Sounds good in theory, doesn't it? Just save a cookie on their end with whatever info you want to save. This is a good way to store data *permanently* about each user — not just during the session.

Say that you want to store information *between sessions* — so that visitors can return to your Web site next week or next year and not have to retype their phone number and address, for example. You could maintain that data in a database, but client-side cookies are one obviously efficient way to do it. Here's an example that stores and then retrieves a cookie on the visitor's hard drive:

```
Private Sub Page_Load(ByVal sender As Object, ByVal e As
            System.EventArgs) Handles Me.Load

Dim PhoneCookie As New HttpCookie("VisitorsPhoneNumber", "434 777-8900")
PhoneCookie.Expires = Now.AddMonths(4) 'destroy it 4 months from now
Response.Cookies.Add(PhoneCookie)


' get the cookie back from the client:

Dim s As String
Dim CookieName As String = "PhoneCookie"

For Each CookieName In Request.Cookies.AllKeys
'keys are similar to variable names

    Dim cookie As HttpCookie = Request.Cookies(CookieName)
    s = cookie.Value & "</br>"
    Response.Write(s)
Next

End Sub
```

Lately, though, using client-side cookies is being discouraged for two reasons:

- First, some users turn off the cookie feature in their computer for security or privacy (unspeakable!) reasons.

- Second, some devices, particularly mobile devices, don't allow cookies at all.

However, in a stable, predictable environment such as a corporation's intranet, cookies remain a useful way to persist data. And, in spite of cookies' restrictions, many Web sites continue to store data in cookies — so it's up to you.

Part V
The Part of Tens

"It's a horse racing software program. It analyzes my betting history and makes suggestions. Right now it's suggesting I try betting on football."

In this part . . .

This part is called "The Part of Tens" because each of its two chapters is divided into ten sections that offer relatively brief tips, techniques, and resources that a Visual Basic Express programmer is likely to find useful. Among the topics covered are these: random numbers, the Upgrade Wizard, keystroke detection, registry access, customized controls, online resources, the menu builder, and other topics. You'll find many useful ideas here.

Chapter 16

Ten Great Visual Basic Express Tips and Tricks

H ere's a collection of tips, tricks, and techniques that are too useful to ignore, but that don't seem to fit into other sections of this book.

Using the Conversion Wizard to Master VB Express

If you're stumped and can't figure out how to do something in VB Express that you know perfectly well how to accomplish in earlier versions of Visual Basic, such as VB version 6, try using the Conversion Wizard, a migration utility built into VB Express:

1. Start VB 6 (you can run it simultaneously with VB Express).

2. **Write the problem programming in VB 6 and then save the VB 6 project to your hard drive.**

   Alternatively, you can simply locate an existing .vbp (Visual Basic Project) project on your hard drive.

3. **Open the file you just saved in one of two ways:**

   • Using Windows Explorer, locate the .vbp file and double-click it.

   If the file extension .vbp isn't already associated with VB Express, you are asked which program to open the file with. Choose Visual Basic Express from the dialog box.

   • Start VB Express, choose File⇨Open⇨Convert, and select VB Project Files (*.VBP, *.VBPRO) in the Files of Type list box in the Open Project dialog box. Find the file you just saved and open it.

As soon as you open a VB 6 project in VB Express, the Conversion Wizard kicks into action, as shown in Figure 16-1.

Figure 16-1:
The Conversion Wizard at your service.

This wizard looks at the earlier, classic, pre-Express Visual Basic programming code and does its best to translate VB 6 into VB Express for you. When the wizard is finished with its efforts, examine the source code that the wizard wrote in the code window. Sometimes this is the quickest way to figure out how to translate classic Visual Basic to VB Express.

Moving from Classic VB or VB6 to VB Express

If you know how to write code in classic Visual Basic, such as VB 6 or earlier, you can probably find the VB Express version of that code in the very large Appendix B, which you can find on this book's Web site. This Appendix is a Rosetta stone for those making the transition to VB Express from previous versions of Visual Basic. (See the book's Introduction for details about this Web site.)

Managing Directories

Here's how to create and destroy directories and subdirectories in VB Express. First, at the top of your VB Express code window, type this:

```
Imports System.IO
```

Then type the following code:

```
Private Sub Form1_Load(ByVal sender As System.Object, ByVal e As
          System.EventArgs) Handles MyBase.Load

Try
    Dim s As Integer
    s = CreateDirectory()
Catch er As Exception
    MsgBox(er.ToString)
End Try

End Sub


Public Function DestroyDirectory()

Dim objDir As New DirectoryInfo("C:\TestDir")

Try
    objDir.Delete(True)
Catch
    Throw New Exception("Failed to delete")
End Try

End Function
```

```
Public Function CreateDirectory() As String

Dim objDir As New DirectoryInfo("c:\TestDir")

Try
    objDir.Create()
Catch
    Throw New Exception("Failed to create new directory")
End Try

End Function

Public Function CreateSubDirectory() As String

Dim objDir As New DirectoryInfo("c:\TestDir") 'parent directory

Try
    objDir.CreateSubdirectory("TestSubDir") 'name for new subdiretory
Catch
    Throw New Exception("Failed to create new subdirectory")
End Try

End Function
```

Press F5 to run this code and then look in your `C:` root directory to see that `TestDir` has been created. Try some of the other functions in this example by substituting their function names for `DestroyDirectory` in the Form_Load event.

Talking to the Clipboard

Sometimes it's useful to use the Windows Clipboard object in your programming. Here's how to bring text in from the Clipboard in VB Express:

```
MsgBox(My.Computer.Clipboard.GetText())
```

To import a picture from the Clipboard, type this:

```
PictureBox1.Image = My.Computer.Clipboard.GetImage()
```

To save the contents of a text box to the Clipboard, use this code:

```
My.Computer.Clipboard.SetText(TextBox1.Text)
```

Randomizing

Generating a series of random numbers has uses in games, encryption, and other programming tasks. To create random numbers in VB Express, you first put this line at the very top of your code window:

```
Imports System.Random
```

Then you can use the random function to get random numbers. Type this code in a form's Load event:

```
Private Sub Form1_Load(ByVal sender As System.Object, ByVal e As
        System.EventArgs) Handles MyBase.Load

    Dim i As Integer
    For i = 1 To 15
        Debug.WriteLine(rand(i))
    Next
End Sub

Function rand(ByVal MySeed As Integer) As Integer
    Dim obj As New system.Random(MySeed)
    Return obj.next(1, 12)
End Function
```

The rand Function returns random numbers between 1 and 12.

When you press F5 to run this example, you see the Debug.WriteLine results in the Immediate window in the IDE. (Choose View⇨Other Windows⇨ Immediate to display this window.)

Although the arguments say 1, 12 in the Return obj.next(1, 12) line, you will never get a 12 in your results. The numbers provided by the System.Random function in this case range only from 1 to 11. I guess some programmers at Microsoft think this isn't a bug. I sure do. But this odd usage has been in VB now for several years, and nobody seems willing to fix it.

Here's an example that illustrates how you can use the NOW command to *seed* (initialize) your random generator. By using NOW, you're providing this function with a random starting point.

Type this code in the Form_Load event:

```
Private Sub Form1_Load(ByVal sender As System.Object, ByVal e As
        System.EventArgs) Handles MyBase.Load
```

```
Dim sro As New coin()
Dim x As Integer
Dim i As Integer

For i = 1 To 100
    sro.toss()

    Dim n As String

        x = sro.coinvalue
        If x = 1 Then
            n = "tails"
        Else
            n = "heads"
        End If

        n = n & " "

        debug.Write(n)
Next i

End Sub
```

Then, at the bottom of your code window, *below* the `End Class` line, type this new class, which tosses a virtual coin and returns a random value in the variable:

```
Class coin

Private m_coinValue As Integer = 0

Private Shared s_rndGenerator As New System.Random(Now.Millisecond)

Public ReadOnly Property coinValue() As Integer
    Get
        Return m_coinValue
    End Get
End Property

Public Sub toss()
    m_coinValue = s_rndGenerator.next(1, 3)

End Sub
End Class
```

Press F5 and see the results in the Immediate window.

Detecting Keystrokes

It's sometimes useful to know what key the user is pressing. You can use the KeyPress event to find out this information. Put a text box on a form and then, using the drop-down list boxes at the top of the code window, create a TextBox1_KeyPress event by clicking TextBox1 in the left list box and KeyPress in the right list box. Then type this into the KeyPress event:

```
Private Sub TextBox1_KeyPress(ByVal sender As Object, ByVal e As
        System.Windows.Forms.KeyPressEventArgs) Handles TextBox1.KeyPress

If e.KeyChar = Microsoft.VisualBasic.ChrW(13) Then
    MsgBox("They pressed the Enter Key")
End If

End Sub
```

Now press F5 to test the program. Type some letters into the text box and then press Enter and notice how the program detects this key press. To see a complete list of all the character codes, use the Help Index feature and type in `character codes`. You replace the `(13)` in this example with whatever character's code you want to detect and react to in your program. For example `(99)` detects the letter *c*.

CStr versus .ToString

It would seem that the `.ToString` method (which many objects in VB Express have) and the `CStr` function do the same job: converting an object or numeric data type into a string data type. If you get an error message telling you that something cannot be converted to a string, you can usually correct the problem by using `.ToString` or `CStr`.

Here's an example:

```
Private Sub Form1_Load(ByVal sender As System.Object, ByVal e As
        System.EventArgs) Handles MyBase.Load

    MsgBox(sender)

End Sub
```

Press F5 to test this code. VB Express displays an error message saying, among other things, `Argument prompt cannot be converted to type string`. (Note that `sender` is an argument prompt; you can see it in the parameter list following `Form1_Load`.)

To correct this, change the code to

```
MsgBox(sender.ToString)
```

`CStr`, however, will not work in this case. It can be used only with objects that can be formatted in more than one way. `CStr` checks to see what locale (such as U.S. or China) is in effect in the current system and then formats the string according to the needs of the local language. `.ToString` executes faster because it does not bother with locale formatting issues.

Simplifying Source Code Two Ways

Programmers usually welcome ways to reduce the *noise* (unnecessary typing and hard-to-read clutter) in source code. VB Express includes two optional shortcuts that most programmers will quickly grow fond of.

Combining the declaration and the assignment

Instead of declaring a variable on one line and then assigning a value to it on a second line, like this:

```
Dim a As String
a = "Hello"
```

you can combine declaration and assignment into a single statement, like this:

```
Dim a As String = "Hello"
```

Avoiding repetition

In previous versions of VB, you could modify the current contents of a variable in only one way: You had to repeat the variable name. For example, to increment variable a, you would type

```
a = a + 1
```

That's not so bad with a simple, short variable name like a. But in VB Express, qualification can make object and variable names huge, like this:

```
Textbox1.Text = Textbox1.Text & objFileRead.ReadLine()
```

Some programmers (users of the C language and its offspring) have been using a set of operators that combine two ideas into one. The fundamental difference is that the C-style code moves the operator (+, -, *, or whatever) over next to the assignment (=) symbol. For example, you can type

```
X += 1 'the new style
```

Instead of

```
X = X + 1
```

This shortcut comes in handy when you are working with longer variable or object names:

```
textbox1.Text += objFileRead.ReadLine()
```

If you want to try out the C syntax, here are the variations:

Classic Visual Basic	*VB Express*
`X = X + Y`	`X +=Y`
`X = X - 5`	`X -= 5`
`X = X * 4`	`X *= 4`
`X = X / 7`	`X /= 7`
`X = X ^ 2`	`X ^= 2`
`String1 = String1 & "ed"`	`String1 &= "ed"`

Understanding How the Registry Works with VB Express

The Windows Registry is downplayed in VB Express programming languages. Microsoft's gurus avoid registration and the idea of a common repository of DLLs by putting any necessary code libraries (assemblies) and other dependencies in the same path (the same folder or a subfolder) as the application that needs them. The idea is that you can deploy (give someone else your VB Express project or solution) by merely copying the folder and its subfolders from where your VB Express application resides to the other machine's hard drive. That's it. No need to register code libraries or worry about which version of those libraries is currently used by Windows.

Instead, your VB Express project relies only on the files it finds in its own folder and subfolders. Oh, well, yes . . . all VB Express projects also need the massive common language runtime (CLR) library that all Visual Studio languages rely on. But the CLR is supposed to be embedded as part of future Windows operating systems; at least that was the promise several years ago. At this point, though, your project will not work on a computer that doesn't have the CLR.

The Windows Registry, currently in disgrace in some ways, is nonetheless unlikely to go away any time soon because too many applications and operating system features depend on the information held in the Registry. It holds everything from user preferences to user identities — and much more. So in the following sections, I explain how to read from and write to the Registry, in case you ever need to do so.

Reading from the Registry

A VB Express programmer may well need to know how to read information from and write information to the Registry. In VB Express, you can query the Registry by using the `RegistryKey` object. Here are examples that show you how to access the Registry with VB Express code:

1. **Start a new VB Express Windows-style project.**

2. **Add a TextBox from the Toolbox to your form.**

3. **Add a Button to the form as well.**

4. **Double-click the Button to get to its Click event in the code window.**

5. **Type this in the Button's Click event:**

```
Protected Sub Button1_Click(ByVal sender As Object, ByVal e As
            System.EventArgs)

Dim objGotValue As Object
Dim objMainKey As RegistryKey = Registry.CurrentUser
Dim objOpenedKey As RegistryKey
Dim strValue As String

' put this next on a single long line
```

```
objOpenedKey = objMainKey.OpenSubKey
    ("Software\\Microsoft\\Windows\\CurrentVersion\\Internet Settings")

objGotValue = objOpenedKey.GetValue("User Agent")

If (Not objGotValue Is Nothing) Then
    strValue = objGotValue.ToString()
Else
    strValue = ""
End If

objMainKey.Close()
TextBox1.Text = strValue

End Sub
```

Note that the complete name (path) of the entire Registry entry is divided into three different locations in the example code. First, the primary key, `CurrentUser`, then the path of subkeys, and finally the actual specific name: `objOpenedKey.GetValue("User Agent")`.

6. **You must also type `Imports Microsoft.Win32` as the first line at the top of the code window.**

   This gets rid of the nasty squiggly lines that show up when you entered the code in Step 5.

   The `Microsoft.Win32` namespace contains the Registry-access functions, such as the `OpenSubKey` method that you need in this example.

7. **Press F5 to run this example and then click the button on the form you created.**

   If your Registry contains the same value for this key as my Registry does, you see a result similar to this:

```
Mozilla/4.2 (compatible; MSIE 5.0; Win32)
```

Writing to the Registry

The RegistryKey class includes a group of methods you can use to manage and write to the Registry. These methods include `Close`, `CreateSubKey`, `DeleteSubKey`, `DeleteSubKeyTree`, `DeleteValue`, `GetSubKeyNames`, `GetType`, `GetValue`, `GetValueNames`, `OpenSubKey`, and `SetValue`.

Drawing Directly on a Control

In VB Express, you can get pretty down and dirty and take charge of precisely how a control from your Toolbox will look to the user. Here's how to frame a Button control with blue — you might like the effect. Put a button on a form and then type this into its Paint event:

```
Private Sub Button1_Paint(ByVal sender As Object, ByVal e As
            System.Windows.Forms.PaintEventArgs) Handles Button1.Paint

Dim g As Graphics = e.Graphics

ControlPaint.DrawBorder(g, e.ClipRectangle, Color.Blue, ButtonBorderStyle.Solid)

End Sub
```

You can experiment with the various parameters of the `DrawBorder` method if you wish. You have my permission.

Chapter 17

Ten Important VB Resources

H ere are some places to go when you want additional information or help with your VB Express projects, plus a few techniques you'll want to master: saving settings, adding menus, and drawing graphics.

Reading the Latest Info

Microsoft maintains Web sites devoted to the latest VB and Visual Studio topics. You may want to visit the Web site at the following address:

```
http://msdn2.microsoft.com/library/default.aspx
```

And also look here for additional information:

```
http://msdn2.microsoft.com/library/2x7h1hfk.aspx
```

Getting Answers to VB Express Questions

Try newsgroups at the following location to ask questions and get (usually) good answers. There are experts here, sometimes willing and able to assist you with a difficult problem:

```
http://msdn.microsoft.com/newsgroups/
```

Keeping Visual Basic Healthy

Microsoft's Visual Basic support sites contain information and, in particular, occasional updates (service packs) that correct bugs.

Check these sites on a regular basis:

- ✔ `http://msdn.microsoft.com/vstudio/downloads/updates/` `sp/default.aspx`: This page offers updates and downloads related to database programming.
- ✔ `http://msdn.microsoft.com/vbasic`: The main Microsoft VB home page.
- ✔ `http://msdn.microsoft.com/vstudio/downloads/default.aspx`: Updates and bug fixes for VB and other Visual Studio components.

Visiting Other Web Sites of Interest

The leading site for information on Visual Studio .NET and related programming is, as you might expect, hosted by Microsoft:

```
http://msdn.microsoft.com/default.aspx
```

Probably the best, most active, independent site of interest to VB programmers is DevX:

```
www.devx.com
```

One of the more active sources of useful VB information is Fawcette Technical Publications, publisher of several programming magazines. Find Fawcette's latest news at

```
www.fawcette.com
```

Also, be sure to visit the following sites:

- ✔ `www.pinpub.com/ME2/Default.asp`: Visual Basic, SQL Server, .NET Developer, and publications from Pinnacle
- ✔ `http://visualbasic.about.com/`

Discovering Microsoft's Plans for the Future of Database Technology

If you want to find out the latest information about ADO.NET, OLE DB, and UDA (Microsoft's initiatives for universal data access), take a look at this site:

```
http://msdn.microsoft.com/data/default.aspx
```

Importing Favorite Settings

If you have more than one preferred IDE (VB Express Editor) configuration, you can easily save them and then import the best one for each situation. The Text Editor, Environment, and other settings you specify in the Tools⇨ Options dialog box can be saved and then imported as needed. Just choose Tools⇨Import and Export Settings to make your choices (which groups of settings you want exported) and save them to a disk file.

Using the Application Test Center

If you create a Web site and want to give it a real run for its money, you cannot simply use the built-in, single-machine testing features available when you work with the version of SQL Server that comes with VB Express. Part IV of this book points out that you can press F5 and your browser pops up and "receives" the Web page you're working on as if that page were sent in over the Internet. That uses the stripped-down, local SQL server version.

However, if you want a more rigorous test involving the large numbers of simultaneous connections that will be made to your site if it becomes wildly popular, you need to check out Microsoft's Application Test Center at

```
www.c-sharpcorner.com/Code/2002/Sept/AppTestCenter.asp
```

It provides a *stress test,* as Microsoft puts it, of your system and software. It not only pretends that you've suddenly reached a huge audience that's trying to connect to your site, but also tests security aspects as well.

Creating Menus via the MenuStrip

What applications don't include menus? Not many. Here's how you create menus in VB Express — it's pretty easy.

Typically, the File menu is the first one on the left of the menu bar, and, equally typically, New, Save, and Open options are located on the File menu. You can create such a menu, with submenus like Save, quite quickly in the new VB Express menu-maker utility. Give the new VB MenuStrip control a try:

1. **Double-click the MenuStrip icon in the Toolbox.**

   This control makes creating a menu structure a snap. The tray opens below your form, displaying a MenuStrip icon. A box at the top left of the form reads, "Type Here." If you don't see that, click the form.

2. **Click the Type Here box to select it and then type &File.**

   As soon as you label a file item, surrounding empty squares open up, inviting you to label them, too, if you want.

The & causes VB to underline the letter that follows it (F in this case), thus providing the user with a shortcut key. The user can now open this menu by pressing Alt+F rather than clicking it.

The menus across the top are called *root* menus (or sometimes *parent* menus). They are always visible. Their only job is to drop down a list of submenu items. In VB Express, these roots already know how to do their jobs, so you don't write any code for them.

Each submenu item, on the other hand, *does* have a Click event for which you must write the programming to respond if the user chooses that menu item:

1. **In the box just below the one you captioned "File," type** &New.

   Note again that various adjacent empty boxes open up, in which you can type additional submenus if you want.

2. **Just below &New, type &Open.**

3. **Then, below &Open, type &Save.**

What I'm calling submenus and secondary menus are referred to officially as *child menus*. Every child menu (or group of child menus) has a parent. Notice that when clicked, parent menu items do nothing except display their child. So you don't write any programming code in parent menus' events — you write your code in child menu events.

4. **Double-click the New item in your menu system to get to its Click event in the Code window.**

   VB provides you with this Click event:

```
Private Sub MenuItem2_Click(ByVal sender As System.Object, ByVal e As
        System.EventArgs) Handles MenuItem2.Click


End Sub
```

Within this Sub named New, you write code to make your application offer the user a "new" whatever it is: an empty text box, a picture box to draw on, or whatever your application does. Likewise, within the Open menu event, you write code to load an existing file.

Protecting Your Intellectual Property

If you're not an intellectual, and some of my friends are emphatically *not*, you can still protect the products of your brain. Writing source code is a form of writing — so you're a sort of author when you tell a computer what to do. Your programming is *intellectual property,* technically speaking.

When you create a VB Express program, people can find ways to read it, even if they can't get ahold of your source code. They can use *decompilers* and other tools to examine your work. This not only makes it possible for them to copy and use your stunning programming concepts, but also to figure out how to exploit any security weaknesses you might have inadvertently left hanging open — *gaping* open might be a more accurate term.

You can make their job tough, if not impossible, though, by obfuscating your code with the Dotfuscator utility. (You know, *obfuscate,* from the Latin for "strong fishy smell keeps them out.")

Read all about it at

```
http://msdn.microsoft.com/library/default.asp?url=/library/
        en-us/dotfuscator/dotf3e5x.asp
```

Graphics Transformations: Kitten with a Whip

I've never really understood why the graphics libraries are included *as defaults* in VB Express projects. They're just not used very often. How many applications need to draw lines, circles, and other objects, fill them with textures and colors, and so on? Not too many. But, after a couple of cold ones, I'll accept anything, however bizarre and ill-conceived. By 5:15 p.m., after happy hour is underway, I'm easy.

If you want to fool around with cartoon-like drawn graphics in VB Express (as opposed to importing photographic files like .jpg or .bmp files, using the BackGroundImage property of a form or PictureBox), here's your chance.

This next code example shows you how to draw in VB Express. From here you can figure out other techniques. This code draws a kitten with a whip; well, the whip, anyway.

Double-click the PictureBox icon in the Toolbox to place a PictureBox on a form. Then double-click the PictureBox itself to get to its Click event. Type or copy this code into the event:

```
Private Sub PictureBox1_Click(ByVal sender As System.Object, ByVal e As
        System.EventArgs) Handles PictureBox1.Click

Dim i As Integer
Dim g As Graphics = PictureBox1.CreateGraphics

g.Clear(Color.WhiteSmoke)

Dim p1 As New Point(54, 12)
Dim p2 As New Point(212, 122)
Dim p3 As New Point(134, 129)

For i = 100 To 400 Step 100
    g.DrawBezier(Pens.BlueViolet, p1, p2, p3, New Point(i, 400))
Next i

End Sub
```

Press F5 to run the program; then click the PictureBox to see the whip. A larger PictureBox obviously produces a thicker, and some will say more threatening, whip.

Appendix A

About the CDs

. . . .

*T*wo CDs come with this book. On one CD, you can find a full version of Visual Basic 2005 Express Edition. The other CD — a Getting Started CD — includes extras to help beginners, such as videos and Starter Kits.

System Requirements

Make sure your computer meets the minimum system requirements listed below. If your computer doesn't match up to most of these requirements, you may have problems in using the contents of the CD.

- A PC with a 600 megahertz (MHz) Pentium or faster processor.
- Microsoft Windows 2000, XP or 2003 Server.
- At least 128 MB of total RAM installed on your computer. For best performance, we recommend least 256 MB of RAM installed.
- A hard drive with up to 1.3GB of available space.
- A CD-ROM drive for the CD.

If you need more information on the basics, check out these books published by Wiley Publishing, Inc.: *PCs For Dummies,* by Dan Gookin; *Windows 2000 Professional For Dummies* or *Windows XP For Dummies,* both by Andy Rathbone.

Using the CD with Microsoft Windows

To install from the CD to your hard drive, follow these steps:

1. **Insert the CD into your computer's CD-ROM drive.**
2. **Click the Start button and choose Run from the menu.**
3. **Type D:\ where D is the letter of your CD-ROM drive.**

4. **Double click the file called License.txt.**

   This file contains the end-user license that you agree to by using the CD. When you are done reading the license, close the program, most likely NotePad, that displayed the file.

5. **Double click the file called Readme.txt.**

   This file contains instructions about installing the software from this CD. It might be helpful to leave this text file open while you are using the CD.

6. **Double click the folder for the software you are interested in.**

   Be sure to read the descriptions of the programs in the next section of this appendix (much of this information also shows up in the Readme file). These descriptions will give you more precise information about the programs' folder names, and about finding and running the installer program.

7. **Find the file called Setup.exe, or Install.exe, or something similar, and double click on that file.**

   The program's installer will walk you through the process of setting up your new software.

To run some of the programs, you may need to keep the CD inside your CD-ROM drive. This is a good thing. Otherwise, the installed program would have required you to install a very large chunk of the program to your hard drive space, which would have kept you from installing other software.

What You'll Find

On the software CD, you'll find a full version of Visual Basic 2005 Express Edition that will help you get started with the program.

On the Getting Started CD, check out all the extras, including

- ✔ **Videos:** The Absolute Beginner's Guide to Visual Basic Express is a video series designed specifically for those interested in learning the basics of creating applications using Visual Basic 2005 Express Edition. You'll find over eight hours of video-based instruction. Go from creating your first "Hello World" application to setting up a fully functioning RSS Reader application.

- ✔ **Card Game Starter Kit:** This Starter Kit is a complete Black Jack card game. The starter kit contains an extensible framework for building card games and a Black Jack game application that is built on top of this framework. The project comes ready to compile and run, but it's easy to customize with only a little extra programming. The section Expanding the Card Game contains a list of some customizations you might make. You are also free to use the source code as the basis for your own card game projects, and share your work with others or upload it to the Internet.

- ✔ **Amazon-Enabled Movie Collection Starter Kit (link):** The Amazon-Enabled Movie Collection Starter Kit is a Windows Form application that uses Amazon.com's Web services to dynamically search for movie titles. This Starter Kit demonstrates technologies, such as calling XML Web services, databinding, application settings, local data storage using SQL Server 2005 Express Edition, and more.

- ✔ **Links to additional resources:** The Getting Started CD also points you to additional resources on the Web. Most of these links will be updated in the future, so you may want to occasionally check them for updated information and resources. Here's a brief introduction to each resource:

  - **Visual Basic Express Edition home page:** This page on the Microsoft Web site provides additional information and links for Visual Basic Express.

  - **Visual Basic Developer Center:** Here you can find the most recent information on Visual Basic.

  - **Visual Basic forums:** Read and post on the many ASP.NET forums.

  - **SQL Server query basics:** Discover how to use the powerful T-SQL language and see how easy and flexible it is for retrieving information stored in SQL Server.

Shareware programs are fully functional, free trial versions of copyrighted programs. If you like particular programs, register with their authors for a nominal fee and receive licenses, enhanced versions, and technical support. Freeware programs are free copyrighted games, applications, and utilities. You can copy them to as many PCs as you like — free — but they have no technical support. GNU software is governed by its own license, which is included inside the folder of the GNU software. There are no restrictions on distribution of this software. See the GNU license for more details. Trial, demo, or evaluation versions are usually limited either by time or functionality (such as being unable to save projects).

If You've Got Problems (Of the CD Kind)

The programs and extras on the CDs were designed to work on most computers with the minimum system requirements. Alas, your computer may differ, and some programs may not work properly for some reason.

The two likeliest problems are that you don't have enough memory (RAM) for the programs you want to use, or you have other programs running that are affecting installation or running of a program. If you get error messages like Not enough memory or Setup cannot continue, try one or more of these methods and then try using the software again:

- ✔ **Turn off any antivirus software that you have on your computer.** Installers sometimes mimic virus activity and may make your computer incorrectly believe that it is being infected by a virus.

- ✔ **Close all running programs.** The more programs you're running, the less memory is available to other programs. Installers also typically update files and programs. So if you keep other programs running, installation may not work properly.

- ✔ **Have your local computer store add more RAM to your computer.** This is, admittedly, a drastic and somewhat expensive step. However, if you have a Windows 95 or later PC, adding more memory can really help the speed of your computer and allow more programs to run at the same time.

If you have trouble with the CDs, please call the Wiley Product Technical Support phone number at (800) 762-2974. Outside the United States, call 1(317) 572-3994. You can also contact Wiley Product Technical Support at http://support.wiley.com. John Wiley & Sons will provide technical support only for installation and other general quality control items. For technical support on the applications themselves, consult the program's vendor or author.

To place additional orders or to request information about other Wiley products, please call (877) 762-2974.

Index

Notes

Notes

Notes

Notes

Notes

BUSINESS, CAREERS & PERSONAL FINANCE

0-7645-5307-0

0-7645-5331-3 *†

Also available:
- Accounting For Dummies †
  0-7645-5314-3
- Business Plans Kit For Dummies †
  0-7645-5365-8
- Cover Letters For Dummies
  0-7645-5224-4
- Frugal Living For Dummies
  0-7645-5403-4
- Leadership For Dummies
  0-7645-5176-0
- Managing For Dummies
  0-7645-1771-6

- Marketing For Dummies
  0-7645-5600-2
- Personal Finance For Dummies *
  0-7645-2590-5
- Project Management For Dummies
  0-7645-5283-X
- Resumes For Dummies †
  0-7645-5471-9
- Selling For Dummies
  0-7645-5363-1
- Small Business Kit For Dummies *†
  0-7645-5093-4

HOME & BUSINESS COMPUTER BASICS

0-7645-4074-2

0-7645-3758-X

Also available:
- ACT! 6 For Dummies
  0-7645-2645-6
- iLife '04 All-in-One Desk Reference
  For Dummies
  0-7645-7347-0
- iPAQ For Dummies
  0-7645-6769-1
- Mac OS X Panther Timesaving
  Techniques For Dummies
  0-7645-5812-9
- Macs For Dummies
  0-7645-5656-8

- Microsoft Money 2004 For Dummies
  0-7645-4195-1
- Office 2003 All-in-One Desk Reference
  For Dummies
  0-7645-3883-7
- Outlook 2003 For Dummies
  0-7645-3759-8
- PCs For Dummies
  0-7645-4074-2
- TiVo For Dummies
  0-7645-6923-6
- Upgrading and Fixing PCs For Dummies
  0-7645-1665-5
- Windows XP Timesaving Techniques
  For Dummies
  0-7645-3748-2

FOOD, HOME, GARDEN, HOBBIES, MUSIC & PETS

0-7645-5295-3

0-7645-5232-5

Also available:
- Bass Guitar For Dummies
  0-7645-2487-9
- Diabetes Cookbook For Dummies
  0-7645-5230-9
- Gardening For Dummies *
  0-7645-5130-2
- Guitar For Dummies
  0-7645-5106-X
- Holiday Decorating For Dummies
  0-7645-2570-0
- Home Improvement All-in-One
  For Dummies
  0-7645-5680-0

- Knitting For Dummies
  0-7645-5395-X
- Piano For Dummies
  0-7645-5105-1
- Puppies For Dummies
  0-7645-5255-4
- Scrapbooking For Dummies
  0-7645-7208-3
- Senior Dogs For Dummies
  0-7645-5818-8
- Singing For Dummies
  0-7645-2475-5
- 30-Minute Meals For Dummies
  0-7645-2589-1

INTERNET & DIGITAL MEDIA

0-7645-1664-7

0-7645-6924-4

Also available:
- 2005 Online Shopping Directory
  For Dummies
  0-7645-7495-7
- CD & DVD Recording For Dummies
  0-7645-5956-7
- eBay For Dummies
  0-7645-5654-1
- Fighting Spam For Dummies
  0-7645-5965-6
- Genealogy Online For Dummies
  0-7645-5964-8
- Google For Dummies
  0-7645-4420-9

- Home Recording For Musicians
  For Dummies
  0-7645-1634-5
- The Internet For Dummies
  0-7645-4173-0
- iPod & iTunes For Dummies
  0-7645-7772-7
- Preventing Identity Theft For Dummies
  0-7645-7336-5
- Pro Tools All-in-One Desk Reference
  For Dummies
  0-7645-5714-9
- Roxio Easy Media Creator For Dummies
  0-7645-7131-1

* Separate Canadian edition also available
† Separate U.K. edition also available

Available wherever books are sold. For more information or to order direct: U.S. customers visit www.dummies.com or call 1-877-762-2974.
U.K. customers visit www.wileyeurope.com or call 0800 243407. Canadian customers visit www.wiley.ca or call 1-800-567-4797.

SPORTS, FITNESS, PARENTING, RELIGION & SPIRITUALITY

0-7645-5146-9

0-7645-5418-2

Also available:

- Adoption For Dummies
  0-7645-5488-3
- Basketball For Dummies
  0-7645-5248-1
- The Bible For Dummies
  0-7645-5296-1
- Buddhism For Dummies
  0-7645-5359-3
- Catholicism For Dummies
  0-7645-5391-7
- Hockey For Dummies
  0-7645-5228-7

- Judaism For Dummies
  0-7645-5299-6
- Martial Arts For Dummies
  0-7645-5358-5
- Pilates For Dummies
  0-7645-5397-6
- Religion For Dummies
  0-7645-5264-3
- Teaching Kids to Read For Dummies
  0-7645-4043-2
- Weight Training For Dummies
  0-7645-5168-X
- Yoga For Dummies
  0-7645-5117-5

TRAVEL

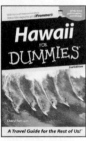

0-7645-5438-7

0-7645-5453-0

Also available:

- Alaska For Dummies
  0-7645-1761-9
- Arizona For Dummies
  0-7645-6938-4
- Cancún and the Yucatán For Dummies
  0-7645-2437-2
- Cruise Vacations For Dummies
  0-7645-6941-4
- Europe For Dummies
  0-7645-5456-5
- Ireland For Dummies
  0-7645-5455-7

- Las Vegas For Dummies
  0-7645-5448-4
- London For Dummies
  0-7645-4277-X
- New York City For Dummies
  0-7645-6945-7
- Paris For Dummies
  0-7645-5494-8
- RV Vacations For Dummies
  0-7645-5443-3
- Walt Disney World & Orlando For Dummies
  0-7645-6943-0

GRAPHICS, DESIGN & WEB DEVELOPMENT

0-7645-4345-8

0-7645-5589-8

Also available:

- Adobe Acrobat 6 PDF For Dummies
  0-7645-3760-1
- Building a Web Site For Dummies
  0-7645-7144-3
- Dreamweaver MX 2004 For Dummies
  0-7645-4342-3
- FrontPage 2003 For Dummies
  0-7645-3882-9
- HTML 4 For Dummies
  0-7645-1995-6
- Illustrator CS For Dummies
  0-7645-4084-X

- Macromedia Flash MX 2004 For Dummies
  0-7645-4358-X
- Photoshop 7 All-in-One Desk Reference For Dummies
  0-7645-1667-1
- Photoshop CS Timesaving Techniques For Dummies
  0-7645-6782-9
- PHP 5 For Dummies
  0-7645-4166-8
- PowerPoint 2003 For Dummies
  0-7645-3908-6
- QuarkXPress 6 For Dummies
  0-7645-2593-X

NETWORKING, SECURITY, PROGRAMMING & DATABASES

0-7645-6852-3

0-7645-5784-X

Also available:

- A+ Certification For Dummies
  0-7645-4187-0
- Access 2003 All-in-One Desk Reference For Dummies
  0-7645-3988-4
- Beginning Programming For Dummies
  0-7645-4997-9
- C For Dummies
  0-7645-7068-4
- Firewalls For Dummies
  0-7645-4048-3
- Home Networking For Dummies
  0-7645-42796

- Network Security For Dummies
  0-7645-1679-5
- Networking For Dummies
  0-7645-1677-9
- TCP/IP For Dummies
  0-7645-1760-0
- VBA For Dummies
  0-7645-3989-2
- Wireless All In-One Desk Reference For Dummies
  0-7645-7496-5
- Wireless Home Networking For Dummies
  0-7645-3910-8

HEALTH & SELF-HELP

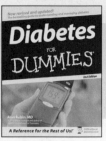

0-7645-6820-5 *†

0-7645-2566-2

Also available:

Alzheimer's For Dummies
0-7645-3899-3

Asthma For Dummies
0-7645-4233-8

Controlling Cholesterol For Dummies
0-7645-5440-9

Depression For Dummies
0-7645-3900-0

Dieting For Dummies
0-7645-4149-8

Fertility For Dummies
0-7645-2549-2

Fibromyalgia For Dummies
0-7645-5441-7

Improving Your Memory For Dummies
0-7645-5435-2

Pregnancy For Dummies †
0-7645-4483-7

Quitting Smoking For Dummies
0-7645-2629-4

Relationships For Dummies
0-7645-5384-4

Thyroid For Dummies
0-7645-5385-2

EDUCATION, HISTORY, REFERENCE & TEST PREPARATION

0-7645-5194-9

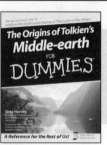

0-7645-4186-2

Also available:

Algebra For Dummies
0-7645-5325-9

British History For Dummies
0-7645-7021-8

Calculus For Dummies
0-7645-2498-4

English Grammar For Dummies
0-7645-5322-4

Forensics For Dummies
0-7645-5580-4

The GMAT For Dummies
0-7645-5251-1

Inglés Para Dummies
0-7645-5427-1

Italian For Dummies
0-7645-5196-5

Latin For Dummies
0-7645-5431-X

Lewis & Clark For Dummies
0-7645-2545-X

Research Papers For Dummies
0-7645-5426-3

The SAT I For Dummies
0-7645-7193-1

Science Fair Projects For Dummies
0-7645-5460-3

U.S. History For Dummies
0-7645-5249-X

Get smart @ dummies.com®

- **Find a full list of Dummies titles**
- **Look into loads of FREE on-site articles**
- **Sign up for FREE eTips e-mailed to you weekly**
- **See what other products carry the Dummies name**
- **Shop directly from the Dummies bookstore**
- **Enter to win new prizes every month!**